No Place To Hide In America

No Place To Hide In America

✦

or The American Misadventures of a Honky White Boy Puerto Rican Mulatto Negro Cracker Syrian Uncle Tom Bastard from Africa

Denys S. Blell
And
Robert D. Kreisher

iUniverse, Inc.
New York Lincoln Shanghai

No Place To Hide In America
or The American Misadventures of a Honky White Boy Puerto Rican Mulatto Negro Cracker Syrian Uncle Tom Bastard from Africa

iUniverse books may be ordered through booksellers or by contacting:

iUniverse
2021 Pine Lake Road, Suite 100
Lincoln, NE 68512
www.iuniverse.com
1-800-Authors (1-800-288-4677)

ISBN-13: 978-0-595-34061-3 (pbk)
ISBN-13: 978-0-595-78847-7 (ebk)
ISBN-10: 0-595-34061-X (pbk)
ISBN-10: 0-595-78847-5 (ebk)

Printed in the United States of America

Contents

Introduction

As we reflect on the development of this book, we cannot help but wonder why Denys especially could not stop writing from the first day. What was the source of the energy that kept him going for days and months until he was finished four years later? Perhaps the energy came from the recognition he had to do something fast to keep others from being hurt by a corrupted system. Perhaps it also came from our passion for civil rights and equality—a movement that has become so corrupted and co-opted over the years that we can hardly identify with it any longer. Having tried and failed to change things from the inside, we decided our only option was to go public with what we knew.

Bob was drawn into the story as Denys' friend and through having worked in higher education watching or learning of many of the sorts of things that happen in this narrative. Had we not experienced and/or witnessed so many of the things that take place in this book, we would not have written it. We watched as a group of top administrators (we would later use them for inspiration in creating "The Cabal") launched a campaign of character assassination against another administrator. They used "diversity" as the excuse for their actions when, in reality, they were merely trying to install one of their collaborators in the position. It was not even a matter of helping out friends. Many of them did not seem to like each other much. The plan was instead to agitate for the promotion of each other. The more power one of them would get, the more power they could wield to help another. We were so horrified by the blatant racial discrimination and the colossal failure of the equal opportunity system to respond that we vowed to work internally to change things and, if necessary, to go public.

This book, however, is not about Denys, Bob, or our experiences in any literal sense. We do not feel compelled to tell either of our personal stories. This is not about us. It is about the corruption and soiling of one of this nation's greatest historical moments. Therefore, we chose to wrap all of these experiences together into an avatar named Samir Dyfan, a wide-eyed idealistic character who is committed to principle at all cost and probably a bit naïve. But we like the juxtaposition of our pure of heart protagonist against the jaundiced antagonists of the book. Although the situations are real and the tensions salient to things we have experienced and witnessed, all of the names of individuals, institutions, and locations of the events have been changed. Any resemblance of this work to any individual or institution is purely coincidental.

Our original intent was to limit its scope to the last four chapters, which paint the biggest, most cynical, and systematic abuses we have ever encountered. But we realized the patterns so vividly enacted there were played out over and over in various settings and circumstances. This recognition led to the development of the other chapters chronicling the politics of diversity in other institutions in order to provide the reader with a sense of the scope and magnitude of those problems

There are two intertwined stories that constitute our narrative. First, there is the story of a nonracial and nonethnic person in the diversity profession during a time of intense racial and cultural wars in American higher education. The second story chronicles the seldom seen inner workings of diversity interest groups and the intra-group and inter-group dynamics they spawn. It may be Denys' unique position as a nonracial and nonethnic person in the diversity business that has allowed him to see many of these dynamics at work. It may also be his unique position as a nonracial and nonethnic person that led to his ultimate failure to find a place in the race and ethnicity system in higher education and in America in general. At its core, it is a system of groups, not individuals. It is a system made for blacks, whites, Latinos, Native Americans, homosexuals, women, and so on. It is not a system that is capable of including individuals. Denys could have fit in as a member of a group. Lacking the ability to identify with one, he never found a place in the institutional system.

People often psychoanalyzed him, trying to figure out his stratagem for asserting no race or ethnicity. Is he trying to play up to everybody, or is he trying to distance himself from someone? What is he up to? What is his angle? Is he just trying to be mysterious? It frustrates many that they cannot figure this out. We have both always felt at home with open-minded, sophisticated people of any origin. And we have never felt at home with closed-minded, self-centered bigots of any color, race, ethnicity, or religion. So he will not say he is black because people then assume he supports "black people." In fact, he has been accused of not supporting "black people". In reality, that is true. He does not support "black people." However, he has been the howling advocate of many a principled hard-working "black persons," as well as quite a few principled, hard-working "white persons," "yellow persons," "brown persons," "women," and "homosexuals."

It is the popular fashion in many areas of the humanities these days to describe one's group memberships to "account" for one's identity. We resist this not because we do not believe our identities are intimately tied with our ways of making sense. We believe they are. However, most of the things that count as identity in academia seem to have little to do with the matter. Maleness, whiteness, blackness, heterosexualness, Midwesterness, religious background (or lack thereof), and such fail to capture identity. So we resist because we resist the politics of definition. As salient as they are, nobody is inherently defined by their race, gender, ethnicity, sexual orientation, or religion—no matter how much others' rhetoric tries to make it so. Utilization of these categories is always an excuse for not knowing an individual as a unique individual. Utilization of these categories is not knowledge; it is a substitution for knowledge wielded by minds not flexible enough to fit another and souls too callous to care.

This is all a rather long-winded way of saying that anyone can identify with the experiences we are writing about. Diversity is one, albeit a very important one, way these relational dynamics come into play. Universities are one, albeit a very important one, place they happen. But this story is not bounded by these variables any more than we are defined by them.

The second story is about our perceptions of what others are doing in the name of diversity. Both stories are, of course, inseparable and dialectical. We have chronicled everything from our perspective, our opinion, and interpretation of things. We do not claim to be right, objective, or impartial, but we have honestly reconstructed the spirit of the things we experienced and witnessed. Is there a possibility that someone else may have a different interpretation, opinion, or perception of the story we have told? The answer is yes. Ours, of course, is a unique story that is told by us.

It is our hope that, by exposing the dark side of diversity interest group politics, we will bring greater scrutiny to a side of diversity initiatives in higher education that is seldom seen or talked about. Finally, it is our hope that greater scrutiny of diversity interest groups will lead to change at all levels of the diversity game. We have a genuine passion for diversity and the principles of equality and democracy. We retain those passions today, especially as we recognize their role in our own successes and opportunities. Denys came to this country and became a citizen because it is truly the land of freedom and opportunity. And he has made the most of it. Bob has broadened his horizons tremendously by being open to people so very different from him, like Denys. However, we are cynical about both the nobility and the success of the way diversity is managed today, especially in higher education.

Denys Blell and Bob Kreisher
Denys and Bob can be reached at denysblell@gmail.com
December 2004

1

Black or White? May I Choose "None of the Above" Please?

Many years ago, I interviewed for a job at Inter-American University for the position of associate vice provost for minority initiatives. The job reported to the vice provost for student development, who told me he was architect of all the programs intended to "integrate" the university. He also said that, if I were hired, I would supervise the directors of several exclusive programs and services, as well as plan and implement events for minorities in the university community. He went on to add they sought someone with experience in managing a diverse collection of directors and someone who could articulate the importance of "minority programs" to the university community. I am convinced his efforts to "integrate" the university were sincere, even if thoroughly misguided.

I also met with the executive vice president, who expressed the university's interest in "fostering diversity and multiculturalism," articulated a deep desire for a day when interest group politics and competition for recognition and resources would end, and spoke of his personal desire for improved group relations on campus. "The key," he said, "is for you to convince key search committee members that you can be trusted with minority interests." He said the student affairs vice provost was under a lot of pressure from minorities to hire the "right person" for the job.

When I walked into the conference room for my interview with the search committee, it became immediately obvious to me that all of the racial and ethnic interest groups on campus had been carefully assembled in the room. It became quickly obvious that various minority advocacy groups wielded a great deal of coercive power over the university's administrators. The interview focused on my relevant experience and my ability to treat all groups equally and fairly.

"It would not be difficult for me to be open and fair," I said, "because I have no particular allegiances to any racial, ethnic, or religious groups." Pressed to

1

explain, I told them I was a nonracial person with no particular ethnic, political, or religious identity. Several committee members became visibly angry. Others seemed puzzled. One declared, "There is no such person in America." It was then suggested I seek professional help because I was in denial about my identity. This interview did not go well. Later I learned I had alienated almost everyone on the committee! It was clear they thought I was dissembling.

They thought I did not want to show my true allegiances in an effort to make them all think I was on their side. This scenario had played out in my life many times. Nobody in this country seemed able to believe I do not play allegiances based on ethnicity, race, politics, or religion. We all profess colorblindness and then gawk in disbelief when we encounter it.

My interview with the president of Inter-American University was the most remarkable of all because it revealed the most about diversity efforts in contemporary America. As we toured the campus, he pointed out what he called the "self-segregation" of students, which he said had grown to such an extent that even the large Latino population was fragmenting into "black, white, and brown" sub-identity groups.

"Why do you think," he said, "there is so much 'self-segregation' on campus? What do you think can be done to reverse this trend?"

"How do your faculty and staff behave on campus?" I asked.

"Just like the students," he replied. "In fact, we have the student equivalent of all the racial and ethnic associations of the faculty and staff. And they jointly plan and develop all of the programs, services, and events for minorities on our campus."

Realizing what I was getting at, he asked, "Do you mean to suggest our faculty and staff are responsible for the segregation of our campus?" He paused and then said, "Of course, they follow the lead of the faculty and staff who create all of these programs, services, and events that tell them to think like a group. That is what fragments and segregates the campus."

As we walked, he pointed out faculty and staff segregation on campus, including segregation of whites.

"Who are the role models on campus?" I asked.

"Faculty and staff," he replied. "So, you are suggesting that changing faculty and staff behaviors to reflect the desired goal of integration will influence students' behaviors?"

"Yes, in fact, isn't that the way it's supposed to work?"

"Yes, that makes sense," he remarked.

Then he dropped a bombshell on me. "Say, do you think that faculty and staff themselves do not feel comfortable in diverse settings and that they design these exclusive programs for their own comfort?"

"Of course," I exclaimed. "That must be the reason why many departments in the university remain all white!"

"Well, it's going to be very difficult to change the current situation on campus," he mused. "The interest groups are very well-organized and entrenched, and they will fight any attempts to change the status quo. I would not know where to begin."

"I guess it would require visionary and courageous leadership in order to *begin* the conversations that would *eventually* lead to change," I offered.

His last words to me were, "I'd like to see you become president of a state university one day just to see how you do it and how long you survive in the job."

Needless to say, I did not get the job. However, the experience helped convince me that "self-segregation" would only end when leaders set an example for others to emulate. It also convinced me that the persistence of this phenomenon could be linked to the lack of visionary and courageous leadership, especially (but not only) in universities and colleges where much of this is learned.

This experience is not unique. Over the past thirty years, I have encountered many similar situations. As a racially and ethnically ambiguous immigrant from West Africa, I have lived, learned, and worked in a nation whose people, institutions, and organizations are preoccupied with racial and ethnic identity as well as the politics associated with those issues to a degree that (to me) seems excessive and pathological.

Over the years, I have faced many attempts to force me to identify myself racially and ethnically. I have encountered those who have categorized me in order to reject me and those who have categorized me to accept me. Those wanting to co-opt me into supporting their political agenda have wooed me. America is so racially and ethnically politicized and polarized with such clearly drawn ideological lines that anyone who fails to join a political camp in this "war" may be attacked by anyone who has declared a political affiliation. The "if you're not with us, you're against us" mentality is alive and well. It is much like the dynamic force that draws city kids into gangs. If you're not a member of a gang, you can and will be persecuted by any member of any gang. Join us. Not only will we no longer persecute you (so long as you behave appropriately), but we will protect you from others who would persecute you. This logic tells us we should join the strongest gang and then go to any length to protect that status.

Much, though not all, of my experience as a person with no racial or ethnic identity or affiliations takes place in a unique context: the American higher education system. However, my experience is neither unique nor limited to this context. Around this fine country (of which I have become a citizen), I meet people who are regularly distressed by the ambiguity of their racial and ethnic background. I meet still others whose race and ethnicity are clear but who are distressed by others' insistence they share their politics, values, and causes if they share their race and ethnicity. However, rather than being members of a new minority called multiracial or nonracial peoples, I would argue for a status as a nongroup. I do not want a nonracial cultural center named after me. My highest aspiration in life is to have no cultural centers named after me!

I have become emotionally fatigued with racial intimidation, rejection, harassment, and retaliation for disloyalty or betrayal to the racial interests others would rather I had. My problem, which I have been told by many people who apparently understand how these things work, is not only that I am racially and ethnically ambiguous or that I claim to have no particular racial or ethnic identity, but that, in addition to these problems, I chose to pursue a career that traditionally thrives on these issues. If only my father had been a bit blacker and a bit less Lebanese or if only my mother had been a bit whiter and a bit less Susu, I could also have the peace and clarity of knowing my place and keeping to my own people. I once heard of a theory that says some people are drawn to careers and even spouses that draw out and accentuate their weaknesses or vulnerabilities. The idea is that you do this subconsciously in order to be faced with situations in which you learn and develop as a human being, that is, you mature by being faced with certain types of existential adversity. It is the only reasonable explanation I can think of for why I have done all of this to myself.

I personally do not think the problem is that I have refused to "identify" with any group. The challenges I have faced are with my refusal to pay the price I have been expected to pay for acceptance by a group. The expectations have always been clear: You are accepted into the group as long as you stay loyal to the interests of the leaders. In my experience of the diversity game, the price of acceptance has often been subservience to the ringleaders, who conceal their personal and selfish aims in racial and ethnic terms. This always leads to someone "outside" the group getting hurt in some way. In this climate, principled, thoughtful individuals eventually find themselves labeled a traitor and a sellout.

It may be that I am simply prideful, arrogant, or idealistic. Although I am all of those things as well, I like to think of myself as independent. I never felt a deep, personal need to belong to anything for a sense of identity or self-affirmation. I only ever wished to be allowed sovereignty over my own choices, my own desires, my own ideas, and my own values.

Before the Beginning of My American Adventure

I was born out of wedlock in West Africa in 1949 to a Lebanese father and a mother of mixed heritage comprised of Susu African, French, and English. Between 1955 and 1965, I lived in ten "foster homes" with Christian and Muslim Lebanese, Afro-Lebanese, as well as African and East Indian Hindu families. As a result, I was raised with no particular racial, ethnic, or religious identity This is because I never lived long enough with any particular family to have developed any particular identity.

When I lived with Lebanese families, I was identified as either African or "mulatto." In African homes, I was referred to as a "Syrian" child. The East Indians identified me as "Syrian" or "malata." The Muslims and Hindus did not involve me in their religious activities because they knew I came from a Christian Lebanese background and assumed this to be my religion. The African families I lived with were mostly nonreligious. Of the Christian Lebanese families, only the Catholic families forced me to attend church with them on Sunday. Some even enrolled me in Catholic schools. In the mid 1960s, I was enrolled in a Protestant boarding "reform" school, the Albert Academy. We were required to attend the Methodist church with which the school was affiliated. No efforts were made to convert me, and I did not live with any of the families for too long. I had also seen too many alternatives in my brief life to easily accept the idea that any of them were the "one true right path." While I learned about many races, ethnicities, and religions, I did not develop any affiliation or group identity during my early childhood years.

During the latter years of my teenage life when I lived with my father, he referred to himself as a "free thinker" and a "free born." (This may explain how he accumulated approximately twenty children with nine ethnically and racially different women, only one of whom was ever his wife) With an adult role model like that as a teenager, none of the diversity of my early years was counteracted. I sometimes used to think I might have been better off if I had grown up an African Christian, a Lebanese Muslim, an African Muslim, a Lebanese Christian, or even a devoutly converted Hindu. At least then I would have been able to identify friend and foe much easier. But I have learned over the years that my lack of a conventional identity is the root of my ability to truly recognize and appreciate diversity in all its forms.

In schools and in the street, I was referred to pejoratively to identify me as "other" in some way. Uneducated Africans referred to me as "white man," which was the least pejorative use. This was mostly an "innocent" description of my skin color (at least in comparison to theirs) and often did not carry a political agenda. The Krios were descendants of the thousands of former slaves "returned" to West Africa despite the fact that most were not from there. Uneducated Krios (returned slaves) used the term "malata" implying dirty. A popular song identified it as "coming from the gutter." Educated Krios, who comprise the vast majority of the educated class of West Africa, would use the term "Syrian." This was the most malicious of the three terms and was meant to deny the Lebanese population any meaningful identity. In 1890, when the French government dumped hundreds of Lebanese in West Africa (promising them it was America), Lebanon was a hostilely held province of Syria. It did not become a country until 1922. Therefore, calling a person of Lebanese descent a "Syrian" was a direct, intentional insult because it was common knowledge they preferred to be called "Lebanese." It would be akin to calling an Afghani "Russian" during the Soviet occupation. When you were called "Syrian," you could not dismiss it as ignorance. You had been insulted intentionally; anyone within earshot knew so.

To add insult to injury, when I prepared to leave for college in the United States, the West Africa government refused to issue me a passport because, as the official-in-charge told me, my father was not black. He explained the laws required that either my father or paternal grandfather had to be a Black African to qualify for citizenship. So, instead of a West Africa passport, he issued me an "Emergency Travel Document" that identified me as a citizen of the British Commonwealth. In addition to not having a racial, ethnic, or religious identity, I now had no national identity! This situation baffled the American immigration official at Kennedy Airport in New York City so much that I was detained for hours until it was determined I could legally enter the country. Even then, I was only allowed to enter because there were no laws or precedents at the time prohibiting my entry. I remain convinced they let me in only because they had no idea what else to do with me. There was no guideline, law, or precedence for denying me entry either! I wonder how immigration officials would regard a vaguely Lebanese-looking man with an Afro, no passport, and no citizenship today!

Soon after my arrival in America, I was asked to identify myself racially in order to secure a driver's license in Raleigh, North Carolina, where I was going to college. I responded by telling the clerk I had no race or ethnicity. Not content with my response, she called a supervisor who asked for my nationality. But, when I responded I did not have a nationality, he proceeded to ask me if I had a passport. Frustrated that I had no passport, he asked me to racially identify my parents. After which, he told me that I was considered a "Negro or black person" in America. My first driver's license listed me as "Negro." In Africa, I was white. In America, I was "Negro." Never the preferred race! The frustration of the clerk, I would learn, was typical in America. When I say I have no racial, ethnic, or even national identity, people have always believed I was trying to make a point, play a game, or just be evasive or unpleasant.

Later, I went to get a new driver's license after losing the original. This time, a different clerk identified me as "white" on the new license without asking. When I mentioned I had been classified as "Negro" in the previous license and was baffled she now identified me as "white" in the new, she called for her department's supervisor. He decided the racial classification should stay, but he wanted it to indicate in their records that I was really a "Negro" that looked white. This notation in the records got me curious.

I asked, "Sir, why do you want the records to have that notation?"

"Well, it's nothing really. It's just so the police would know what to look for if they are looking for you for any reasons," he explained.

"How does that work?" I asked.

"Well, as I said before, if, for example, they have a warrant for your arrest, the system will tell them they should be looking for 'Negro' who looks like a white man. Now that's not hard to understand, is it?" he responded.

"Well, it is confusing, to say the least," I explained.

"Well, it would be even more confusing to the police if we classified you as a 'Negro' when you look really white. Because they would be looking for a 'Negro' or a black person. This way, they would be looking for a white person and not a black person. Anyway, this has nothing to do with you. I don't even know why I am even explaining all this to you. That's the way it is, sir. Thank you," he explained as he walked in a back room and disappeared. This means that, in one year, I had gone from being white to being black to being white again. Amazing. What was even more interesting to me was that, a few months after I was issued the new driver's license identifying me as white, I found the original one, which identified me as black.

I decided to keep both licenses because they could come in handy with the girls I dated, who always wanted to know whether I was black or white before they dated me. The white girls were shown the license saying I was white (except for one that I sensed wanted something a little dangerous). Black girls were shown the license saying I was black. Those licenses were also very useful during college in Raleigh, North Carolina, because I was enrolled in a historically black college where the students always wondered (often aloud) whether I was white.

I moved to the Midwest during 1973 to enroll in a joint masters and doctoral program in African history and received a master's degree one year later in 1974. I was accepted into the doctoral program a year later and continued with my studies until 1978 when I returned from doing fieldwork for my dissertation on "Afro-Lebanese Identity in West Africa." Returning home after many years, I discovered that I was still white—no matter what one of my American driver's licenses said.

2

Who the Fuck Are You?

When I returned from doing my dissertation research in 1979, I was offered an opportunity to live and work as a graduate assistant at the Black Cultural Center at Midwestern State University. The director of the Black Cultural Center was an African-American, but he did not hesitate to hire me for the job as his assistant because he said he had confidence in my ability to do the job and that was more important to him than whether I was clearly black or white. I was from Africa, and I was a doctoral student in African history and Afro-American studies. And that was what he required for the job. I raised the issue of my racial ambiguity with him because I was aware the Black Cultural Center had always had an all-black staff and the students had expressed a desire to "keep the center staff all black." Unfortunately, a few months after he hired me for the job, he accepted a new position at another university and left town.

Nonetheless, I continued to live and work at the Black Cultural Center and excelled at most aspects of my job. In fact, things were going quite smoothly with the staff and operation of the BCC until some of the students who used the building began to attack me verbally every time I tried to enforce the center's policies. They had never done that before when I enforced these very same policies. To this day, I wonder what changed that. The building was an old fraternity house with approximately twenty-five rooms as well as two large living room areas and a large dance floor in the basement where dances were often held on the weekends. I was one of five student assistants who, on a rotating schedule, supervised the functions held in the building. Our job was to ensure the sponsors adhered to university policies and rules for the use of the facilities and to ensure that students' safety was not compromised.

I lived in the basement off to the side of the dance floor. If there was fighting, regardless of who was on duty that night, I was always the first on the scene. In the late 1970s, drugs and alcohol were plentiful on campuses. Midwestern State University was no exception. Fights were, unfortunately, a weekly occurrence, usually around 2:00 AM on Saturday nights. If I could get to the fight fast enough, I could stop it before it really disrupted the dance. However, if the fight had degenerated into a brawl, I had to declare the dance over, make everyone leave, and lock down the building. Being the guy who turned off the music and announced the end of the dance over the public address system made me an easy target for the anger that was typically still boiling in some individuals at this point. Being racially ambiguous provided them a target to direct this anger at.

On many occasions, some students refused to leave the building and challenged my authority to close down the center.

"Who the hell are you to tell us to leave? This is our center, and it is for black people."

"I am the staff in charge, and I'm closing down the building because the violence endangers the safety of students," I would respond.

"Why are you even here? You are not black; you have no goddamned right to drive us out of our center," they usually responded.

The new director was always very sensitive about the image of the BCC in the university and the community. He did not want the police called unless our physical safety was in danger or someone was badly hurt. I had to be patient but firm and hope they would leave peacefully. Sometimes, they did. Many times, they refused to leave and verbally assaulted me. Most frequently, however, they hung around to call me "goddamned Puerto Rican," "whitey," "honky," "cracker," or simply "motherfucker" to try to bait me into fighting with them. Even then, I really did not take offense at these epithets. I realized they were focusing on my race not because it was actually important, but because they were angry, violent, and looking for an excuse to express it. I knew then (as I do now) that it had a whole lot more to do with the personality and character of the individuals that would antagonize me than with my race or character.

After a while, they started to actively question why a white boy was living in a center for blacks. Black student leaders lobbied to have me expelled from the building and replaced by "someone who was black." When they were told I was from Africa, they insisted I was "white" because I did not "look black." The new director mentioned to me that leaders of the Black Student Union had gone to the office of the vice president for student affairs to complain they did not consider me to be black.

"Did you hear black students are demanding that only real black people should be hired in the Black Cultural Center?" he informed me, half-jokingly.

"What does that mean?" I asked, smiling. I did not realize his comment was in reference to me.

"They are pissed off at you and are charging you are an interloper in the Black Cultural Center that does not belong there," he responded.

"Me? How did it get this far? They have made such comments before, but I did not think they were that angry to have gone to the extent to pressure the vice president to push me out," I commented.

"Am I going to be pushed out of the center? I need to know so that I may look for somewhere else to live. Please let me know," I pleaded.

"Well, just be careful with them. My advice to you, in order to avoid any further confrontation that may escalate to demands for your removal, is to let the black staff members deal with black students when problems develop, particularly during their social events at night," he cautioned.

"Well, unfortunately, my room is on the same basement floor as the dance floor, just around the corner. I am the first person out on the floor soon after fighting breaks out late at night. What if no one comes down and there is an emergency? What should I do?" I asked, trying to get clarification.

"Well, just go fucking upstairs and get someone. I can't spell out every scenario for you. If you want to keep your ass in the center, then use your fucking head. These fucking niggers can get your sweet ass kicked out of here if you mess with them again. Leave them alone. This is coming from the vice president. I mean, man, just leave them alone, and get someone else to deal with them," he barked.

"Well, I have done nothing wrong, and now I feel as if I am somehow being made the problem when I was doing the right thing," I said.

"I don't give a sissified shit how you feel. Just keep the fuck away from these niggers, or they are going to kick your ass. And that will get my black ass fired. Do you hear me?" he responded.

"Sure. This is pandering in the worst sense," I said as I walked away in disgust. The following week, a black graduate student acquaintance approached me, warning me to be careful with the BSU members because some of them were threatening to "take me on" the next time I tried to prematurely end their party. I took the warning seriously and decided I would not intervene directly the next time fighting broke out during dances at the center. My plans were to either call one of the other student staff members or campus police, even though the latter may cause problems for the director. I was consistently counseled not to call the police because it would contribute to stereotyping of black students as unruly and violent. A police report would also create problems for the director with the university administration and may give them reasons to close down the center. Most of the time, the other staffers were able to handle the conflicts. However, because their rooms were not as close to the dance floor as mine, the fights had usually devolved into brawls by the time they got there. Thus, because of a few students' protests, the dances were prematurely ended more often than before—but by someone more satisfyingly black.

Although the facility was named the Black Cultural Center, it was not exclusively for blacks. All of its meeting rooms and social spaces were open to any member of the university community. Nonetheless, most people were under the impression the building was exclusively for blacks. In fact, blacks used it ninety-five percent of the time for their events, and the director was reluctant to advertise the fact the center was open to all because of the fear that increased use by others may make it difficult for black students to use the spaces when they needed them.

By the early 1980s, the number of Hispanics and Native Americans on campus had grown significantly as had their use of the BCC. By the beginning of the spring semester 1980, several Hispanic and Native American students began to complain to me that some black students were being hostile to them—apparently because they felt the center was no longer exclusive to blacks. Indeed, it had begun to feel more like a multicultural center than a Black Cultural Center. I advised them to speak with the director about their concerns. When they did, the director advised them that, if they followed the policy of reserving the space in advance, they had nothing to worry about because the facility was open to any member of the university.

But things went from bad to worse as increased numbers of other minorities began to use the building for their activities. Some black students became increasingly frustrated and resentful because of competition for use of the meeting rooms and dance floor. When the director told them they could not permanently reserve any space exclusively for blacks, their frustration led them to become increasingly more confrontational with the other students. Some even threatened to disrupt non-black events during prime times when blacks had used the spaces before. And this was precisely what happened one evening when I was on duty.

It was around 7:00 PM when I heard a loud argument, stomping feet, and sounds of slamming doors coming from the second floor of the building. I was sitting at the front desk when a handful of black students walked past me and up the staircase to the second floor. A second wave of black students briskly followed them a few minutes later. Soon after, I heard commotion coming from one of the meeting rooms on the second floor. I rushed upstairs to find a Hispanic student standing inside the room, confronted by the black students who were standing outside in the hallway and forcefully holding the door open as the two groups of students argued about the use of the meeting room.

As I approached them, I asked both groups of students to back off from the door and to ease the confrontational posture each side had taken.

"But we are not the problem here," pleaded one of the Hispanic students inside the room.

"Oh yeah? This is the Black Cultural Center. It's our meeting room. We've been using it for years," one of the black students demanded.

"We made reservations for the use of this room three weeks ago, and we are not leaving until the meeting is over," a Hispanic student inside the room responded.

I told the black students they could have the use of the room after the Hispanic students' meeting was over. I also reminded them that priority for the use of the facilities was given to those with a reservation. I reiterated the policy on reservations and recommended that, in order to avoid confusion in the future, they should make a reservation.

"Who the fuck are you to tell us to make reservations? This is the Black Cultural Center. Black students should not have to make reservations, and we should have priority."

"Why are you always against black people on this campus?" said another.

"You are not even black, and you are living for free in the center we fought for," he continued.

"You are taking the space and job that should have gone to a black student. We want you to get the fuck out of this center before we kick your motherfuckin' honky ass out of here," someone else concluded.

As they left the building, one of them said, "We better not have problems with the use of the dance floor for our annual Halloween dance."

I opened the schedule for rooms and almost fainted when I saw LASA (Latin American Student Association) scribbled across the calendar on Halloween night. At this point, I thought the best response would be to tell them to call the director the next day to confirm their reservation. This would give me enough time to forewarn the director of potential trouble.

As they left, one of them said, "If we can't have the dance floor on Halloween night, no one else can have it."

"And we are going to demand that, when we meet with Vice President Stone, they get your white, honky ass out of our building," said another.

The following week, Hispanic students wrote to the president detailing their grievances with the black students' attitude regarding the use of the Black Cultural Center. They demanded the university provide them their own cultural center. In response, the vice president came to the center to meet with the director and the staff to discuss the problems between black and Hispanic students and to solicit suggestions regarding possible solutions. I recommended he consider broadening the mission and name of the center. As one possible solution, I also suggested the building be renamed a Minority Student Center with a diverse staff. He thought it was a good suggestion, but he wondered how the more vocal black students would react to those changes.

The other staff members did not like my suggestions because they believed black students would view the changes negatively. All of them threatened to resign if my suggestions were implemented. They also promised they and other black students would fight any changes in the mission of the center. They suggested the Hispanic students be given their own separate building. But the vice president was not inclined to do that because of the financial cost. He informed us he would announce his decision in the following week.

A week later, the vice president announced the facility would be changed to the Minority Student Center beginning in the fall of 1980. He also announced the facility would be renovated during the summer and would have a diverse staff representative of all minorities on campus. Among the residential staff, there would be two blacks, two Hispanics, two Asians, and two Native Americans. He also informed me I would continue as the "international" graduate assistant to the director.

Many black students, faculty, and staff at Midwestern State denounced the decision and chided the vice president, who was black, as a "sellout." Many vowed to boycott the new center and threatened to burn down the building if the university painted over the black, green, and red emblem symbolizing the black liberation flag, which was painted in the front of the building. The administration decided not to paint over the flag in order to avoid problems with the BSU. For as long as I worked in the center thereafter, non-black students and staff protested the presence of the black liberation flag in front of the building. As far as they were concerned, the presence of the flag signified that, as one Hispanic put it, "Blacks will always see the center as theirs, and Hispanics will always feel cheated."

Over the summer of 1980, the director and I worked on reviewing the applications from minority students and selecting student representatives for the new staff of the center. The new student staff we selected comprised of two blacks, three Hispanics, one Native American, and one Asian. Among their duties were staffing the building when it was open, program planning, and development for each of the constituent minority groups on campus. The new staff began arriving in late August 1980, just before the fall semester began. My job was to welcome them as they arrived at the Minority Student Center, usher them to their respective rooms, give them each a set of keys, and provide each a detailed orientation to the center, its programs, policies, and their job responsibilities.

Despite all odds, the fall of 1980 turned out to be the happiest times of my life. It all began on a Wednesday around 8:00 PM As I was getting ready (both physically and…uh…spiritually) for reggae night at the University Union, a beautiful, young woman literally walked into my living room and announced her presence. She was the first of the new staff to arrive at the center.

My first words were, "Thank you, Lord, for this delectable delivery."

"How did you get into to the building?" I asked.

"I came through one of the open windows in the back of the building," she replied.

"Why?" I responded.

"Because the doors are locked and you couldn't hear me knocking because you're playing your music too loud," she smirked.

"Oh, I am sorry. I forgot you were arriving this evening," I said, smiling (probably too broadly) at her.

"What is your name?" I asked curiously.

"Marisol," she replied.

"That's a beautiful name," I said.

"Would you please help me with my luggage? I have them just outside the back door," she asked.

"Sure, sure. I would do anything you want," I grinned dumbly as I stumbled into the armrest of my couch.

"By the way, which group are you here to represent?" I asked.

"I am the president of the Graduate Hispanic Social Work Student Association," she replied.

"But you look American Indian-ish. Apache, are you?" I asked.

"Well, I am really Tejano. You know many people who identify as Hispanic from Texas have Mayan blood, Chiricahua Apache blood, or both running through their veins," she explained.

"Sure, that's exotic! Brown sugar. I like it already," I said in utter excitement.

I followed her to the back of the building to get her suitcase and helped her to her third-floor room. As I left the room, I invited her to reggae night as my date. She agreed with an approving smile. We agreed to meet in my suite at 9:00 PM. That was it. I was in love with her from the moment she walked into my room.

We continued to date until we were told in the summer of 1981 that the new policy of the center prohibited dating and cohabitation between staff members. That was when we moved out of the Minority Student Center into graduate student housing. We were married that fall and moved away in the summer of 1982.

3

150 Minutes to Come up With Some Bullshit to Impress Them

My dissertation had run into a little snag in 1982. My advisor had resigned to take a position in Nigeria. There was one other professor at MSU that would be appropriate for me. He reluctantly agreed to take me on, adding I would have to scrap the three chapters of my dissertation I had already written and the year of fieldwork in West Africa I had done. I would also have to take several of his courses and then start my dissertation over. I began, instead, searching for permanent employment immediately.

My journey from Midwestern State University to New England State University (NESU) began with a telephone call in late April 1982 from NESU's executive dean to offer me the position of director of the Educational Opportunities Program (EOP). The $32,000 they offered me in 1982 was a phenomenal amount of money to a third-world immigrant who had been living on graduate student stipends.

The position reported to the dean of student affairs, and my first task was to design and develop a comprehensive retention program for minorities. This program was intended to incorporate a smaller student retention program developed by Darlene Mossey, a master's degree student in the counseling program at NESU. When I was hired, she was already the part-time director of that program, which had been supported by a grant for three years.

My other primary task was to incorporate a state-supported summer residential program for incoming freshmen minority students who failed one or more components of the placement tests in math, reading, and writing. The idea was for the EOP to evolve from these two separate, limited programs into a comprehensive, orchestrated effort to retain minorities. My instructions were to have the new program designed and developed to receive the first cohort student group by the following fall in 1983.

I applied for jobs before finishing graduate school because my situation at MSU had become untenable, and I was tired of not having money. I had applied for this particular job because I had been working at MSU in positions that directly supported students and enjoyed it. I never really intended to get a position supporting only minority students. However, in the United States, it seems there is an unintentional tracking of minorities into positions working with minorities. It is as if there is an assumption that, if someone is black, they are by nature committed to and competent for only "black" causes and interests. There is also an assumption that there is something wrong with them if they are not so committed and interested.

Some critics have called this kind of professional-cultural tracking a form of discrimination. Supposedly, the fact that blacks are some of the strongest supporters of this viewpoint does not change that fact. They are "Uncle Toms," or they are good brothers and sisters who have been brainwashed. Then others say we have to stick together and look out for each other. That is why a successful black man has to dedicate himself to serving blacks. Supposedly, this leads to solidarity rather than the realization of the Jim Crow mantra of "separate but equal." I cannot speak for the logic the administrators at NESU used when they hired me. All I know is that people are always much more interested in my race and ethnicity than I am.

I have already made it clear that I have no race. But, back in those days, my frustration with race and ethnicity had not yet reached a critical mass. I would tell anyone who cared to listen that I had no race, ethnicity, or religion. But I didn't shout it from a bullhorn or wear a sign that said, "Move along. No race or ethnicity to see here." Okay, so I don't do that now either, although I am much more outspoken about it. But somehow, I do not know if it would make a difference if I did shout it from a bullhorn or wear a sign.

In any event, I realize now that NESU must have hired me for that position on the assumption that I was black or clearly a minority at the very least. My vitae, of course, reflected that I grew up in Africa, studied African history, and had played soccer for a historically black college when I came to the United States. Back in those days, I also wore my hair in an Afro. Nonetheless, NESU did not *seem* the least bit interested in my race or ethnicity when they hired me. That would quickly change.

As Darlene and I reviewed the university's student attrition and academic probationary data, we realized the university had a very serious problem retaining students that went beyond minorities. In addition to a high dropout rate for all students, we discovered a significant number of all students were on academic probation every year. The connection between the dropout rate and probation numbers became clear to us and compelled us to advocate the development of an even more comprehensive and inclusive retention effort. Consequently, we proposed the new EOP be a major retention program open to all students who failed one or more parts of the university's placement tests. We also recommended a large and more comprehensive student services office be developed in order to bring together other related programs as well as to develop new retention programs.

By spring 1983, the university administration enthusiastically endorsed our proposal for the development of a more comprehensive retention strategy, despite the fact it would require a moderate budget and staff. Nevertheless, not everyone was happy with the proposal to broaden the mission of both of the existing programs to include other students. Several black faculty members strongly opposed the proposal. One of them had been an applicant for my position and was said to be bitter about not getting the job. Others who opposed the changes were known for advocating continued segregation of races on campus by establishing separate services and programs for minorities.

Over their objections, the president approved our proposal and appointed me the new director of student services. He also reassigned the disabled students services office, the veteran's services office, and the international student services office to report to me. I had been hired to get the EOP up and running in one year. Six months later, I had managed to not only get a promotion but a much bigger task to accomplish. And I only had six months left in which to do it.

Because of my promotion, I had to hire a replacement for myself, along with several part-time positions to administer the respective budgets for several new retention programs and services. After the EOP design was approved, I developed a job description for the director's position and began the search process. Just before I advertised the job vacancy, I spoke with the director of affirmative action. I told him I believed Darlene Mossey had shown initiative and commitment in the creation and development of the previous program and had worked part-time as program director for the past five years. I also mentioned she was instrumental in the designing of the new EOP. I already had a good working relationship with her, and I would like to hire her now if I could. It was also important for me to hire someone immediately because we needed to have the program up and ready to receive the first class in the fall of 1983, which was now less than six months away. He advised me I did not have to advertise the position if I really wanted to hire her for the position and approved the search waiver for me to hire Darlene as the director of the new EOP program.

I was much relieved that I could now work with Darlene to hire the counseling staff for the program and work to develop the EOP processes and accompanying forms, letters, and program literature. Little did I know that, in less than a week, there were going to be major distractions from business. As it turned out, several black faculty members had gone to talk with the university's president to protest the waiver. A few individuals who had expressed interest in the position felt slighted because they were not given an opportunity to compete for the position.

These individuals agitated the Black Student Union (BSU), who staged a demonstration on campus protesting the hiring of a "white Jewish woman" over "more qualified blacks." A black administrator who supported the programmatic changes I had made informed me that one of the protestors had expressed disappointment over the decision to hire Darlene instead of doing an open search for the director's position. He advised me to ignore comments about my race and ethnicity that certain individuals were making.

He added that some students had told him they had overheard someone at the demonstration declaring, "A black director of student services would not have made the same decision. Let's face it. Someone black in that position would not have hired a white, Jewish woman when so many black folks wanted that job."

A few weeks later, the president invited me to a meeting with the BSU to talk about the "plans for the new student program we were developing." He asked I meet with him to discuss some of his ideas before our joint meeting with students.

As I walked into his apparently empty office, I heard him somewhere saying, "Samir, you have nothing to worry about because you have the support of Tom, Sarah, and Vinny. Those who are trying to go after you have no supports, but they are formidable because they have the backing of the local NAACP president, who, by the way, was an applicant for your position. And he is jealous of you." I then saw him tying his necktie inside his office's restroom.

"I am going to announce in the meeting with the BSU that a new office of minority student services will be created in the fall of 1983 to complement the new programs you will be developing. What do you think?" he asked.

"Why would you want to make that announcement?" I asked.

"Because it will get them off our assess for a while. In fact, the president of the BSU, the Black Muslim kid, is a senior. That means he won't be around next year to make trouble, and that will give us breathing room," he responded.

"What will be the purpose of this new program?" I asked

"That's where you will come in. You have 150 minutes to come up with something that will impress them. You are really good at this kind of bullshit. Really good actually. Impress them with all that same bullshit you sold those bastards in the undergraduate curriculum committee last week," he urged me.

"But remember that, whatever you sell them, you will have to pay for from your current budget. There will be no additional allocation of new funds. My advice to you is to stick to generalities. Don't give them any specifics. You can promise to give them specifics later," he added.

"Where and at what time do you want me to meet you before the noon meeting?" I asked.

"Meet me at 11:50 AM in the basement lounge of the library," he responded.

"I will do my best. But there's one thing that I will not do, and that is change the central philosophy of program development to support diversity and inclusion. I will not develop any segregated and exclusive programs, services, or events," I responded.

"I know you won't. I have full confidence in you. Just give them some bullshit that will shut them up. You know how they are," he assured me as he walked back into the bathroom.

As I left the president's office, I started to have mixed feelings about the whole thing. On the one hand, I felt good the president had confidence in my ability. On the other, I felt disappointed that he sounded like a flimflam man and that I was being put in the untenable situation of flimflamming the BSU members in the upcoming meeting. I was also somewhat concerned that he thought my ideas were "bullshit." Did he really think I was serving some secret goal of his while telling people what they wanted to hear? I could tell there was a great disconnect between the president and I. I was acting on principles while he seemed to have some kind of agenda I could not quite grasp just yet.

I went straight from the president's office to see my boss, Paul Daniels, the dean of student affairs. He informed me the president had not spoken with him about it and said he was not surprised. He encouraged me to talk with one of the BSU leaders, Janie Musser, whom he felt was a reasonable person, to find out what the students wanted to accomplish at the meeting with the president. He believed this information might be helpful in formulating my thoughts.

As I left the dean's office, I ran into Janie at the entrance of the president's office and talked with her briefly about the purpose of the noon meeting. She told me the BSU members wanted an office that dealt with the needs of black students on campus. She said this was in response to my attempts to integrate all the programs, services, and events that fell within the student services office.

"Some of the students feel betrayed by your efforts and are adamant about their demands for an office of black student affairs. There are others, like myself, who are willing to settle for what President Gallo is proposing. A Minority Student Services-type program that will incorporate other minorities," she said.

"What types of services would you want a Minority Student Services program to provide to the students?" I asked.

"Budget and administrative support for the minority celebrations, mentoring, advisors for their organizations, bus tours, and field trips. That sort of thing," she said.

"Thanks, I'll see you at noon," I said.

As she left, I realized she had just been to see the president. That is how she knew about the MSS proposal. The trick now for me was what I should tell the students when the president called on me to explain the purpose of the new MSS program. I did not want to lie to them, and I did not want to make any specific commitment before I knew what they wanted. So, it occurred to me to just go in there, ask a lot of questions, listen carefully to what they had to say, and promise to consider their concerns and suggestions in formulating the design of the new service.

This actually seemed to work quite well. The meeting went very smoothly. The president was pleased; the students were pleased with the exchange of ideas. Some promised to bring me their individual ideas about the new program in the following weeks. I felt good because I now would have time to consider all of my options for the program's development. I had at least bought myself some time to figure out how to get out of this bind with my integrity intact.

As we walked out of the library toward the Administration Building, the president put his arm around my shoulder.

He said, "Paison, the ball is now in your court. run with it. You have the gift of gab like a good Italian. I admire that in you. It will serve you well in academia," he mused.

"Gift of gab?" I thought. "All I did was listen."

By fall of 1983, we had developed most of the student retention programs, including the EOP, the Campus Tutorial Center, and the Campus Writing Center. These new programs brought the total number of programs under the student services administration structure to six. The now-integrated EOP program had taken its first cohort group of students during the fall. About one-third of the 150 students in the new EOP program had gone through the residential summer EOP program for students who failed all three components of the university's placement test in reading, writing, and math. But not everyone was pleased.

Some black faculty and staff were not pleased and continued to oppose the program.

By mid-January 1984, I had designed a program called Minority Student Services. It was administratively located in the student services office and would provide black and Hispanic students assistance with planning their celebrations and events. President Gallo was delighted and praised me for having an "imaginative mind."

A few weeks after he approved of the program design, he announced the new program as a major initiative and mailed copies of the program description to the individuals who had written to him in the fall proposing the creation of a minority affairs office at NESU. The students accepted it, but some faculty and staff could see through the "smoke and mirrors" and reacted angrily because they knew the administration did not really support their proposal. It failed to create services exclusively for black students, which was what they had wanted all along.

In March, Paul Daniels asked me to develop an academic retention program for all students in the residence halls who were on academic probation. He asked that I submit a proposal entailing all of the above by May because there was a high probability that it would be funded. Most importantly, if it was approved by June, it could be put into operation before the students arrived on campus by August. He emphasized that developing this program was a major university priority and encouraged me to give it my best.

Working with a small group of my staff and people from the university housing offices, we designed the Residential Educational Program (REP) and wrote a proposal to house it in the largest freshman hall, along with a comprehensive set of academic support services for all students available until 10:00 PM The program was cost-effective because the design called for hiring high school teachers and guidance counselors as well as graduate student interns in the College of Education's counseling program. It was enthusiastically received by the administration and pronounced "futuristic" by the housing staff. In June, the president approved both the design and budget and instructed us to have it operating by August of that very year.

Sometime in June 1984, Marisol was offered an opportunity to serve as the director of the largest co-ed residence hall with 500 residents. This was a great personal and professional opportunity. On the professional side, Marisol also functioned in the capacity of resident therapist. (She was doing limited psychological counseling with the students in the hall.) It was also the residence hall in which the REP program was situated. The location was perfect for me because I could keep track of the program's development from close proximity. We moved into the five-room suite allocated to the hall director in early August and set up shop, ready for the start of the fall semester.

A few months after hiring Marisol for this fabulous position, the director of housing, Angelo Rossi, approached me, saying he had a serious problem with a senior female faculty member. He said this faculty member had alleged in the Faculty Senate that he was misspending and misappropriating housing funds. This faculty member also alluded that corruption was the reason the housing office had been audited twice in the past couple years. Now, he said he had thought up a plan to discredit and silence her once and for all. He needed my help.

"Do you know Janet Macaulay in the Advising Center?" he asked me.

"Yes, I do. I have worked with her on a number of projects," I replied.

"Good. You know she's the one who has been running her mouth in the Faculty Senate and has threatened everything we've got here. She is on a personal vendetta against me. And I think she is in league with Benny, the former fire marshal, with whom I've had some problems," he said.

"Now, you know I have helped you out many times because of my connection to President Gallo. I got you significant salary and budget increases, gave your wife a job, free housing, and office space for the REP program. I can be of tremendous help in the future if you'll do me a favor," he added.

"It depends on what you're asking me to do," I replied.

"Well, how well do you know Vince Richards in the College of Education? The black faculty member who runs the Summer Opportunity Program (SOP). That's Vinny, isn't it?" he asked.

"Yes, you know he is a good friend of mine. Why?" I asked.

"Very good. Here is the plan. I was told by someone who was present at the time that, during the summer registration of SOP minority students, Janet Macaulay was very rude to black students in the Advising Center. I heard she was particularly very abusive in her treatment of black students. Here's what I think you can do for me. Can you tell Vinny about Janet's behavior toward black students? I've heard you know Vinny very well, don't you?" he asked.

"I know him very well. But I can't go along with this. I also know Vinny will never agree to do it. He is a man of integrity. In fact, he is a minister and teaches part-time theology in a seminary," I replied.

"I know. That's why if he, being black and a man of high integrity, condemns her as racist it will have more of a sting than if it were you or Darlene who condemned her," he responded.

"Well, I have many problems with what you are proposing. Does the president know about this? What does he think about it?" I asked.

"I am working through Dean Bunker on this. We need to shield the president from direct involvement in it. You know, because he is the president, each one of us is expected to cover his ass, even if it means diving for the bullet. But he knows what's going on."

"I have a lot of problems with this. But I have to go now. I'll be in touch later. Let me find out first what really happened in the Advising Center with the SOP students." I ended the conversation, having bought myself some time to think. I also began to realize how this group had built a web of deceit and was trying to ensnare me in it.

That afternoon, I received a telephone call from Vince Richards. He said he had received a call from Angelo regarding "the racist mistreatment of black students by Janet Macaulay in the Advising Center." Vince said Angelo had told him I had asked he report the incident to him because he was the program director. He also said Angelo had said I would be calling him to discuss the situation and a response strategy. And, before I could say anything, he informed me he was familiar with what happened in the incident Angelo was referring to and had already dealt with the matter. He said that he could not even imagine what Angelo was up to, but he did not want any part in it. That is when I told him everything Angelo had told me, but I quickly added I had told Angelo that, not only was I not interested, but I was certain that he, Vince, would never go along with it. Before we hung up, Vince mentioned he might leave NESU for a permanent position at a theological seminary in South Carolina. I was relieved that my assessment of Vinny had been accurate and that I was out of the frying pan for now. But I also knew that it was to be only a temporary respite.

The next day, I went to talk with Angelo about my decision and Vince's reaction to his proposal. He said, "Don't back out on me. I took a lot of risk asking you to do this. Don't let us down. You owe us this one. We need you. Don't betray us like this." He went on and on until I stopped him.

"No. No. No. Angelo, I can't do this. I will go and talk with President Gallo about my decision," I replied and left his office.

The next day, I went to talk with the president about my concerns regarding my conversations with Angelo and the possible repercussions for his administration. He listened intensely to what I had to say.

He then said, "Samir, thanks for coming to talk to me about this. You know I have known Angelo for over forty years. We were boyhood friends, went to NESU as students, and worked here until I became president. Angelo is my buddy. He is like a brother to me I tried to stop him, but I could not. You know how strong-headed he is. You are the only one that can stop him. Help me. Angelo has a lot of respect for you, and I think you can persuade him to stop by telling him what you just told me. Tell him about what this might do to my administration if it gets out or backfires."

"I will do what I can, but I will look to you for cover if he turns against me or gets angry because I know how malicious he can get. I may have to tactfully confront him to drop the matter before it is too late," I responded.

"Please do. I'll cover you. I'll even talk with Dean Bunker about this," he promised.

"Okay, I'll try," I promised.

A week later, I was summoned to Dean Bunker's office for a meeting. I found him standing beside his desk, shuffling through stacks of papers and folders as he looked for something when I arrived. As I tried to take a seat, he instructed me to continue standing because he was not going to be long with me. He proceeded to reprimand me for going directly to the president regarding my concerns about Angelo's behavior. He referred to everything I had said to the president as "hearsay and assumptions" and warned me to be careful about where I repeated false rumors because he said he had become "very thin-skinned" about my behavior. I told him that I did not appreciate the way he was talking to me and walked out of his office.

The next day, I went to talk again with Angelo about abandoning the idea of going after Janet Macaulay. I mentioned I had talked with both the president and Dean Bunker about his proposal. Neither was in favor of it. He said he had already spoken to both of them about it. He said, "Dean Bunker was acting like an asshole." He said Dean Bunker was trying to pull rank with him. He proceeded to tell me Dean Bunker had recently crashed his brand-new Audi 5000 on his way home while driving drunk one evening. He was under investigation for leaving the scene of an accident, and that is what was eating him up.

"If he doesn't watch it, someone in the police department might find out about his drinking that night because there were witnesses to the accident. At any rate, just forget about it. I will find another way to deal with that old witch."

Sometime in October, my wife Marisol, told me that, of late, she had noticed Angelo had become more authoritarian in his dealings with her. He had even yelled at her about some minor issue the other day. She said she did not tell me about it because she was not sure about it at first. But, she said he had done it several times since, and she was now certain he was taking his anger with me out on her. She felt strongly we should start looking for opportunities to leave because she feared for our safety. We both recognized we were caught in the web of a corrupt administration—what many faculty members called the mafia administration of NESU.

In November, Angelo called me to talk with me about allegations that my wife was a drug abuser. He informed me he was trying to "kill the complaints a number of students had filed against her." He needed me to come by his office to discuss the matter with him. I asked him why he was calling me when the allegations were made against Marisol. He said this was a matter we needed to talk about—"man to man." So, I walked over to his office to find out what he was up to this time. When I arrived, he was very friendly as he offered me a cold beer and talked about working closely again together. He assured me, like a good friend, he had buried the complaints against Marisol. He said his recent stern behavior toward her was the result of the other director's complaint that he was giving Marisol preferential treatment because she was his "best friend's wife." They felt he never came down hard on her when she messed up, so he started to pretend he was coming down hard on her to keep them off his back. He expressed his hope she understood what was happening and did not take it personally.

I told him that both Marisol and I were tired of playing power games and were not interested in being part of the family he always spoke about. I also informed Paul Daniels that I was planning to move on professionally because I could no longer accept the behavior of Angelo and Dean Bunker. I asked for his support as a job reference. He agreed and promised to help. He assured me he fully understood my concerns, particularly about Angelo.

By spring of 1985, I was trying desperately to leave NESU. Marisol was scared to be in the residence hall director's apartment by herself throughout the Christmas holidays because she was aware that Angelo had the master key to all the residential buildings. I installed extra locks on the front door to provide additional security. In March of that year, to the relief of my family, I received a job offer from Traditional Tech University in Ohio.

Before I resigned my position as director of student services in April, I went to talk with the president again regarding my concerns about Angelo's behavior and the problems they were creating in the university. He thanked me for having "done an excellent job." He thanked me for my efforts to help him with Angelo. A week later, I received a general letter of reference from him, without my asking. A few days after that, I received another letter of reference from Dean Bunker and a note of appreciation for my service to the university. Why were *they* kissing *my* ass? It seemed clear they were happy I was leaving and wanted to facilitate that.

They also did not want me leaving pissed off and trying to cause any trouble for them.

4

Will the Distinguished Gentleman Please Shut Up?

We moved to the Midwest in June 1985, and I started working at Traditional Tech University (TTU) as associate dean for minority programs in June. The university was a private and conservative institution with one of the oldest medical colleges in the nation. The new president, Anthony Jurgens, was a former provost at a conservative Ivy League school during a period of racial turmoil in the early 1980s. He had become very sensitive to diversity issues by the time he arrived at TTU in 1984. One year after his arrival, he announced a major minority affairs initiative and created the position of associate dean for minority programs to lead the initiative.

My first priority that fall was to design minority recruitment and retention programs along with budgets and a major grant proposal directed to fund the office's programs. It took me about a month to become settled and hire a secretary before I could begin any work on the design of the Minority Retention Program (MRP), as it came to be called.

By September 1985, my boss, Alice Taylor, dean of student affairs, was polishing the final draft of the program design and the grant proposal for $1.5 million addressed to the Metropolitan Community Foundation for the university. By October, the proposal was at the foundation's office. By November, after a revision, the proposal was approved and scheduled to begin by June 1986. The difficult question that now needed to be answered was who would be the director of the new program. Sarah David, director of the Multicultural Engineering Program (MEP), believed the new program should be under her supervision with a separate director. She also believed she should be made assistant dean for minority programs and actively lobbied for it. I recommended the new director report directly to me (and not Sarah) because of my concerns she would politicize the new program as she had done with the MEP. Many faculty and administrators had urged me to keep the new program away from her, or the MRP would lack credibility on campus. I was told she frequently mobilized students against faculty and the administration to get her way and was not trusted in the administration. It was this negative image of her that worked against her when she applied for the position for which I was eventually hired (which I am sure started us off on good terms).

As the administration deliberated about what to do about the MRP, Alice Taylor received a letter from a group of black students outlining their concerns the university was not responsive to their needs and demanding a meeting with the dean. I attended the meeting with Alice and black student leaders from the MEP, who had a list of grievances and some suggestions about how the university might respond both to the individual and the overall concern. The underlying agenda in all of the "suggestions" was that Sarah be given supervision over MRP. It was quite clear to Alice and me that Sarah orchestrated the meeting. It was meant as a warning shot to the administration, and the warning shot was heard loud and clear. Within a few weeks, the new MRP was handed over to Sarah. I was told the president did not want any trouble with blacks on campus or in the community. Needless to say, I was very disappointed about the decision. My goal for the program was successful at retaining minority students. The president's goal, however, was appeasement of political tensions. I was very worried that Sarah would bury the program's genuine purpose in service of her political and personal goals.

In October 1985, I was invited to attend the Black Faculty and Staff Association (BFSA) meeting by one of the officers of the organization. The purpose was to introduce me to their membership. At the lunchtime meeting, I was asked to say a few words about my primary focus for the first few years of my administration. I spoke broadly about the need to increase minority representation in the student body, faculty, and administration. I emphasized the need to focus on women, blacks, and Hispanics for the first few years. I mentioned the university was doing well in terms of Asian faculty and students because of their significant presence in the technology programs of the university, which accounted for a substantial portion of the students and faculty.

At the end of my comments, Dan Silver, the president of the BFSA and an associate professor in the School of Dentistry, expressed grave concerns about my comments. He said he was frustrated with the fact that my "priority lacked focus." He suggested I visit the archives and read some of the reports he authored. He added, "Let me say this. Go to the archives and get copies of two reports I've written in the past twenty years that have dealt with these issues. On two different occasions, I chaired two different committees that wrote two different reports that addressed these issues. Neither of which were implemented. Read them, and you will find the focus you need. Then you can come back and tell us about your primary focus."

"Thank you, we intend to make this an open and inclusive process and look forward to future dialogue about BFSA concerns as we develop a strategic plan," I replied, trying my best to show indifference to his tone.

A week after the BFSA meeting, Kathy Rivers, director of the Upward Bound Program, and I went to lunch to talk about the progress in the "minority initiatives." At the end of lunch, she said to me that Dan Silver had spoken to her about his concerns that, when I speak about the minority affairs agenda, I should focus on blacks as the primary focus. She said the focus of those reports that Dan was alluding to in his comments focused exclusively on blacks. She advised me that, in order to avoid conflict with Dan in the future, I should refrain from mentioning the other minorities when I speak to the BFSA. I thanked her for the feedback, but I affirmed that I would not permit Dan Silver to censure my speech. Besides, the mission statement of the office and my job description were clear about the focus of this initiative. It was inclusive and named all of the other groups he did not want to hear about.

In December 1985, Tom James, the associate dean of the College of Medicine, said (almost as an afterthought) that I was to attend the next BFSA meeting with him. He said he had not been active in the association, but he was interested in this particular meeting because they were asking to hear from him about the minority affairs program in the medical school, particularly about the large grant he had just received from the Robert Wood Johnson Foundation. I debated whether I should warn him about Dan Silver's edict against talking about other minorities, but I did not want to bias his perception of Dan or the BFSA, so I chose not to warn him. James' presentation went well, and no one said anything about his references to other minorities.

Everything was going well at the meeting until Dan got to the BFSA Christmas Party item on the agenda. He announced, "There are three things we must decide today. First, do we want to host the party on or off campus? Second, do we want to invite white folks? And finally, who wants to volunteer to help plan it?"

"Well, as I see it, the question about whether we invite white folks depends on whether we have it on campus. If we do it off campus, there is no question about it. I don't want them there," someone in the audience said.

"Well, yes. But, even if we have it on campus, we don't have to invite them if we don't want to," responded Dan.

"I have a question. What do you suggest to BFSA members whose spouses are white?" I asked.

"Well, we are not going into that because that is their personal problem. They knew what they were getting into when they chose to marry a white person. They need to figure that out for themselves. That's the kind of problem they create when they do that sort of thing," responded Dan to my question.

"My wife is white. What do they expect me to do? This is terrible," Tom James whispered to me.

"Let's get the hell out of here. I have to leave. These individuals are just a bunch of angry people. I can't be associated with an organization like this," Tom said as he walked out of the meeting.

As we left the meeting, I now chose to mention my experience with Dan Silver and his behavior at the BFSA meeting at which I spoke in October. He again asserted he would never again attend their meetings as long as Dan remained president.

A week later, I received an invitation to the BFSA Christmas reception to be held in a large, on-campus meeting room. I was told, as a compromise, they were planning two different Christmas parties: one off campus for black folks and the other on campus that would be inclusive. Apparently, someone had talked with Dan regarding concerns that his rhetoric was tarnishing the image of the BFSA. The Christmas party on campus was well-attended with many senior white administrators present in attendance. I showed up for fifteen minutes and left as the socializing began just after all of the obligatory speeches of goodwill and so forth.

A day after I had conducted a presentation to students on the diversity goals of TTU, a student who had been very argumentative and had voiced his concern we "not sacrifice quality for quantity" during the presentation came to speak with me at my office.

I recognized him as soon as he walked in to my office. As I welcomed him, I asked jovially, "What can I refuse to do for you?"

"Well, I am not here to argue the merits or demerits of diversity but to ask your advice on a problem I am having," he replied.

"I hope I can help. But first, let me ask you a question What was really bothering you at the presentation the other day? You dominated the conversations with your concerns and left some in attendance with the impression you were against having blacks at the university. You were very articulate and assertive about your position and spoke with authority about your concerns that the university not discriminate against white students in the admissions processes. Are you opposed to admitting blacks at TTU?" I asked.

"Oh, no. I went to school with many blacks in Indiana and played basketball with them. I have many black friends and believe in equal opportunity for all. I am not a racist—far from it. I was speaking as president of the Student Senate. The Student Senate had asked me to attend your presentation to represent their concerns, and I committed to do so to the best of my ability. Some members of the Senate might have been influenced by prejudice in their concerns, but not me—far from it. In fact, I am here to ask for your advice about a related problem I am having with my parents," he responded.

"What can I do for you?" I asked

"Well, I am having a difficult time with my father because my fiancée is Korean. He doesn't want me to marry her and has threatened to disown me if I do. He keeps referring to her as Chinese and believes marrying her is an act of racial suicide. He claims we'll have 'Chinese kids and not white' and likens it to marrying a 'nigger.' He is adamant about it and keeps saying that. When a white person has a child with a 'nigger,' the kids are 'niggers not white.' He wants me to marry a good white girl from Indiana and keeps asking me, 'What's wrong with white women? Your mother is a white woman.' It has gotten so bad that I don't even go home anymore to visit. In fact, I am moving to Canada, where Kimmi's parents, live to get away as far as I can from my family," he added.

"How do you get along with the girl's parents?" I asked.

"Fine. They have no problems with it. If they do, they at least have not said anything to me or her," he responded.

"How does your mother feel about it?" I asked.

"She never argues with my father. All she says is 'Listen to your father; he knows what is right for you,'" he responded.

"How do you think your parents will react to moving to Toronto?" I asked.

"My father is a strong-willed person. He probably will never speak to me for marrying Kimmi and moving to Canada, which he considers a communist country," he responded.

"How was your relationship with your father before this issue involving your fiancée?" I asked.

"It has never been good. He is an alcoholic and abusive of my mother and everyone. That's the reason why I chose to attend college far away from home," he responded.

"It sounds like you are rebelling against your father and everything he stands for. Did you know your father did not like Asians before you met your fiancée?" I asked.

"Yes. Like Archie Bunker, he hates anyone who isn't white and Protestant," he responded.

"Why do you think you weren't influenced by his views about non-whites?" I asked.

"Well, first thing you should know is that his abusive behavior turned us off against him and everything he stands for. I suppose that is what you mean when you suggested I was rebelling against my father. But I am not trying to spite him by wanting to marry an Asian woman," he reasoned. "Maybe that's why, but I love Kimmi. If that makes him mad, then that's too bad. Frankly I don't give a damn what he thinks. I can't wait to move to Toronto."

"Is that what you want to do?" I asked.

"Well, as I said earlier, I am going to marry her and move farther away. I hope I could convince my mother to move with us," he responded.

"Well, if that's what you want to do, why does my advice matter?" I asked.

"I wanted to be sure I am making the right decision. What do you think?" he asked.

"These are difficult decisions to make. My advice is to do what you think is best for you. It sounds like you are asking me to assure you that, if you marry her and move to Toronto, everything will eventually turn out right. Isn't that what you're really looking for?" I asked.

"Well, now that you have said that, yes. I didn't think of it that way, but yes. Yes, I am confused and needed to bounce it off someone else to be sure I am making the right decision," he responded.

"Well, I'm not a professional counselor. But I can tell you that there's no way you can be absolutely certain the outcome of any action will be exactly as expected. But my advice is to be certain of your motives and intents. Make sure they are honorable and you are doing it for the right reasons. When you do that, you can be at peace with the decision—whatever it is. My other advice is to seek professional help to clarify your motives and intents, just to be sure," I responded.

"Well, thank you. Do you know any counselor I could contact? It sounds like I need to do that," he asked.

"Why don't you begin at the Counseling Center? They may be able to help you," I advised.

"Thank you, Mr. Dyfan. You have helped me tremendously. I appreciate it. I will be in touch again," he said as he left my office.

I never again heard from him. However, a year letter, I received a wedding invitation from him with a Toronto address. And, for several years, I received Christmas cards from him, keeping me abreast of how he was doing. (Quite well, in fact.)

To this day, I am struck at how well this young man and others like him who I have met dealt with diversity in his life compared to people like Dan Silver. The only difference I can see is that he dealt with it at a personal level instead of an institutional or political level. He dealt with its effects on himself internally. I don't think for a minute that institutional change need not happen sometimes, but, when people have not dealt with their problems at a personal level, whether they be cancer survivors, victims of discrimination, survivors of sexual abuse, or whatever, their anger will make them ineffective at changing institutions, practices, and, most importantly, winning over hearts and minds.

By spring 1986, the MRP had been funded, and key staff positions were being filled. The first cohort class of students was being accepted into the program. The various program components, including the mentoring, tutoring, advising, and student financial aid matters, were being put into operation so that the first class could be on campus for the summer academic enhancement component of the MRP.

In late February, I received a telephone call from the associate dean of student affairs in the law school regarding a racial incident involving a white student. The dean asked if I would be willing to intervene on behalf of Dr. Howard, dean of the law school. He also informed me Dean Howard had written an open letter to all law school students reiterating the school's policy prohibiting racial and ethnic intolerance and behavior, in reaction to the racial incident at the school. But first, he suggested he and I meet to discuss the incident and my role in the intervention process. During the initial meeting with the dean and assistant dean, I was given a copy of the official complaint and asked to meet with all of the parties to determine the facts with the purpose of making a set of recommendations to the dean regarding the disposition of the case. I agreed to intervene and promised to move expeditiously.

The "Racial Incident Complaint" was filed against a white male student who was an acquaintance and classmate of the two white students that had filed the complaint. The complaint alleged the offending student had referred to the Black Law Society (BLS) as the "primate society" during a conversation about the upcoming Black History Month program. The students who filed the complaint of "racial intolerance" also mentioned to me they had reported the incident to the BLS President and BFSA because they felt the law school would do nothing about their complaint. My meeting with the two students lasted about twenty minutes. It was short and to the point as the complaint had stated.

During the meeting with the students, they mentioned they had never before heard the accused student use racial epithets and were, therefore, very surprised when they heard him referring to the BLS with "racial epithets."

"Why did you report the incident to the BLS and BFSA?" I inquired out of curiosity.

"Well, we thought some of the black students who were sitting nearby had heard his comment and wanted to protect ourselves. We did not want them to think we supported his racist comment," one replied.

"Also because I, personally, was offended by his comment because my boy-friend is black," said the other.

"Is he a student here at the law school?" I asked.

"No, he's living in Chicago. That's where I'm from," she replied.

"Did he know your boyfriend is black?" I asked again.

"Yes. In fact, he has been trying to get me to go out with him for months, and I've told him many times I have a boyfriend I love. And he knows he is black. That's why I don't understand why he would say what he said in my presence. Maybe he was testing me. I don't know why," she added.

"What do you want as an outcome of your complaint?" I asked them.

"Well, I think he should have the book thrown at him, shouldn't he?" she asked.

"What does that mean?" I asked.

"Whatever he deserves. This is a serious offense. Throw him out. He is a rac-ist. At least, that's what the BLS students are going to demand when they write to the dean," responded the other student.

"Thank you for reporting this incident. I will make a recommendation to the dean in a few days," I added before they left my office.

The next day, I met with the offending student to discuss the incident and his motivation. But, to my surprise, he turned out to be very contrite and scared to death of what might happen to him as a consequence of his action. As soon as he walked into my office, he started shaking and crying. I sat quietly and listened to what he had to say.

"I am so, so sorry for what I have done. I did not mean to hurt anyone. I never would say what I said in the presence of an African-American. I am not a racist. I don't hate them or want to hurt them. I don't have anything against them. In fact, my roommate is black. You can talk to him about me, and I get along fine with him. Please believe me. I have worked very hard to go to law school, and I am doing well. Please don't kick me out of law school. It will destroy me forever. I am in my final year. I am willing to apologize to the BLS if I have to, but please don't expel me," he said, sobbing and wiping his nose as the tears ran from his eyes.

"Tell me. Why did you do it?" I asked.

"I don't know. I was trying to be funny, I guess. But I am really not a racist," he responded.

"Trying to be funny at the expense of others?" I asked.

"You see, sir, I know how much bigotry and intolerance hurts and should have known better because, as a Jew living in the Ukraine in the Soviet Union, I suffered the same type of treatment. That's why my father moved us to the United States so that we won't have to put up with intolerance and discrimination. I deeply regret the comments that I made. Please let me try and make things up with the students. My roommate has agreed to help me," he pleaded.

"What specifically are you willing to do?' I asked.

"As I said, I am willing to write a letter of apology to the students involved and African-Americans, if needed. I am also willing to do anything else you want me to do," he added.

"Okay, why don't you draft a letter and bring it by next week as I deliberate on my recommendations," I suggested.

"I will be back next week to see you. Will you have your recommendations ready by then?" he asked.

"No, I will wait until I read your letter before I make my recommendations," I replied.

"Thank you, sir. What if I have it ready before our meeting date? Can I leave it early for you to read?" he asked.

"Yes," I replied. I received the draft letter in a few days with a note attached asking me to "make any recommendations for changes I deemed necessary." The draft letter was well-written in a tone that suggested contrition and specifically asked for forgiveness for what he termed a "serious error in judgment and unprincipled behavior."

I was sufficiently satisfied he was sincere and contrite to decide on a set of recommendations to send to the dean of the law school. My recommendations to the dean were the following: He should send a letter to all students in the law school apologizing for his behavior; he should spend one hour a week for four weeks with me exploring his feelings about the incident; and he should attend a seminar on the causes and effects of prejudices and intolerance.

The dean asked for a meeting with his assistant to discuss my recommendations before any decision was made on whether he would accept the recommendations. When we met a few days later, he appeared hesitant to accept my recommendations because he wanted to explore black student reactions to the recommendations with his assistant dean.

"How will black students react to these recommendations?" he asked his assistant, who was black.

"I'm not sure, and I don't know if it really matters," he replied.

"Do you think we should consult with them in advance in order to avoid negative reactions from them?" he asked again.

"I'm not sure we really need to ask them anything. Let me tell you what my concern is. Suppose we ask and they reject the recommendations as being too lenient. Won't we be giving them vetoing power over something that is within the prerogative of the administration? Why do we want to give students the power to dictate to us how we handle student discipline? As the assistant dean with responsibility for student discipline, I don't want to have students approving or disapproving my decisions regarding discipline. It would set a very dangerous precedent. I think that would just be bad policy. We are paid to make principled judgments," he responded.

"What if the BLS students reject the recommendations? What would we do then?" asked the dean.

"Too bad. What we need to do is determine if the recommendations are just in relationship to the offense and have the convictions to stand behind them," he responded.

"I understand what you mean, but I don't want trouble. I am not sure what to do," he added.

"Why don't we do this? Consult with BLS students, and get their feedback without telling them what we're thinking of doing. Then we'll meet again to discuss our course of action. How about that?" he asked.

"I can go along with that," I responded.

"I don't have any objections," the assistant dean replied.

As we left, the assistant dean informed me he would not be at the next meeting because he was seriously thinking about leaving the university.

"I am fed up with this patronizing crap. These guilty white liberals are always trying to prove they love black people and are not racist. I have to put up with this shit every time something involves black students," he said.

"You sound like you've had it," I responded.

"It has gotten so bad that, if a black student gets a grade of 'D' in any class, all he has to do to get the grade changed to a 'B' is to threaten to file a discrimination complaint against the instructor. I am so sick of this crap that I am leaving. I have an offer from a private law firm," he responded.

The next day, I received a telephone call from the dean asking me to add forty hours of community service in the NAACP to my recommendations and resubmit it to him as soon as possible.

I did not have a problem with this. So I sent him the revised recommendations the next day.

A few days later, he called me to ask that I have the student send the letter of apology to all students in the law school. He stipulated the letter be sent addressed to each student, sent via United States Postal Service, and paid for by the offending student. The letters went out as demanded by the dean. A few days later, I received a call from the dean's office that he and the leaders of the BLS wanted to meet with me regarding their concerns.

The meeting went fairly well even though they were not pleased with my recommendations. They expressed concerns we had "trivialized" the offense and failed to consider their demands the student be expelled from the law school for his "racist and offensive behavior."

I responded that we had considered their demands, but, in the end, I felt the recommendations were just and adequate relative to the offense. They were not happy, but they accepted my recommendations with "deep reservations."

To my surprise, I did not hear again from the dean or any of his assistants about the disposition of the case. It was as if they were afraid to be associated with the recommendations and, to some extent, me. I felt betrayed and I suspected this feeling might have been the very reason the previous assistant dean had resigned his position at the law school.

In the end, the student completed all of the requirements and graduated a year later, having learned a hard lesson I believed served him right as an individual and as an attorney in a diverse society.

In March 1986, I was invited to attend a meeting at United States Congressman Les Frost's office by the BFSA Executive Committee and a group of concerned African-American citizens. The purpose of the meeting was to discuss strategies to pressure TTU to be more responsive to the needs of the black community. I was told that a total of ten people would be at the meeting and my job would be to present the facts about the status of minorities at TTU. They wanted data regarding the number of black students from the local community in recent freshman classes, numbers of black faculty and staff, and the number of black studies courses offered each year for the past ten years. Dan Silver and Ron Taylor, who was a member of the TTU Student Services Advisory Board, led the group.

I arrived early and had an opportunity to chat with Congressman Frost and Ron Taylor before others arrived for the meeting. During that time, I was asked to provide the congressman with the relevant data regarding black representation at TTU.

After he reviewed the numbers (which were dismal), the congressman turned toward me in an angry voice and announced, "I am appalled. This is unacceptable. It means you have failed as the dean of minority programs. That's why they should have hired someone black from this city with strong connections to the black community and public schools. Someone like Ron Taylor, a retired high school principal. Traditional Tech needs someone like him to help them with this problem."

"Well, Congressman Frost, I have been on the job for less than one year. Besides, we are aware of the problems and are working on it. But it is my understanding you have never once made it your concern to inquire about the status of minorities or blacks at TTU in all your dealings with the institution during the past twenty years. Why is it all of a sudden an important issue for you?" I replied.

"Well, I didn't know that things were this bad in the institution. Nobody brought it to my attention until today. If I had known, I would have done something about it. I've signed off on millions of research dollars for that goddamned institution over the past twenty years. If I had known, I would have held their feet to the fire until they did something to about it. Why did you wait this long to come and talk with me?" he asked me.

"Please don't get self-righteous with me, Mr. Frost. It is not my place to bring you information. I don't work for you nor did I vote for you. I am here today because Ron invited me to this meeting, which has turned out to be a setup. Moreover, I am not responsible for reawakening your conscience or commitment to the community you represent in Congress. It is interesting that, in the twenty years you've been signing off on millions in federal grants for TTU, you never thought on your own to inquire about these issues," I replied.

At this point, the congressman's assistant announced the rest of the folks were there for the meeting. As they sat down, the congressman asked those present to introduce themselves. Then he went on to tell them we had been talking about black representation at TTU while we waited for them. The congressman said it was one of the things that had led to the meeting in his office and that he wanted to continue talking about it. Toward the end of the meeting, he assured everyone that he now had a good understanding about the problems. He announced, "I now know what the real problem is, and I will be talking with the president about it. I think they need someone over there that is sensitive and responsible for these matters at the highest level of the administration. Someone who understands the community and someone the community can identify with."

After the meeting, I talked with Ron Taylor about his take on what Congressman Frost meant about this last comments regarding the need for someone "sensitive and at the highest level of the administration." He felt my position should be maintained and I had done a "fine job" since my arrival. But he felt, above and beyond my position, someone else should be at the top, advising the president about policy matters.

He then added, "Someone like me, who is black, from the community, and a former high school principal. I know the community, and I understand the needs of the people and the school system. They need someone like me in that position."

"I heard you had applied for my position when it was vacant last year. What happened? Why didn't Alice hire you for the position?" I asked.

"I don't know. It was Alice's call, and she preferred you for the job. And that's fine. I am not after your job. Don't worry about that," he promised.

"I am surprised that, along with your experiences, you are also a member of the Student Services Advisory Board and have worked closely with Alice for years. So I cannot understand why you were passed over for the position. You seem to be the ideal candidate," I prompted.

"Well, my concern now is with the need for a special assistant for minority affairs position. I think your office should administratively be part that new office. That's what the congressman is going to demand. He had told me that new federal research monies somewhere between $60 and $160 million slated for TTU awaits his signature. So he feels what we are asking for is pittance. He believes he will get it, or he will delay the money for their biomedical building and other initiatives," he informed me.

"Well, will you be interested in the position if and when it is created?" I asked.

"Well, it depends on a number of things. You should be aware this is an issue that will come up during the next Student Services Advisory Board meeting. I have already talked with May Johnson about this issue, so be prepared for it. It's not going to be a very nice discussion like most of the meetings we've had over the past few years," he warned.

After the meeting, I talked briefly with Alice Taylor about the meeting with Congressman Frost and his promise to raise black concerns with the president when they met. I also mentioned that one solution the congressman might propose is the creation of the special assistant to the president for minority affairs, similar to the position at the nearby State University. He promised to talk with the president as soon as possible and mentioned he may want to talk with me himself.

In May, Alice talked with me about the upcoming advisory board meeting and asked if I would do a thirty-minute presentation about progress in developing the Minority Programs Office and some of the new programs, including the MRP. She wanted me to make the presentation because she felt the board should be kept informed by me in recognition for all the "great work" I had done in just one year on the job.

The meeting was well attended by board members and student services directors. The president and provost were present and reaffirmed their commitment to hire more minorities in the faculty and staff and increased recruitment of black students from the city. My presentation was slated for late morning, immediately after the mid-morning break, around 10:00 AM During the break, Ron Taylor and May Johnson approached me to discuss the content of my presentation. They insisted my presentation include not just a report of my activities but also a detailed analysis of the problem with lots of data. They wanted a serious critique of the problems at TTU. I promised to do my best.

When the meeting reconvened, the chair invited me to give a "brief report about the minority initiative at the end of the first year." I began my presentation with a detailed description of the status of minorities at TTU and a plea to the board, president, and provost to pursue institutional diversity as an imperative of excellence and to embark on a major strategic initiative rather than waiting for political pressure to force change. "The situation was so dismal," I told them, "it undermined any claims to excellence in the liberal arts and, indeed, in the institution as a whole." I emphasized the failure to address these issues in a meaningful way amounted to dereliction of duty and gross failure of responsibility to think strategically and systemically. My final remarks focused on the financial cost to the university of continued failure to address these concerns. I mentioned that the immediate cost may be the loss of the long awaited two hundred million dollar Federal Grant for the university's biomedical laboratory. I concluded the presentation with a list of recommendations that I promised to put in writing. I went on to add a brief report of my activities during the past year and emphasized the need to broaden the mission of the office, relocated in the appropriate administrative area commensurate with a university-wide mission.

At the end of my presentation (which lasted ninety minutes), the next speaker, May Johnson, thanked me for a very enlightening presentation and for framing the issues in terms of excellence in the cornerstone of institutional mission. She went on to add that she looked forward to the written report. And then, she turned our attention to what she termed institutional failures that went back twenty years—when she was a student at Traditional Tech—and connected her experiences to those failures. She expressed deep frustration at the fact the institution offered no courses in African-American history and thanked me again for teaching courses in those areas, even though teaching was not in my job description nor was I being paid extra for teaching. But the real problem, as she pointed out, was the failure to hire faculty to teach those critical courses. She said such failures leave the university vulnerable to charges of racism and loss of Federal research grants.

After she spoke, Ron Taylor endorsed everything May and I had said and added he did not know how the institution got away with neglecting minority issues in the past because he was a student there forty years earlier. But he vowed TTU would not get away with neglecting minorities any longer. He promised the president and provost they would be hearing more often from the black community. He blamed himself and his son, a recent graduate, for not tearing up the university when they were students in order to force change. But he said the community was ready for the appointment of someone at the senior most level to address these concerns—before it was too late.

By the time Ron Taylor ended his comments, it was close to lunchtime. So the advisory board chairman hurried through the agenda (after he thanked me for my presentation) so that lunch could be served. At the end of the meeting, before lunch was served, I noticed all of the senior administrators were deliberately avoiding me. Those who spoke to me thanked me for a candid presentation and offered their support should I need it. I began to feel as though I was in trouble and needed help. One person advised me to keep my "résumé fresh." I decided not to stay for lunch and left early for our scheduled out-of-town trip.

When I returned to work on Monday, I was told Alice Taylor wanted to talk with me as soon as possible. So I went immediately over to her office to talk with her. She was busy when I arrived, but she promised to talk to me as soon as her meeting was over.

In the meantime, a couple of white student services directors came by to talk to me regarding their concerns about what they termed my "unprofessional conduct" at the board meeting. They felt I had undermined everything they had done in the past few years to change things at the university. They accused me of "being in league with black radical elements who do not understand that change is a slow but deliberate process." One of them, claiming to be a close friend of Alice, said I'd be lucky if I didn't get fired when I met with her. He said that, if he was Alice, he would fire me for not adhering to the time allotted to me during the meeting. He also accused me of preventing him from making his presentation about the wonderful things he was doing for minorities in the Career Center.

I thanked them for letting me know how they felt about my presentation and urged them to suspend judgment until they have heard the reasons for my actions. I promised to meet with them again after I talked to Alice in order to explain the reasons to them. I then warned the director of the Career Center to watch the choice of words he used in expressing his frustrations to me. I did this because he was beginning to get a little personal with his frequent use of "you" in reference to me. I had a strange feeling when they left that I had not heard the end of this because one of them was on an ego trip.

Alice called me into her office as soon as the director left. She was sitting in one of the sofas in her office when I arrived. The first thing she said was to let me know she was no longer angry with me for what happened at the board meeting and made it clear that were it not for the president's intervention, she would have fired me. She added that the president had called her the evening of the board meeting to ask her to thank me for my courage and honesty and to say he would like to see me immediately that afternoon. She said that, over the weekend, she had time to think about what happened at the meeting and got over her anger. Now, she said that all she wanted to know was "why" and added she could see me through the opening in the curtain in an animated discussion with Ron Taylor and May Johnson outside the conference room during refreshment break of the board meeting last week.

She asked, "What was all of that about? It looked very intense."

"Alice, all I did was present some unpleasant but accurate data regarding the status of minorities at TTU," I replied.

"You added your interpretation and commentary to some of the data, didn't you? You even said, to quote you, 'the curriculum stinks.' Didn't you? Do you think that kind of language is acceptable? Well, I don't," she replied.

"Alice, I wanted to preempt a nasty scenario of racial confrontation between white and black board members. I had hoped that, by presenting the data and framing the issues as central to institutional excellence, the conversations would be less rhetorical, more meaningful, and civil," I replied.

"Do you mean to tell me May and Ron were going to do something confrontational and that was what you were preempting?" she asked.

"Yes, this is not going to be the last of it either. There are efforts going on in the community to rally black support to pressure State University and TTU to hire black senior minority affairs officers in each institution. There's a feeling that both institutions have failed to address minority issues and concerns and will not address them until there's political pressure for change," I said.

"Do you know what State University is doing in response to political pressure?" she asked.

"Yes, they've just created a minority affairs office of that is being led by the new vice president for minority affairs. It is being staffed by an associate and assistant vice president and three support staff," I replied.

"Have you met him? Where is he from?" she asked.

"Yes. He was recently hired from Bender University, where he was the director of the Black Cultural Center. He is black and a native of this city. He appears well-connected in the community," I replied.

"Samir, I recommend you make an appointment to speak with the president about this please. I think he should know what's going on," she advised.

"I'd be delighted to," I responded.

"I will talk to the president immediately so that he is aware you will be going to speak with him. Thank you, Samir. You've been a great help. And don't worry. You're not going to be fired," she promised.

That afternoon, I scheduled a meeting with the president for the next day because it was an important meeting in the eyes of the president's secretary. I believe the president put a high priority on the meeting because he understood who the major players were in the political push for change. He told me Congressman Frost had not talked with him yet, even though they were together recently at a Metro Roundtable reception He then informed me he was in the process of appointing Stan Gordon, chairperson of the mechanical engineering department and longtime resident of the city, as the special assistant to the president for minority affairs. He asked me if I felt that would be well received in the black community. I told him I was not sure, but I knew many blacks on the campus and in the community had said they did not trust him because his wife was white.

He then added the provost had recently appointed a black lawyer on loan from an industrial firm for one year as special assistant for minority outreach. His responsibility, I was told, would be to focus on minority outreach for the university. That meant he was also in charge of developing and maintaining the university's relations with the black community, schools, colleges, businesses, as well as federal and state agencies. I was told his efforts in those areas over the next year would relieve me of those responsibilities so that I could focus more on students. Nothing in all of this was as discouraging as being passed over twice in a row. The president was quick to add these two appointments were in no way a reflection of dissatisfaction with my work. But he added, "These are highly important moves symbolic of the challenges the university faced."

In June 1986, I received a call from the director of the Black Cultural Center at Land Grant University (LGU) in Indiana, requesting my services as a consultant. He said he also represented the BFSA and wanted to know if I'd be interested in advising the BFSA in its fight with the university administration over the hiring of a white female and avowed lesbian from Liberal State College as vice president for diversity. He suggested they would retain my services under his center's budget as a speaker for a number of days if I would, in turn, be willing to work with them (confidentially) to help push out Suzy Rich. He mentioned I had been highly recommended by an old friend and colleague, John Rogers, director of minority programs in the medical school at TTU and former dean at LGU.

I mentioned to him I was an applicant for the same position for which Suzy Rich was hired. But that didn't mean that I harbored ill will towards her. He emphasized that all they wanted me to do was read and critique a number of documents with the purpose of discrediting the concepts and authors. He was clear they were looking for ammunition to fight and push out Suzy Rich and the new provost who hired her. He repeated his emphasis that they would do something with the information I provide them. He also promised that, if I helped them push out Suzy Rich, he would push for my hiring—something he said they were fighting for in the first place. He mentioned that, through John Rogers, they had known about my work and me, but the chair of the search committee, a black female lesbian faculty member who chaired the search committee had pushed for Suzy. He mused the chair of the search committee had mistakenly "committed racial suicide by putting her gender and sexual orientation before her race interests."

He told me to expect a packet of information by express mail to read, and he promised to call me back in a week to discuss my reactions to his offer. Just before he hung up, he mentioned he was Cuban ethnically and black racially and had no confusion about his race interests. He must have thought I was a black African because all John Rogers told him was that I am "from Africa." I wondered how he would feel were he to see me in person or what he would think if he found out I had no racial identity or interest to protect and promote. But I decided not to say anything at this point.

A few days later, I received a packet containing several documents, including a minority affairs report from Suzy Rich plus several memoranda between the BFSA, Suzy, and the new provost dealing with the status of minorities at LGU. After I read the documents, I decided I did not want to be part of any attempts to sabotage Suzy's work nor was I interested in being part of an organized conspiracy against someone because of the person's race or sexual orientation. What I was being asked to do went against everything I believed. Therefore, I declined the offer to work with the BFSA at LGU. And that's exactly what I told the director of the Black Cultural Center when he called me back. But he wouldn't accept my decline of his offer. Instead, he offered to double my fees if I would reconsider and promised to call back in three weeks when he returned to work after eye surgery. But when he called again, I was even more adamant about my refusal. After that, I never heard again from the BFSA at LGU. I have no idea what unfolded, but I do know that Suzy Rich continued in that position for many years to the general satisfaction of the LGU community.

In July, I went to a job interview at the Justice University (JU) for the position of vice president for multicultural affairs. The local NAACP president, who was also a faculty member of the Social Work department at JU, chaired the search committee. He had been instrumental in forcing the university to respond to the needs of blacks and minorities at the university. The key problem, it appeared, was retention of black students, who dropped out in record numbers because of being academically underprepared. After I met with the search committee, I appeared at an open forum that was attended mainly by black faculty, staff, and students. The main question to which they wanted me to respond was if I believed "poor, white students from Appalachia" should be included in minority student retention efforts at the university.

Apparently, this issue over the extent of inclusion was a hot topic on campus and had been hotly debated before my arrival for the interview. My response was direct I told them that, from the standpoint of an administration, inclusive programs that meet the needs of a broad range of students tend to have broader support and more resources than exclusive ones. I was more philosophically predisposed to inclusive programs because of their sociological value to the education process. But they would have none of it. Some even suggested the university create a separate program for "poor, white students" instead of including them in the program for black students, a statement that was roundly applauded by the audience.

After the public forum, I was told the executive committee of the BFSA was hosting a reception for me at a member's home. On the way to the BFSA reception, the search chair confided that some of the characters at the reception are overly simplistic about race. He advised me to ignore them if they say anything inflammatory. He promised they mean no harm by their comments. He explained that some of them are that way "because of the ignorance that prolonged isolation creates." He emphasized the reception was an informal social and not part of the official search process. He advised me to relax and be myself. But I knew better to be cautious.

As we climbed the stairs to the top floor of a two-story house sitting on the side of a small hill, the chair told me to continue up into the house as he ran back to get something from his car. I approached the door carefully and knocked on the open door, but no one heard the knock because of loud laughter coming from inside the house. I entered into the first room and decided to wait for my escort. As I waited, I could hear the conversation.

One of them said, "I don't trust anyone who says he is Afro this or Afro that. What I want to know is: Are you black or white? Don't give me any of this Afro-Hawaiian, Afro-Lebanese, or Afro-Japanese stuff. Where I come from, you are either black or white. That's the problem I have with people who are trying to hide their racial heritage."

"Well, wait 'til you see this guy. You really can't tell what he is. He is the brother from another planet," said another.

"They say he claims he is from Africa. Therefore, blacks in America should have no problems with him. But I have. We want someone who, when you see him, you know he is black. Not someone you need to go around telling folks he is black before they know he is," said another.

By this time, the chair returned from his car with several bottles of wine for the reception. Neither he nor the individuals in the living room were aware I had heard the conversations, and I did not say anything about it. There were five black males in the room when we entered a large area overlooking the hill on the backside of the house. My escort gave me a general introduction. After which, each person made a personal introduction of himself. That is when I found out, to my chagrin, they were all faculty members. I was given a warm welcome by the reception's host, whose distinctive voice I recognized as one of the ones I had heard earlier when I was waiting in the other room. It was also interesting that each one identified himself as "black" during their introduction in some way.

After about twenty minutes into the reception, one of the guests asked me to say a few words about myself.

He announced, "Now, welcome everyone this evening. Let's extend a special welcome to our guest and candidate for the vice president for multicultural affairs position at the university. Mr. Dyfan, perhaps the best place to begin this evening is for you to tell us about your background. I mean your heritage, cultural, and racial—as well as your professional experience."

"Thank you. I am originally from West Africa and immigrated to the United States in 1970. I was educated at a historically black college in North Carolina and at Midwestern State University. I was formerly employed at New England State University as the chief retention officer. Currently, I am the associate dean for minority programs at Traditional Tech University," I concluded.

"You see, Mr. Dyfan, down here in the south, the world is either black or white. We don't have half-worlds. This is West Virginia, not New York or California. So, what we want to know is if you are one of us. This position is going to represent us blacks. We don't have Hispanics or Asians down here. Even if you include—forgive me for saying this—poor, white Appalachian trash in the programs, minority affairs down here, baby, means blacks. We fought for it, and it's ours. Nothing is gonna change that," said yet another.

"You see, Mr. Dyfan, we are confused about you. You are from Africa. You attended a black college. Your academic background is black studies. You are in minority affairs, but you don't look black. We are not even sure you will identify with us sufficiently enough to even join the BFSA, if you were hired," said another.

But, before I could respond, the host's spouse walked into the room and interrupted the conversation to invite everyone into the dining room to try out the buffalo wings and potato salad she had just prepared. As we walked into the dining room, one of the guests walked up to me and whispered he knew that I had not yet completed and returned the EEO data card. He advised me to fill one out before I left town. The food was delicious, and the conversation changed from focusing on me to jazz and sports. It never again returned to the position or me. I suspected the chair of the search had signaled caution regarding questions about my racial identity. But it never came up again until the end of the reception at 8:00 PM when I was reminded to return the EEO form.

I met the next morning with the university president, who assured me of his deep commitment to minority issues. He then invited me to a breakfast meeting with the vice presidents. After a brief introduction, I was asked a few questions about my job experience, educational and academic background, and so forth. None had to do with my race or ethnicity. At the end of the meeting, one of the vice presidents asked me if I was a Methodist because he recognized I attended a

Methodist secondary school, the Methodist Academy, in West Africa. He informed me he was, at one time, on the board that funded the school and recognized it as soon as he saw it on my curriculum vitae. Without going into too much detail, I told him I was one of the few non-Methodists at the boarding school.

The interviews ended at midday on the second day of my visit. Upon my return home, I telephoned the president to inform him about my concerns regarding the appropriateness and legality of the questions regarding race and religion I was asked during the interviews.

The president's response was to assure me that none of the questions about my race or religion would influence his decision. But he reminded me the BFSA reception was not an official part of the interview process even though he admitted "the presence of the search committee chair made it appear official." As for the "dumb-ass vice president who asked the dumb question about my religion," he would be told such questions are illegal. He reassured me that he would make a fair selection when he decides whom to hire.

The next week, I received a letter from the president apologizing for discomfort that I may have experienced during the interviews and reassured me his decision to hire someone else for the job was not affected by any of the inappropriate questions. He concluded with "best wishes in your job search." I was not surprised that I did not get a job offer, but, then again, my interest in the position had wavered after the open forum session during the first day of the interview.

A week later, I received a telephone call from the president of Justice University, thanking me personally for taking the time to visit the campus. He also reassured me again that neither race nor religion played any part in his selection of person whom he had hired, who, he pointed out, just happened to be black. I thanked him for his fairness and openness and assured him I did not intend to take any legal actions against his university. But I also emphasized that he needed to put an end to such behaviors. He thanked me for my understanding and promised sensitivity training for all administrators in the university.

By December 1986, I had decided I wanted to leave TTU by the end of the fall of 1987. My wife and I agreed I should start the search process in January. Sometime in late January 1987, I saw a job announcement for assistant to the president for diversity at Fiesta College in the Northeast that was advertised in the *Chronicle of Higher Education*. I was not interested in the position at first because of my interest in finding a job in warmer climate. But the more I found out about the college, a prestigious, private liberal arts college, the greater my interest became in the position. After a week or two, I decided to apply for the job.

In late February 1987, I received an invitation to visit Fiesta College for a job interview, scheduled for mid-March. The interview went well, and I was very impressed by the institution's traditions, size, location, and established commitment to liberal arts. The new president, Father John Macarthy, paid me a courtesy visit and offered me the position upon his return a few days later with August 1 as my starting date. In April, I turned in my letter of resignation with a final date of July 31. So, as to avoid surprising Alice Taylor, I discussed my decision to accept the offer from Fiesta College with her before I turned in the letter. A week later, she told me the president wanted to talk with me before my departure. She said the president was concerned I was leaving because I was upset or felt pushed out by blacks. I promised to follow through on the diversity recommendation before I left the university.

Sometime in May 1987, I received a telephone call from a reporter at the local newspaper who wanted a reaction from me about Roy Whiplash's firing from his recent position as vice president for minority affairs at the state university. He informed me that he was writing an article about the whole story and had a few questions for me. I told him that I did not know anything about it and did not even know Roy was having any problems at State University. After he realized I did not know much about the reasons for Roy's sudden firing just eleven months after he was hired, the reporter promised to call back for follow-up stories.

The next day, the story was on the front page of the local newspaper. State University was now fully embroiled in racial turmoil with students, faculty, staff, and people in the black community outraged at what they saw as blatant racism in the firing of Roy Whiplash. There were calls from some prominent black leaders for the president's firing. Others called for federal and state investigations of the university. Still others wanted Roy rehired. The story was front-page news for two months, particularly after a dozen students staged a prolonged occupation of the administration building to protest the university's refusal to reinstate Roy Whiplash.

About two weeks after the story first appeared in the newspaper, I received a telephone call from Roy Whiplash himself, urging me to give an interview to a sympathetic black reporter about racial problems at TTU. He also urged me to make a symbolic gesture of support for him by visiting the student demonstrators. And finally, he urged me "to strike while the iron is hot" and join him in a press conference where he intended to expose specific instances of racism at State University. He believed I should do the same to put the spotlight on TTU and expressed concern that, while State University was being scrutinized in the local newspaper, TTU was "getting away with murder." And that, he said, was unfair. I told him I had already accepted another job at Fiesta College and would be leaving town in a few weeks. Therefore, I would prefer to leave it up to the two special assistants for minority affairs at TTU. It was their job now; let them take care of it. I politely declined his offer.

A deeply disappointed black faculty member I knew at State University told me that Roy Whiplash had alienated everyone in the administration within a few months by his frequent use of allegations of racism against members of the senior staff and the deans. He was reputed with having called the dean of the College of Law a racist. And indeed, he was said to have accused the president of racism for only giving him a cost of living raise of one percent. The president, it was said, was dissatisfied with Roy's performance, particularly his aggressive and confrontational style during his first year in office. So, when Roy referred to his performance evaluation and the decision regarding his raise as racist and rejected the offer, the president had no choice but to fire him.

The conflict at State University lasted for over six weeks and was featured in the *Chronicle of Higher Education* It did not end until Bender University, his previous place of employment, rehired him later that summer. The subject came up in my conversation with President Jurgens a week after. He thanked me for not becoming involved in the mess and hoped that I was not leaving TTU disappointed. He assured me that he and the university administrators were all very pleased with the quality and extent of my work and urged me to reconsider my decision. But he offered no incentives. I told him the position at Fiesta College was a promotional opportunity for me. But, before I left, I submitted a comprehensive diversity report to the president—as I had promised during the advisory board meeting earlier that year. He appeared surprised when I handed him the document. He promised to read it and, when possible, to implement many of the recommendations. Then he thanked me again for not going along with Roy Whiplash's invitation to join him in his desire to drag TTU into their mess at State University.

5

The Bishop's New Clothes

Fiesta College was perhaps the only institution—of all the places I have worked—where my lack of any particular racial or ethnic identity did not create many problems for me. Most of the problems I experienced at this institution were either gender/sexual orientation or ideologically based. Perhaps this can be attributed to the very small numbers of minorities in the student body, faculty, and staff. In fact, the total number of black and Hispanic students was so small that they decided to create one student organization called the Black and Latin Students Union (BLSU). When I started, the college had only three black faculty members, two Asians, and one Hispanic in a total faculty of 200.

On the other hand, the college had done well in its recruitment of women—both in the faculty and the administration. With this increase in the representation of women also came an increase in the number of lesbians and feminist among the faculty and staff. As a result, the movement for increased diversity included among others, a significant number of feminists, gays and lesbians, pacifists, and "multiculturalists." There was only one vehicle for change on the campus for a long time, and that was the Women and Minority Affairs Committee (WMAC) that began as an advisory committee to the vice president for academic affairs. By the time the new president arrived on campus in 1986, WMAC had succeeded in changing its reporting line to the president. However, by then, it had lost its credibility because of its confrontational and aggressive style. The president appointed a new diversity transition committee chaired by the assistant vice president for academic affairs, Rich Walton.

The Transition Committee developed the college's first action plan for diversity that included among its urgent goals the creation of the position of assistant to the president for college diversity. (I was hired for this position in 1987.) The Transition Committee was the group I was told to work with very closely when I first arrived at Fiesta College. My office was located in the academic affairs suite, next door to the vice president's office. My office was also next door to Rich Walton's office, which made frequent consultations possible. But, to my surprise, there was strong opposition to the location of my office in the academic affairs suite from the WMAC. As the president explained it to me, the academic affairs office was viewed as "enemy territory because the vice president for academic affairs, Daniel Bowl, had refused to go along with the political agenda of the women and minorities." They pushed for a more "neutral location" because they were concerned that being in the academic affairs suite would make me vulnerable to bad influence by Daniel Bowl and Rich Walton.

The president, on the other hand, decided to temporarily put me in a vacant office in the academic affairs suite until he could find another location for me. I ended up staying in that suite for almost two years. By the time I was moved down the hall, next door to the president's office, I had become so "tarnished by the prolonged exposure to bad influence" that the WMAC declared me an enemy. This issue of location caused such a problem that the president once told me that putting me in the academic affairs suite was the greatest mistake of his presidency.

About three weeks after my arrival at Fiesta College, I was invited to lunch by the outgoing chair of the WMAC, Ellen Beane, and the new chair, Valerie Dale. The meeting was supposed to be a "get acquainted" lunch that provided them with an opportunity to bring me up to speed on their work, major accomplishments, and plans for the future. But what I got was a political agenda and an ultimatum from the two women. From the moment Valerie Dale picked me up in front of the Administration Building, I was bombarded with warnings about my association with the people in the academic affairs office. As we drove off in her car for the fifteen-minute ride to the restaurant where Ellen was scheduled to meet us, Valerie zeroed in on the vice president, Daniel Bowl, as enemy number one of women and minorities. She lamented the decision to locate me in the academic affairs office and referred to the decision and rationale as "stupid." She said that decision by the president "disappointed everyone and raised serious questions about his fitness for office."

As we arrived at Denny's restaurant, she promised an earful from Ellen, whom she referred to as "the mother of the WMAC and more familiar with multicultural issues on campus." Ellen arrived and started the meeting soon after our orders were taken by saying, "Two hours is not enough time for me to lay it all out for you, honey. I mean the institutional racism, sexism, ageism, and homophobia that we've had to fight in this college is amazing. They talk about preserving their Franciscan traditions, that very racist, sexist, and homophobic tradition we need to change."

"How are the Franciscan traditions racist, sexist, and homophobic?" I pleaded. "Help me understand, please."

"Well, where should I begin?" she replied. "Let me give you one example of the homophobia and the hypocrisy of the fucking Catholic Church, the bishop, and their goddamned Franciscan traditions, forgive me for saying that. When Louise Delray, a professor in religious studies, decided last year she wanted to get pregnant by artificial insemination because she is a lesbian, the goddamned friars went through a fucking holy fit. Some of them even demanded her firing. I mean we had to go to war with the Catholic Church and the fucking bishop, who himself is rumored to be an active homosexual. But you don't have to look very far. Half the friars at Fiesta are gay. Many of the priests in the Catholic Church are gay. I mean you can't have a bigger fucking hypocrisy than that."

After thinking for a moment, she added, "Boy, I don't even want to go into this. Have you seen the way the bishop wags his ass when he walks? Well, if he isn't gay, I don't know what he is."

She continued, "I mean wiggling his ass like a woman, honey. I tell you, I don't know what he is. You know it wouldn't be so obvious if he didn't wear a frock, or what do you call the dress they wear…a habit? As for the sexism issues, the friary, which was built with institutional monies, has nothing but men living in it. We have a Catholic nun on this campus, but they won't let her stay in the friary because she is a woman. She has to drive thirty miles away to live in a convent because of their sexist policy."

"What you don't understand, Samir, is these men who run this college…the friars, I mean…they don't know how to live and work with women because their sexist world is all male. The church segregates them and then as administrators. They don't know how to handle women's issues because they don't know anything about women. The only women they have ever related to are their mothers and that was forty, fifty, sixty years ago," finished Ellen.

"How are the Franciscan traditions racist?" I asked.

"Well, I feel disappointed I have to be the one to educate our diversity officer. Forgive me for saying this, but it is not my job to educate you. If you can't figure that out after what we've told you here today, then that's one of the things you will have to figure out for yourself. That's your job, mister. You are the assistant to the president for college diversity," said Ellen.

"Now, what have they told you about us…or me in particular? I would like to know," asked Ellen

"I have only been at Fiesta for two weeks, and no one has said anything to me about you," I replied.

"Let me be specific," she added. "What has Daniel Bowl or Rich Walton told you about me? You've been in that suite long enough with them that I'm sure they have already said something about us or me in particular. I know they don't like me because I won't let them hijack the diversity agenda when we've been the only ones fighting for these issues for years. These Johnny-come-lately administrators think they can just waltz in and take over these issues. So what have they told you?"

"They have said nothing personal about you or anyone else." I replied. "I have spoken to them about issues, not personalities."

"They've probably referred to me as a bitch and a witch, haven't they?" she asked.

"You see, Samir," she continued, "we can make matters very difficult for you if you allow them to influence your decisions or outlook regarding these issues. It's your choice, but beware that, if you go with them, we will not allow you or them to hijack the multicultural agenda. We are a very powerful group of faculty and staff with an already established agenda. What we need from you is to help us implement it."

"I am not going to beat about the bush," she added. "As far as I am concerned, the president has already sided with them by hiring you. The person we wanted was a black woman who is a diversity consultant in New York City. They wanted you and prevailed. Don't get me wrong. We are willing to work with you, but it's up to you. We will be watching you."

"Well, I'm flabbergasted," I replied. "You've given me a lot to think about. One thing is certain; however, I intend to work closely with everyone to find common ground. That's my style."

By the time lunch arrived, I had lost my appetite. All I wanted to do was to leave, but I did not have my car with me. I ate a little piece of my steak sandwich and put the rest in a doggy bag. Not much else was said for about fifteen to twenty minutes while we ate our lunch. Ellen was the first to leave, immediately after she finished eating her salad, because she said she had a multicultural studies class to teach. We left soon after her. But, before Ellen left, she made a point of telling me she hoped they had not overwhelmed me and that all they wanted to do was to let me know where they stood on the issues

I spent the rest of the afternoon processing what was said, the experience, and their implications for me and for the college's diversity initiatives. The more I thought about it, the more the experience felt like I have been given an ultimatum of "play ball with us, or we will destroy you." After consulting with a number of individuals who were not directly involved with either group, I decided to talk with the president about my findings so far and my concerns as well. I was forthright with him and simply narrated everything I had heard and observed since my arrival at Fiesta College and my assessment of the situation in terms of its potential for serious conflict between the college administration and the WMAC.

The president was "surprised" by what he had heard, particularly the denigration of the Franciscan tradition and the allegations against the bishop. He advised me to be careful in my dealings with them and encouraged me to involve others in my work. He was also clear that I not allow Daniel Bowl and Rich Walton to dictate directions. What he wanted me to do "was to steer for the middle ground between both groups and avoid becoming exclusively associated with any one of them." I reassured him I would strive to remain open to both sides as we searched for common ground.

A few weeks later, I was invited to a meeting with the director of the Education Opportunity Program (EOP), Angela Lopez. The meeting was scheduled at the EOP main office, where her office was also located, with the intent of introducing me to the program staff and students. After the introductions and tour of the program, which was conducted by the administrative assistant, I ended up waiting in the student lounge for over twenty minutes to meet with the director. When she finally emerged from her office, she said, "I'm sorry you had to wait for so long. I had to take care of an urgent problem that took longer than I expected. Please come into the witch's cove, as my office is usually referred to these days."

"Well, some of my closest friends are witches," I replied with a smile.

"I should have said the bitch's cove because that's what I am said to be lately," she added with an intense look on her face.

"Angela, are you trying to tell me something?" I asked her.

"Excuse me for a moment here. I will be back in a minute," she said and walked out of the room, closing the door behind her.

While she was away, I looked around the office and the congestion caused by excessive piling of papers and folders on the floor and on all the chairs in the room. Her desk was also covered with piles of papers and file folders fifteen inches high. In fact, she had to move a pile from one of the chairs to make room for me. She was gone out of the office for about five minutes before she returned with another apology for the interruptions. As she reentered the room, she said, "Now I can talk. You know it's not easy being an advocate for my poor students in this institution. I have to go to war almost everyday with that overdressed bimbo that is in charge of financial aid."

"Whom are you talking about?" I asked.

"That bimbo," she replied. "Sylvia Dupont. Have you met her?"

"No, I have not," I cautiously responded.

"Well, all of that aside, I'm glad you're here. Now I will have an ally in this struggle. You were my first choice in the search. But, even though I missed your interview, I voted for you because you have been a former EOP program director and you know what the struggle is like down here in the trenches. Unlike some people, who claim to be advocates for women and minorities, I voted for you. They wanted the black woman from Troy, New York, because she is a fake feminist, like many of them in that committee," she added as her face turned red with an angry look to it.

"I'm totally confused now. What are you talking about? What's going on?" I asked with some frustration.

"Well, I can help you, but you are going to have to work very closely with me because I've got the students with me. They don't, and that's why they are both jealous of me. You are caught between the racists in the academic affairs office and the fake feminists in the WMAC. Neither one of them knows anything about minorities. In fact, they have no minorities in their group except for that sycophant, John Akpan, a Nigerian faculty whom you may be able to wean away from them because you're from Africa," she answered with a forced smile on her face.

"Let's start with each group separately. Tell me about your relationship with the WMAC. What happened?" I asked.

"Well, I was a member of that committee many years ago, and I was the only minority, a Puerto Rican Latina, for a long, long time," she explained. "I had to put up with a lot of ignorant crap from people like Ellen Beane and her male-dependent, so-called feminist lesbian followers in the committee. They met separately and decided on a course of action before committee meetings. Then they expected me to go along with their agenda without any input or questions. My only role was to garner support among students of color When I protested their mode of operation, I was called a 'fucking bitch' by that brainless, stammering witch, Ellen. They called me divisive and accused me of undermining the work of the WMAC. In response, I stopped attending their meetings many years ago."

"She is a tenured, full professor. Why do you refer to her as brainless?" I asked.

"Well, she had half of her brains removed a few years ago during brain cancer surgery. At least that's what I heard," she replied.

"What about your relationship with the folks in the academic affairs office?" I asked.

"Well, the problem started with Daniel Bowl's insistence that all academic-related matters pertaining to EOP students must be cleared with that office. I wanted the authority to make those decisions without having to go to the great white *massa* for permission every time I was dealing with students. To make things easier, I recommended the EOP be transferred to the academic affairs office so that I could have the authority to make the kind of decisions I need to make without going for permission every time I am dealing with a student problem. They refused, and that's how they alienated me. You see these are the reasons why we need you in this college. These are the things that you will have to help us with," she ended her comments with another smile of anxiety.

"What other problems do you think I will have to deal with and where?" I asked.

"Well, to tell you the truth, there is one other person, if I were you, that you will need to watch out for. And that's a black, incompetent faculty member in the political science department, Awilda Mack. She is a black racist and has turned some of my students and staff against me," she replied.

"What happened?" I asked.

"Well, she is a really pathetic woman, whose boyfriend dumped her soon after she had a baby last year. I grant you that she was badly beaten by him, but what she is doing with her anger is destructive to the students and the program. She has been trying to organize black students and my staff against me under the guise of concerns about fairness and equity in the EOP," she said.

"So, are you saying that black students in EOP are alleging unfairness in the program?" I asked as I tried to understand what else might be going on.

"Yes, but only after they've been co-opted and coached by that bitch, Awilda, and, I must admit, the WMAC. Both are trying to use black students against me because I wouldn't go along with their preordained agendas."

"Are you suggesting that Awilda is in cahoots with Ellen and the WMAC?" I asked.

"No, they hate each other. She's had some of the same problems I've had with them when she was in that committee last year. They don't like her because she refused to play along with their white, patronizing behavior. But, when it comes to this office and me, they separately try to negatively influence black students' perceptions. They have been using the black students to make trouble for me for years," she explained with expressions of sadness in her face.

"How are black and Hispanic students getting along?" I asked.

"Well, there are two groups. One group comprises the black and Latin student organization. They are the ones that want to do coalition building and work together. They are mostly students from EOP. There is a second group that has been agitating for separating the black and Latin student into separate organizations and is influenced by both Awilda and the WMAC. You know, the classic divide and conquer tactic," she mused.

Before I could say anything else, the door to her office opened, and a male student who introduced himself as Bryan Soto, president of BLSU, walked in. As he introduced himself, Angela walked from around her cluttered desk and led me out of her office while thanking me for a wonderful meeting. I then figured the meeting was over and walked out of her office into the lounge area. There I ran into Jim, the assistant director of EOP, whom I had met when I came for the job interview earlier that year. As he introduced himself to me again, he mentioned he made an appointment to speak with me about some of the challenges from his perspective because he said he was sure I had heard about the problems in the college. I asked him to think about some possible solutions to the problems as well. He agreed.

A week later, Jim and I met for about an hour to discuss his insights to the problems. But, to my surprise, he only wanted to speak in generalities and refused to discuss problems within EOP. He insisted he had no authority to discuss EOP and preferred to leave that up to Angela Lopez because she was the director of the program. He proposed the creation of a multicultural programs planning committee (MPPC) that would bring together all the various factions in the common pursuit and coalition building. I promised to support the effort if he would articulate the idea in writing and agree to be the first committee chair. He agreed and promised to bring his ideas in writing in a week.

In the meantime, I kept the president informed about the problems as I discovered them in the many meetings I attended with faculty, staff, administrators, and students. He was familiar with most of the problems, though not the details and intensity of many of the interpersonal conflicts. He was particularly upset they were using students as surrogates in their respective political struggles. He encouraged me to do what I could to resolve the conflict and wanted me to work separately with the students to defuse some of the separatism that had emerged because of some of the faculty and staff struggles.

In late September 1987, I had a surprise visit from the chairman of the economics department, who introduced himself as Forest Sawyer. He said he was waiting for a meeting with Daniel Bowl and said he just wanted to ask me a few questions. He started by telling me he was a doctoral candidate at Catholic University and his wife was also a doctoral student in Marxist economics at a nearby university. He also informed me he was due for tenure review and the absence of his doctorate was creating some problems getting tenure. He explained his wife, Trish, had been an instructor in his department for several years and the position was going to be permanent the next academic year after a national search. But he felt the department should just award her the position because she had done an excellent job.

He insisted he was against a national search because he felt his wife did not have a chance in an open search because there were many qualified minorities with PhDs. He also said his wife was a Marxist economist in a department whose priority was business economics. He added that, because his wife just had a baby, he did not think she had any prospect of finishing her doctorate any time in the near future. He added he had tried to work things out quietly in his department, but he had failed to convince two members of a department of four. As such, it was important for him to stay involved in the search process. At this point, I cautioned him against conflict of interests and nepotism. He informed me that, if he abstained completely from the search, the vote would be "two against and one in favor for his wife."

He then proceeded to discuss the internal politics of the department. At which time, he referred to two members of the economics department as "conservative, old–fashioned, and sexist." He added that one of them, Dr. Basie, had long passed the point of retirement and called him a "senile Neanderthal." But he spoke highly of another member of his department, Aaron Phillips, whom he called liberal and an ally. He then concluded by assuring me he knew what he was doing and that, one way or another, he was going to get his wife Trish hired.

Just before he left for his meeting with Daniel Bowl, he asked, "Say, are white women considered minorities? Do they contribute to diversity in an all-white male department?"

"Well, the concept of diversity is broad and inclusive," I replied.

"Would you push for the hiring of a white woman in a search scenario in which she is the only female among a group of white male applicants in an all-white male department? And hear this, a white woman married to a handicapped man with no hands and feet," he asked me, holding up his arms for me to see.

"I don't expect to be involved in decisions regarding faculty hiring because of faculty governance issues," I replied.

"Will you support my wife, Trish, if the vice president sought your advice?" he asked again.

"Well, I am not sure. Let me think about it," I replied as he left for his meeting with Daniel Bowl.

A few days later, I asked Daniel Bowl about the position vacancy in the economics department and the problems associated with Forest Sawyer's involvement in the search process. He assured me there was going to be an open search and he would closely monitor the search process because he recognized the potential for problems. He then asked me to work closely with him on that particular search because. He said, "Forest had already brought up the issue of diversity in his advocacy for his wife."

The first meeting of the MPPC that Jim had proposed was scheduled for the first week in October. Approximately thirty faculty, staff, and student leaders were invited to the meeting to discuss programming issues for the upcoming year. The list of people invited to the meeting included faculty and staff that were involved in program development and students from the BLSU. The meeting started with a very good turnout with almost everyone present when Bryan Soto entered the room with all guns blazing. As he entered the meeting room, he demanded I conduct "sensitivity training for all the whites at the meeting" before he was willing to sit in the same committee with them. Pointing at each nonminority person in the room, he insisted they leave the meeting until they've gone through "cultural sensitivity training."

Such grandstanding was unacceptable. I informed him that I had little tolerance for foolishness and asked him to withdraw his comment before he sat down. His refusal to apologize forced me to ask him to leave the meeting. As he walked out of the meeting room, someone commented that he, Bryan, was the one that needed sensitivity training most. As he walked out of the room, he asked the other Latino students to follow him. I also followed them out to encourage they stay for the meeting. But they refused to be part of the committee because the WMAC faculty were involved. Bryan told me he would not return to the committee until the white WMAC faculty attended racial sensitivity training.

I tried to continue with the meeting, but I was unsuccessful because, as soon as I returned to the meting, I encountered the WMAC faculty just walking out in protest of Bryan's behavior. Needless to say, I was very frustrated. The few people who remained at the meeting and I talked for a while about ways we can promote better understanding and collaboration between the various groups on campus. In the end, those who stayed for the meeting were not hopeful the MPPC was a workable vehicle for improving collaboration. Some frankly told me they would attend future meetings only after Bryan apologized to everyone for his disrespectful behavior. All of my efforts to get Bryan to recognize his behavior was wrong failed. On the contrary, he believed he was right and being truthful. He saw no need to be contrite or to apologize for anything.

The next day, the president told me that several Latino students, including Bryan, had come to speak with him about my failure to support them against the WMAC. He said Bryan complained that Latino students did not see me as an ally because I was always against them. At the end of our discussions, the president assured me he was certain Angela had put them up to it. He encouraged me to be careful and to ignore the student's complaints because he was certain they were doing Angela's bidding.

In early December 1987, I had a surprise visit from someone who introduced himself as chairman of the economics department, Aaron Phillips. I was surprised because I thought I had recently met someone else with that same title, Forest Sawyer. He informed me he was the new chairman because Forest was on sabbatical. I introduced myself and offered my services. He hesitated for a while and appeared uneasy, but he left me with the impression he wanted to talk about something. I then closed my office door, asked him to relax, and offered him some water.

After a while, he said, "I would like to talk with you and get your guidance on something that has been bothering me for some time now. I hope you can help me."

"If there's something that I can do, I will certainly help," I responded as I pulled my chair closer to him.

"The reason why I am uneasy about this is because Forest is a friend of mine and I don't want to do anything to harm him. But then, I don't want to do anything illegal," he said.

"I will do whatever I can to help," I assured him.

"Well, the problem began the day we learned the department would permanently fill the vacant faculty line that Forest's wife, Trish, now fills as an adjunct. He began to lobby immediately for his wife the minute he heard about it," he said.

"Yeah, he talked to me about it several weeks ago. He even asked me if I would support his wife for the position," I replied.

"He did? Well, he hasn't left me alone since this search began. And I am fed up about it. Even though he is on sabbatical, he has insisted on staying actively involved in the search. He even followed me last week to the National Economist Conference in Washington, DC, and involved himself in the interviews of prospective applicants at the conference," he said with a troubled look in his face.

"What was his role during the interviews at the conference?" I asked, sensing conflict of interest in Forest's involvement in the process.

"He insisted on being involved in the name of *fairness* for his wife. But I don't feel comfortable about the whole thing," he added.

"I don't blame you!" I responded.

"What did you do or say to him about his involvement?" I asked.

'He refused to listen to me when I objected to his involvement," he replied.

"But that's not all," he added. "Throughout the train trip to and from Washington, I was under intense pressure to exclude minorities from the final pool of candidates. In fact, he has been pressuring me to exclude an Asian woman with a PhD from Berkley that I interviewed at the conference. Forest claimed Asians are not minorities and should not be considered under the concept of diversity. But I am not sure about that, and I need your expert advice on that issue. What is your opinion about that?" he asked.

"Well, Forest is wrong on both counts. I will advise you to stop involving him in the search," I replied.

"Well, I believe Forest wants a scenario in which his wife will be competing with white males so that he can raise the diversity issue on behalf of his wife," he confided to me.

"I know, he even alluded to that the first time I met him, and I am very concerned and feel very strongly that you and I must speak with the dean and vice president about Forest's behavior," I added.

"If you think we should, then will you set up the meeting?" he asked.

"Yes, I will be in touch very soon," I promised.

At the meeting with the dean of the School of Business Administration, the vice president for academic affairs, and me, Aaron repeated what he had told me about Forest Sawyer's involvement in the search and the pressure he was under to eliminate minorities from the candidacy pool. He said they had interviewed four candidates for the position, including an Asian woman, and indicated a white male was the leading candidate. He asked if I would be willing to review all of the applications to ensure that no qualified minorities had been overlooked. The dean and vice president were very clear about keeping the process fair and free of undue influence from Forest.

A few days later, I received approximately 300 applications for review. As part of the review, I used generally recognizable information that applicants disclosed, including information such as names, school attended, professional memberships, civic affiliations, subjects and topic of interest in publications, thesis and dissertation topics, lectures, and relevant reference in letters of applications, recommendations, and nominations. I identified seventy-six minorities in the applicant pool for a second review by the search committee. A few days later, Aaron

Phillips informed me the committee had reviewed all of the applications and was convinced the process had been fair. He informed me his department had offered the position to a white male of Palestinian descent, Amir Majnuni.

By the spring semester of 1988, my honeymoon was over. The various factions on campus felt I had done enough listening and it was time for me to take action. Each group expected me to side with them and take action against others, particularly against those they had identified in their respective discussions with me. But what had emerged from my experience during the first semester was a picture of what each of the groups was contributing to the diversity-related problems in the college. My role, as I saw it, was to work with each group to educate them about the part of the problems for which they were accountable. This way, I had hoped they would become more aware of their behaviors and, as a result, take responsibility for their actions. But, as I attempted to have serious conversations about the problems each faction was creating on campus, I began to experience what I have come to call the "exorcist's effect," that is, all the bad spirits united against the exorcist who is now their common enemy.

It was not long into the spring semester that the first shots were fired. By the end of the fall semester of 1988, each side was accusing me of "blaming the victim" and of "being unfair and offensive." I was even called "stupid for playing psychological games" with them by a staff member in the Counseling Center who identified herself as a "feminist psychologist." Another even had the nerve to accuse me of being "divisive" and of practicing "divide and conquer tactics" against women and minorities in the college. So, you can see how surprised I was when, soon after the Martin Luther King celebration in mid-January, the first shot was fired. It came in the form of a memorandum from Jim in the EOP and it was addressed to the president of the college. It was filled with diatribes against the college administration and its Catholic traditions, as well as allegations of institutional racism in its failure to diversify the student body, faculty, staff, and the curriculum. But the hardest criticism was reserved for the person who designed and printed the MLK Celebration booklet that was distributed during the program.

The focus of the criticism was a photograph depicting poverty in Mississippi. A black mother and her two young children were sitting on the porch floor of a plantation shack and were eating scraps of food. The "offensive photograph" was reproduced from a pictorial book on Martin Luther King. The photographs were reproduced in the program guide the MLK Birthday Committee had developed for the celebration. It was this photograph that Jim referred to as racist, stereotypical, and highly offensive to minorities. The MLK committee included the photograph in the program guide because it represented the wellsprings of King's moral authority—what he was fighting to change in America. The memo appeared in the student newspaper the day after the memo arrived in the president's office.

Soon after, the memorandum appeared in the Op-Ed section of the *Oracle*. I went to talk with Jim about my concerns. He agreed to speak with me after a short wait.

"Jim, can you explain what's going on with this memo?" I asked.

"Yes, I had intended to write an open letter to the Fiesta community regarding my deep disappointment about the hypocrisy in the college. To shame a college that claims to hold Martin Luther King in high esteem to the point of celebrating his thoughts and actions, but, year in year out, they continually fail to live by its ideals. I wanted to call attention to the hypocrisy with the hopes of spurring greater diversity at Fiesta College. But Angela asked me to make it into a memorandum to the president, condemning the racist picture the WMAC put in the MLK Celebration booklet. So I decided, as a courtesy, to send it first to the president before I published it in the *Oracle* Is he angry with me? Oh well, it doesn't matter anyway. I am leaving for a postdoctoral at Harvard this summer, so I am not worried. That was my parting shot," he responded with a laugh.

"Did it occur to you that perhaps you should have verified your assumptions?" I asked him.

"Well, the part that you are referring to is Angela's. She asked me to add the part about the picture because she said black and Latino students have complained to her that it is stereotypical. You should talk to Angela about that," he replied.

I walked about twenty-five yards into Angela Lopez's office and asked if I could speak with her. She invited me in.

She asked, "Can I help you, Samir?"

"Yes, Jim told me you had asked him to include in his memorandum to the president the concerns regarding the photograph in the MLK booklet?" I asked.

"Yes, black students in the EOP complained they find the picture insulting and racist. Whoever did it should be reprimanded for gross insensitivity. You don't know what a picture like that can do to the self-esteem of students of color on this campus," she replied.

"Can you arrange a meeting for me to talk with them about their concerns?" I asked her.

"Well, no. They are afraid of talking to anyone else. I am their advocate on campus. You talk to me, and I'll tell them what you have to say. It is more effective when it goes through me because they trust and respect me. So tell me what you want me to tell them," she replied.

"Tell them the photograph at issue was reproduced from a pictorial book on the life of Martin Luther King. I was the one that recommended its inclusion in the booklet. The MLK committee felt that, if it was included in a book on King's life, then it must be okay to include in Fiesta's program booklet. Tell them the WMAC had nothing to do with it. Also tell them I will be willing to meet with them individually or collectively to talk about their concerns," I urged her.

"I will tell them. I'll help you out this time, but I don't know for how long I can continue to hold them back. They are really angry at all the abuses they've had to take from this institution. They trust me, and I am like their mother. They will listen to me. But, like I said earlier, I am helping you out this time, but they want results," she threatened with a frown on her face.

"Angela, are you threatening me?" I asked.

"No, no, no. I am not. I don't control these students. They are intelligent and know what is going on in the institution. They have a mind of their own," she replied.

"It sounded as if you were threatening to use the students against me if I didn't go along with your agenda. Is that right? I understood your comment 'next time' as a threat. I hope I am wrong because I don't have time for foolishness. I hope you understand that." I responded as I walked out of her office.

The next day, I talked with the president about my discussions with Jim and Angela. He advised me to talk with Barry Ray regarding Angela's behavior. I met with Barry for about an hour and told him what I have heard and observed about the level of ethnic and racial tension on campus and her role in it. He informed me that Angela had been doing that for many years and explained all of his efforts to get Angela to stop had failed. In frustration, he explained he and Daniel Bowl had brought a Harvard-trained Latina, Estella Meija, from Buffalo College to assess the situation. After the visit, he explained that she wrote a scathing report that Angela had become a cynical, negative influence on the students in the EOP and in the college as a whole.

"What did you do then?" I asked.

"What can I do? If I touch her, she will use the students to come after my ass, not yours," he responded.

"Have you talked with the president about your concerns that she might use the students against you? Because he is wondering why this problem had not been dealt with," I advised him.

"Did he say something to you about it? Is he angry with me because of Jim's memo?" he asked.

"He is concerned about Angela, not Jim. Barry, I am willing to work closely and support you, but you will have to take the lead because she reports to you. I am willing to be present when you speak with her because this is a diversity-related problem, but I am not willing to take the lead," I offered.

"Well, I might take you up on that. I will set up the meeting right now," he said as he picked up and dialed Angela's number to set up the meeting. The meeting was scheduled for the next day in his office. It lasted one hour, and, to my disappointment, Angela was let off the hook. Barry appeared uneasy and tentative whenever he spoke to her about the concerns. I decided to add my voice to the discussions, hoping Angela would get the message that we wanted her to stop using the students to threaten and attack other members of the college community. She denied ever using the students to threaten or attack anyone, and said, as an advocate for the students, she was blamed for everything they did on campus. And she told Barry she had helped me out when the students were angry with me. That was when I told her several students had told me they had not heard anything about the allegations she made about the photograph. I repeated my offer to meet with the students to discuss the matter, but she declined the offer again. At that point, Barry suddenly ended the meeting by announcing he had to go to another meeting downtown. But, before he left, he asked Angela to work closely with me to resolve the problems. She promised to do her best.

In March 1988, I attended a meeting of the Martin Luther King Task Force that was comprised of dignitaries from the community as well as faculty and administrators at the college. Its charge was to commemorate MLK's birthday, and it met monthly to make plans for the upcoming celebration. Both Daniel Bowl and myself were members along with three members of the WMAC. This particular meeting was notable because I overheard Ellen talking about their efforts to organize opposition among faculty against Daniel Bowl during his upcoming evaluation by the faculty.

I arrived early for the meeting to help set up the hors d'oeuvres and juices for the guest. They had been talking for about ten minutes before they realized I was in the room. When they finally saw me, Valerie Dale signaled for me to go over and help them set up the room for the meeting.

As I helped her with the tablecloth, Valerie asked, "So, how are you getting along with Daniel Bowl, your next-door neighbor in the academic affairs office?"

"I've enjoyed working with him. He has been very supportive of the projects I have initiated in the past few months," I replied.

"How can you really say anything good about him when everyone is tired of him? He is so slow and undisciplined. I can't stand him. I have written to the president about his absence from these meetings. The task force charge stipulates the vice president for academic affairs must represent the president during our meetings, but he has not attended any of the meetings since 1987," she said as she pounded the ice prongs on the table to each syllable she uttered.

"Now, you can be of help to us in our efforts to have him pushed out so that we can get someone in that office that is more in tune with the needs of women and minorities," Ellen said as she walked over to me while eating some of the grapes she had taken from the fruit tray.

"I don't have anything to tell you. I will not be part of any conspiracy to harm anyone. I don't operate like that," I responded as several task force members, including Jane Dope, the President of the NAACP, arrived for the meeting.

But they didn't stop talking about Daniel Bowl even after several people arrived in the meeting room. That was when I intervened and stopped Valerie and Ellen from continuing with their attacks on Daniel. I reminded them we were there for the King Task Force meeting and suggested we might best serve King's memory by trying to adhere to some of his principles as we conduct business in his name and memory. I suggested that, at the least, we should try to be fair and respectful of each other. After the meeting, Ellen angrily accused me of reprimanding her and Valerie in the presence of everyone on the task force and demanded an apology from me.

My response was simple, "I meant what I said at the meeting. I felt it was unfair and disrespectful of you and Valerie to be speaking about Daniel Bowl in the manner in which you two were carrying on in the presence of community members. It was mean-spirited and antithetical to everything for which Martin Luther King stood."

"I am going to deal with you by talking with the president about this tomorrow," she replied as she walked out of the meeting room to her car. The next day, the president stopped by my office on the way off campus to tell me Ellen had stopped by his office at 7:00 AM that morning to "rant and rave" about the incident at the King Task Force meeting. He was laughing as if to suggest he was pleased with what I had done. He added he was fed up with her histrionics first thing in the morning. He said she sometimes came to speak with him in his office at 6:30 AM After I told him what she and Valerie had done, he thanked me for having the courage to confront them. As he left, he promised to talk about it with me when he returned in the afternoon.

When he returned that afternoon, the president called and asked me over to talk. We discussed a number of items: the King Task Force incident, Angela Lopez's meeting with Barry Ray, and Daniel Bowl's evaluation by the faculty. I told him I believed the results of the faculty evaluations would be skewed because the WMAC was organizing faculty against Daniel Bowl. But he assured me he knew how to handle what they were doing. I was not to worry. He said the evaluations were confidential and required the evaluator's signature. That, he said, sometimes has a moderating influence on what people wrote down on paper. He promised not to read any unsigned evaluations.

By May 1988, the evaluations had been mailed out to the faculty, completed, and returned to the president's office. By June, Daniel had been asked to leave his position as vice president for academic affairs. During a campus-wide meeting about the status of the college, Daniel announced he was resigning his position and would not be around "to be kicked around like the football." He was reassigned to the president's office as a special assistant and given a year to find another job. He left Fiesta College a year later to assume the position of provost at Brandy University.

After he left, I discussed my disappointment with the evaluation process that precipitated Daniel's departure. I felt the president had allowed himself to be unduly influenced by a highly organized faculty lynch mob that went by the name of the WMAC. I have always believed the WMAC saw Daniel's departure as a victory and, as a result, felt more empowered in their politics of personal destruction. I also knew I might be their next target and had no illusions they had the power and mean-spiritedness to target me and succeed at pushing me out of my position.

Soon after Daniel's departure, Valerie Dale and Ellen Beane began to openly criticize everything I did on campus. I was now on their list of enemies to be destroyed and crushed. Valerie Dale became more aggressive toward me and frequently expressed "disappointment with the quality of my work and educational programs." The president and I had frequent conversations about their expressed concerns because they went to complain to him about everything I did on campus. They were frequently unhappy or angry about something I had done or failed to do. He urged me to not be distracted by their criticisms and to continue with the course I had set for the college. He assured me that he intended to ignore their criticisms of my work because he had received positive feedback from other faculty and staff regarding the quality of my work and educational programs.

The search for the vice president for academic affairs began during the fall of 1988 and continued until the position was filled in the summer of 1989. The interviews began during the early spring with five candidates for the job. One of them was Tom Mann, an internal candidate. Tom was chairman of the allied sciences department, a former Faculty Senate chairman, and also interim vice president for academic affairs during the fall semester of 1988. He gave up the interim position at the end of the fall in order to be eligible to apply for the permanent position.

During his tenure as interim vice president, he was a big supporter of Angela Lopez and had tacitly permitted her a free hand to make academic decisions that previous vice presidents were unwilling to do. Angela was telling anyone that would listen about her excellent friendship with Tom. Whenever EOP or Angela's name came up in senior staff meetings, he was unwavering in his support for the program and of Angela. He felt Angela's behavior was a reflection of the hostile environment in which she had to do advocacy for her program and students. He felt she was always under assault from many who did not really want the EOP program or students of color on campus. Those whom he felt "wanted to keep the college the way it had always been—lily white." Aside from his blind support for Angela, he was a person I had grown to like since I first met him as a member of the search committee that interviewed me for the job.

And so it was when I met with Tom as a candidate for vice president for academic affairs in early spring of 1989. The interview process involved individual interviews with each of the senior staff of the college. The hour-long interview was a remarkable experience for me. We began with the perfunctory questions. And then, somewhere during the conversations, he turned his attention to his "commitment to diversity and multiculturalism." He reiterated his strong support for my office and EOP. He promised, if hired, to "put the WMAC folks out of business." He assured me he would fully support and protect me from the women and minorities whom he described as vicious and racist. He also proceeded to warn me to watch my back because he said Valerie, Ellen, and others in their cabal were quietly building support among faculty and staff for my removal. And he promised to put a stop to it as vice president and asked for my support. I promised to think about it and get back in touch with him.

In the end, he did not get the job because the WMAC fought against his candidacy. They feared him. He was a highly respected man with strong convictions and with the courage to deal with them. And they knew it. For that reason, they were opposed to him and used their network to oppose his candidacy. Instead, they threw their support for another candidate from another small, New England liberal arts college, Dan Nastop, who got the job.

In March 1989, I received a telephone call from the dean of students about racial problems in one of the residence halls. She said that, against college policy, a group of four black female students had moved together into one room after two of the black females had antagonized their white roommates into leaving. Two black females had moved in with them to create an all-black room. Now, she said the two white girls were complaining about the all-black room. She said that, in addition, the same four black female students had recently made racial harassment allegations against five white male students on their floor. She explained the problem started when a group of white students who were playing handball in the hallway, which was against residence hall policy. The ball bumped against the door of the black students' room several time that evening. She added the encounter between the two groups of students degenerated into a racial confrontation.

"SO, WHAT I CAN I DO TO HELP YOU?" I ASKED HER.

"Well, we have disciplined the white male students who were playing handball in the hallway against residence hall rules. But the black female students are not happy with that decision. They want the boys disciplined for racial harassment," she replied

"What evidence do they have to justify a charge of racial harassment?" I asked.

"None. They are charging the only motives the white male student could have had for playing handball in the hallway in front of their dorm room was to harass the room's occupants because they are black. One of the black females reported she had been in unpleasant encounters with one of the white male students earlier that week and felt targeted by them," she replied.

"What was the encounter about" I asked

"It appears that one of the black female students overheard one of the white male students complaining to the residence hall staff about the room with all black girls on his floor. She got angry and called him a 'white racist.' He became angry and called her a 'black racist and a bitch.' That's why the black female students felt like they had been targeted for harassment by the white male student and his buddies," she replied.

"What about the issue of the all-black female room? Is that against college policy?" I asked

"Yes. In fact, that is why we need your help. Two of the black females were reassigned to other rooms. Two other students (a Latina and a white student) were then assigned to the room. But the black females are refusing to leave the room. And we don't want to create a racial incident by forcefully removing them from the room," she said with deep frustration in her voice.

"Where are the white girls who moved out of the room living now?" I asked.

"They moved out of the residence halls."

"On which particular policy did you base your decision to reassign the black females to other rooms?" I asked.

"Well, only the housing office can assign and change student's room assignments. No one authorized the room changes for the two black female students who moved into the room after the two white female students moved out. We really need your help. Will you please intervene and ask them to follow the policy?" she asked.

"Is that the only reason?" I asked.

"No, it goes against our policy of deliberate integration of all residence hall rooms. We don't permit racially and ethnically segregated rooms. That is the reason why we don't permit students to choose who they room with at Fiesta College," she assured me.

"Okay, I'll see what I can do to help. I will be in touch with you as soon as I talk with the students," I promised.

The next day, I met with three of the black female students to discuss the concerns of the housing office. But they were adamant that attempts to separate them were motivated by racism and refused to obey the reassignment orders. Instead, they moved out entirely from the residence halls into Awilda Mack's house for the rest of the semester, a situation Awilda used to her advantage after the college refused to renew her teaching contract because she had failed to complete her doctorate in five years as her contract stipulated. She claimed Fiesta College was pushing out blacks from the college and cited the situation involving the four black female students who moved out of the residence halls and her predicament in the political science department as evidence of "widespread racism at Fiesta College."

Summer brought a new surprise. In early June 1989, Awilda Mack came to talk with me regarding problems in the political science department. She said the chairman of the department had informed her they were not going to renew her teaching contract because she hadn't completed her doctorate in a timely manner. She believed the real issues were racial and suspected the WMAC and its allies were trying to push her out because she had refused to align herself and black students with that group in its fight against Angela Lopez. She even expressed concern that Angela's allies may also be working to push her out because she had refused to align herself and the black students with her Latino side against the WMAC. What a tangled mess!

She was also very angry about what she termed the racial climate in the department. She explained the chairman had reprimanded her for missing scheduled department meetings and alleged they had deliberately scheduled meetings on days when there were community programs commemorating Martin Luther King's birthday. She said all of her attempts to convince her colleagues not to schedule department meetings on the week of MLK's birthday had failed. She thought their refusal was motivated by racial insensitivity and added she had expressed these sentiments to the department chairman. She appealed for my intervention to keep them from pushing her out of the college. I promised to look into the matter and to get back in touch with her.

My conversations with the president and vice president for academic affairs did not go well for her. The president told me Awilda had already gone to talk with him about her concerns, but there wasn't anything he could do because the central issue is the completion of her PhD. He emphasized that, if she were to get the PhD tomorrow, she would be fine.

"She has one year to finish her dissertation. If she completes it before the end of the year, then she should be fine. Please encourage her to focus on the dissertation because that is the concern, not all the other stuff she's talking about."

But, when I relayed the response to Awilda, she was not pleased because she felt there was no way she could complete the dissertation in a year with an infant baby and a full teaching load. She was not pleased with the response and threatened to sue for discrimination.

In early August, a faculty member from Nigeria, John Akpan, who taught African history, came to speak with me about some concerns he had about the attitude and behaviors of some of the individuals in the WMAC. I had become acquainted with him when I first arrived at Fiesta College and had interacted with him a number of times at college-wide events. He was always cordial but distant, and I respected that. He was different, however, on the day he came to speak with me regarding his concerns about the level of animosity toward me among some of the leaders of the WMAC. He said that, of late, Ellen Beane, Valerie Dale, and others have been particularly angry with me. He informed me he had felt trapped with them ever since he joined the WMAC when he first arrived a few years ago because they needed a minority in the committees.

He wanted me to know that, even though he was friendly with them, he did not support everything they were doing in the name of diversity. He said the reason he had stayed close to them was because they could be helpful with his application for tenure. He informed me he had not said anything before about their behavior because he did not want to offend them and hurt his chances for tenure. But he wanted to make me aware of what they were saying and doing behind my back. He also informed me he had heard many positive things about my work in the community. In fact, he said someone he ran into that worked in New York State government spoke very highly about a presentation I gave to the New York State Training Council. He assured me he would keep me informed about whatever they were saying or planning to do about me. Just before he left, he advised me to watch my back because some of them had been complaining about me to the president. I, in turn, informed him the president had been talking with me about their complaints.

During the next few weeks, I began to wonder whom the WMAC cabal had targeted for destruction. John had hinted they might be targeting me, and I agreed with him. But, after my encounters with Ellen Beane and Valerie Dale in a number of events, I began to wonder if it was not the president they were after. The first event was at a college-wide meeting the president had called to discuss budget issues and the endowment. After the meeting, I overheard Valerie and Ellen telling other faculty that "Father Macarthy sounded so stupid, and his memorandum to faculty was poorly written." Valerie kept making that comment repeatedly to anyone that would listen. She kept saying how she was "extremely disappointed with the president's performance." Ellen would encore her sentiments with "that whole office is stupid," almost as if it was a call-and-response performance between them.

My next encounter with Valerie Dale was at the meeting of the Human Resources Advisory Committee in early September. During the discussions about the college's diversity initiatives and the issue of whether the college should develop an affirmative action policy and plan, Valerie continually referred to the president, who was not present, as stupid every time she mentioned his name or his office. At one point, I asked her to refrain from doing that because it was inappropriate and disrespectful. But she refused to stop. Instead, she referred to my comments as stupid and declared, "I am not afraid of you or Father Macarthy. All he has that I don't have is a little brown penis. That's the same way I feel about you as well, Samir. I am not afraid of you either. If you don't want me to call you and him stupid, then you should stop doing and saying stupid things."

"Is that what Freudian psychology refers to as penis envy?" I asked her.

"That's another stupid question," she replied.

"You know, Valerie, if you really need one, there are substitutes you can buy. Some of your closest friends know where they are sold," I responded.

I have to admit my response probably antagonized her unnecessarily. I was so angry over her hostility that I went over the edge when she referred to his "little brown penis." I thought of all kinds of smart-ass remarks, and the one I made was probably the mildest of them. But I wasn't going to let her devolve the meeting into a sophomoric attack.

My third encounter with Valerie Dale was soon after a panel discussion on affirmative action that she facilitated in early March. The discussion began well with questions and answers until she and some of the panelists started to make judgmental statements about students who disagreed with some of the positions of the panelists. From that point on, the discussions degenerated into a political debate between the left and the right. The event was billed as "an educational program to shed light on the issues" and even labeled a "dialogue." But it was the farthest thing from a dialogue, particularly after the racial, ethnic, gender, and sexual orientation blaming and name-calling began. At one point, I intervened by reminding everyone the objective of the session was "understanding," and this requires listening to and respecting others. I implored everyone to refrain from invectives and personal attacks.

After that comment, everyone backed off, and things calmed down. At the end of the discussions, Valerie walked over to me and said, "That was a really stupid thing that you did a little while ago. You are such an embarrassment in this place. Take my advice, Samir. Maybe you should not say anything in public when we are discussing these issues because your comments are sometimes so stupid."

"I don't know what psychopathology drives your behavior, but I do think you owe it to yourself to find out. You should search for a very experienced psychologist because you have serious problems. Now get the fuck out of my way," I replied.

"Stupid, stupid, stupid," she kept whispering to herself as she walked away.

After this experience, I became more convinced I was the one they were after and not Father Macarthy as I had suspected. My suspicion was later confirmed by John Akpan. He believed they were confident they could not successfully take on the president, so they were focusing on pressuring him to get rid of me. The strange thing was, after the last encounter with Valerie, they never again said anything negative in my presence or to my face. They went underground, quietly organizing their forces against me to pressure the president for my removal from office. I kept the president fully informed about all of my encounters with them, and he discussed with me their concerns and activities. He recognized what they were up to and assured me I should not be concerned that he would go along with them and fire me.

A faculty member in the religious studies department had approached me in October 1988 with a suggestion of Ancient Egypt as a thematic focus for the upcoming Black History Month (BHM) programming. It was an idea that other members of the small BHM Planning Committee endorsed. We spent the next three months planning a calendar of events, which included lectures, music, art, and food. The keynote event was a debate with a slideshow presentation between Ted Snow, a black classicist at Federal University, and Robert Rendall, a historian at the New England Museum of History. The topic of the debate was "The African Origins of Egyptian Civilization: Fact or Fiction?" Ted Snow was a renowned scholar with many books to his credit, including *Blacks in Ancient Times* His reputation as a major black scholar was a big attraction to the black community. Turnout for the event exceeded the capacity of the auditorium (400), and some people left because of room capacity.

Problems developed soon after Ted Snow began his presentation. A small group of black males standing at the back of the auditorium became increasingly agitated as Snow spoke. They began to heckle him after he suggested the ancient Egyptian civilization was a multicultural civilization. The heckling grew worse after he concluded there was no evidence that Ancient Egyptian civilization was African before 2,500 BC. I had to intervene several times to ask for civility and respect when things began to get out of hand. By the end of Snow's presentation, the tension in the room was palpable. The question and answer session was full of personal attacks and name-calling. One of the black participants in the back of the room referred to the presenter as "a sellout and an Uncle Tom."

As the next speaker prepared his slides for the second part of the presentation debate, I went to the back of the auditorium to speak with the group of black males who were responsible for most of heckling and interruptions during Snow's presentation. I asked them to refrain from disrupting the speakers and to conduct themselves in a civil and respectful manner. As it turned out, I recognized several members of the group. The leader of the group was Nathan Abrasive, the director of the Liberty Program. Another was a graduate student at the state university and a former Fiesta College football player. They promised to refrain from personal attacks, but they "promised to ask a lot of tough questions."

The next speaker, Robert Rendall, was not as controversial at first. He was a white Africanist historian and believed there was ample evidence that pointed to the "African origin of Egyptian Civilization." His presentation was given a lukewarm reception by the audience, particularly from the group in the back of the auditorium. Many of the questions at the end of his forty-minute presentation were rhetorical with most of them aimed at Ted Snow. But the one question that sparked the most heat was asked by one of the individuals at the back of the auditorium.

"How can the whitey see the evidence so clearly while the Uncle Tom claims he can't see any evidence of a Black African origin of Egyptian civilization?"

Stepping up to the podium, while rolling up his shirt's sleeves as if he was getting ready for a fistfight, Snow replied, "You come down here and call me an Uncle Tom to my face, and I will punch out your black ass. I am eighty-three years old, but I can kick your dumb, black ass," responded Snow

"All I have to do is kick your dentures down your ass, old man. Down your Uncle Tom ass," said a voice at the back of the room.

At this point, the audience had started to leave the auditorium in disgust. I stepped in and asked the group at the back to leave. As I walked toward the stage to speak with Ted Snow, Jane Dope, president of the local chapter of the NAACP, stopped me.

She said, "Where did you find the old Uncle Tom and the white racist?"

"Jane, what you are doing is inappropriate and irresponsible," I replied.

By then, the group of black males at the back of the room moved closer to her as if to surround her in support of her position.

"It's not just me that's upset at the racist intent of this program. It's all of these people as well. They are my guys, and I am proud of them for standing firm on their cultural heritage. And talk about being fair, where is the fairness in this program? Getting a whitey to make the case for black people is not fair. It's racist. You should have brought Dr. Ben, an Afrocentric Egyptologist, to represent our side of the issues," she declared at the top of her voice.

"Well, I disagree with your opinion about the program, and I am disappointed with your behavior this evening. Particularly the behavior of your so-called 'guys' during Snow's talk," I responded as I walked toward the stage.

As I approached the stage, I could hear Ted Snow saying, "They want Dr. Ben to speak on Egypt. He is not a scholar. He is a charlatan and an idiot who doesn't need evidence to support his claims. He is the one who believes that only racist and Uncle Toms need evidence before they will believe the ancient Egyptians were black."

"You are the idiot, you old fool. You are the idiot, not Dr. Ben. You are an Uncle Tom and an old fool," responded a young black male that was with Jane Dope earlier.

"Come close, and say that. I'll then kick your dumb, black ass," responded Snow.

I stepped in quickly and led both of our speakers into another room where we were having a reception for them. As Jane Dope and her entourage approached the reception room, I politely asked them to stay away from the reception to avoid further problems. She was angry and threatened to call the president about me.

A week later, the president and I had a conversation about complaints from Jane Dope about what was termed insensitivity to blacks and expressed concerns from Sally Mello that I may be damaging the "excellent relations they had developed with the black community over the years." But, even the president recognized that what Jane Dope and her entourage had done during Snow's talk was inappropriate and "not a sign of excellent relations." The president even thanked me for the courage to tell Jane Dope her behavior was disappointing. He said he would have done the same thing had he been there. He wanted me to meet with Sally to discuss their concerns, but he wanted me to ignore Valerie Dale and Ellen Beane's comments about racial sensitivity.

A week later, I met with Sally Mello, chairperson of the religious studies department and King Task Force member. She accused me of undermining the excellent relationship with the African-American community that she and others had worked hard and long to build. She said Jane Dope had called to complain about lack of racial sensitivity to the black community in the Ancient Egypt lectures. When she was through, I politely explained to her my interactions with Jane Dope and her entourage's behavior during the Snow presentation. They admitted they did not have all of the facts, but they were hopeful their relationship with Jane Dope could be salvaged. I assured them I had no intentions of prolonging the matter and promised not to do anything else about it. But she wasn't pleased with my response.

In May 1990, the president informed me he would be conducting a public review of my performance in office as assistant to the president for diversity and asked I provide the names of faculty and staff I had worked with over the part three years. I gave him a list of over forty names, including those of the WMAC cabal. He eliminated their names from the list because he said he had already heard from them many times. The evaluations were returned, and the president and I discussed the findings. Most of the feedback was supportive and favorable. The major concerns were about the failure to end racial tension in the college. But the president was familiar with the problems. My overall performance evaluation was between very good and excellent. He said, in general, faculty and staff were pleased with my work and the educational programs I had developed in the past three years.

After we finished discussing my evaluations, the president then turned his attention to another matter. He informed me the college was facing a big discrimination lawsuit that might cost the college a bundle and wanted me to know that John Cabbot, Fiesta College's attorney, might be talking to me about it.

"What's the suit about?" I asked out of curiosity.

"Well, it's Trish, Forest's wife. She is suing us for gender discrimination over a faculty search a few years ago. It was the search that led to Amir Majnuni's hiring in the economics department," he replied.

"Oh, Father, that case was a setup by Forest Sawyer," I said. "In December 1987, Aaron Phillips came to report to me that Forest was pressuring him to eliminate all minorities from the pool of finalists in order to create a scenario in which Trish was competing with white males for the position. I scheduled a meeting the next day with the vice president for academic affairs and the dean of business to discuss the matter."

"Well, Samir, this is good news," the president said. "I want you to contact John Cabbot about this. You know this information has yet to be mentioned throughout this lawsuit. Well, both Daniel Bowl and Dan Lee are no longer with Fiesta College. But Aaron Phillips is still here. Why hasn't he said anything?"

"Perhaps he has forgotten about it or is afraid or too embarrassed to say anything," I said.

"No, Aaron is trying to cover his ass," replied the president.

The next day, I called John Cabbot, and he was surprised to learn about Forest's behavior. He then informed me that he would like me to testify as a witness in the case. He then asked me to write down for him everything that transpired between myself, Forest Sawyer, Aaron Phillips, Daniel Bowl, and Dan Lee. I did it and mailed it to him a week later.

In July 1990, I was called to give a sworn deposition in the case. My testimony must have been a surprise to Forest's attorneys because I did not believe Forest or Trish had ever told them anything about Forest's shenanigans on behalf of his wife's application. I was not even sure how much Trish knew about Forest's activities. There was a deep sense after my deposition that the case was over. Forest certainly was not pleased with my testimony and made it clear to me when I ran into him in the hallway of the administration building that very afternoon. As we approached each other from opposite directions, he moved to the other side of the hallway and looked away. It was clear to me that he was angry with me for telling what I knew.

A week after the July deposition, I heard from several sources that several of the WMAC faculty who were friends with the Sawyers were very angry with me for my deposition. I was told that Valerie was openly calling for them to put additional pressure on the president to remove me from office. They were particularly "incensed the chief diversity officer of the college would testify against a female in a gender discrimination case. To add insult to injury, she was also the wife of a 'disabled self-made faculty' with whom the women and minorities had close affinity." John Akpan confirmed to me they had gone from not liking me to hating me. To them, I had become the enemy that galvanized their deepest and meanness impulses for personal destruction. He warned me to be careful of them because they were out to get me. They organized letter-writing campaigns in the community against me.

In early May 1990, the president asked me to work closely with Leticia Sayers, associate director of the Greenwood Association of Colleges and Universities (GACU), to revamp the Cultural Diversity Committee that had become ineffective. My role was to lead a small workgroup of committee members to develop a statement of committee charge as well as relevant processes, procedures, and policies. The committee had not been able to do anything meaningful because, instead of the senior diversity officers attending the meeting, many were sending subordinates to represent them at association meeting. In some cases, different individuals were sent in consecutive order to represent the senior diversity officers. This situation created problems with continuity and delayed decisions to allow for consultations with the senior diversity officer before a decision could be made. The problems were paralyzing, resulting in apathy and low turnout for meetings.

It was a challenging task given some of the characters I had to work with. Early on, I recognized the only way the workgroup would complete the task in a timely way was to keep them focused. I also recognized that, as chair, my role was to facilitate the discussions, and I was determined to do that even though I knew it would upset some. There was a tendency to drift into long sessions of complaining, blaming, and invectives against whites and white society. On several occasions, I had to confront certain behavior by some of the workgroup members, and this was sometimes unpleasant for everyone at the meetings. I accepted upfront that there was going to be some degree of bitching because I recognized that was part of the culture of diversity professional. But, on the occasions when raw bigotry reared its head, I felt compelled to respond.

Unfortunately, most of the bigotry came from one person, Nathan Abrasive, director of the school and community relations at the GACU. He was a black nationalist and Muslim with strong racist views about whites that he openly expressed during meetings. He was also one of Jane Dope's "guys" at Snow's talk who was heckling and calling him an Uncle Tom. He was a quiet but very angry person, and he interacted with me only when he had to. Even then, he was always short, abrupt, and matter-of-fact. I knew he was hostile toward me. I accepted that and tried not to bother him.

The problem with Nathan's behavior deteriorated as we were completing the workgroup's task related to revamping the Cultural Diversity Committee. He came into the last meeting of the workgroup angry and steaming about racism against him at the Greenwood Association.

"It's whitey again. Always out to put down an assertive and proud black man," he announced as he walked into the meeting room.

"What's happening, man?" asked William Stills, director of diversity at Rosary College.

"I just had my performance evaluation that amounted to a racist put-down of a successful black man. I mean the whole thing was so offensive and insensitive. It was a racist attempt by the racist new director to push me out so that they can hire another whitey or Uncle Tom. All the criticisms were personal and about what they call 'my general attitude and behavior,'" he declared.

"I know what you mean, man. I am going through the same thing at Rosary College. That's the way white folks are. They don't like black men with a strong sense of identity confidence. They want us all to be 'step 'n fetch it' before we are good enough for them. You practically have to be an Uncle Tom for them to promote you," added William Stills.

"Yeah, man, I know what you mean. I have seen some of it at Regency College. But they leave me alone 'cause they are scared of me because of my physical stature," said Abel Sigfried.

"These motherfuckers even criticized the small, knitted black, green, and red skullcap I wear to work. They don't think it's professional, but, if a goddamned Jew wore a skullcap, I bet it would be okay. I've had it with these white dogs, man. Whitey is always out to put us down, man," added Nathan.

"Well, I am looking for another job. I have an offer from the Social Work Institutes, but I am not sure if I want to work again with all those crackers over there. It will drive me fucking crazy. You should see this loudmouth, midget Jewish bitch I have to deal with, man. I had to listen to her fucking talk about her personal diversity—that she is of French, Jewish descent," said Nathan.

"What's the job?" asked William Stills.

"Director of diversity. It's one of the largest, oldest private social services organizations in the country. Here at the Greenwood Association, all I have to do is deal with are three or four whites at the most. But out there, I will have to deal with dozens of them and lots of loudmouth and opinionated Jews. I don't know if I can take it," responded Nathan.

"How is the salary? Is it good?" asked Abel.

"When has whitey ever paid a black man an honest salary? It's about the same as what I make here. Whitey is whitey everywhere, man. They pay only slave wages, man," replied Nathan.

"Man, I've got to say this, but we sound just like the bigots we condemn out there. I believe we need to have a serious conversation about our own behavior and values. I'm not just talking about Nathan's behavior, but our acceptance and support that allowed him to continue with racist comments," I announced.

"What the fuck are you talking about?" asked William Stills.

"Well, I am talking about the tone and racist nature of the conversation that went on between you, Nathan, and Abel. I am also talking about those of us who said and did nothing even though we realized it was wrong. Why didn't we say something to stop the conversation? I am including myself in this, you know. Why didn't I say something immediately after Nathan used the first racial epithets? Why did I wait 'til the end before I said something? I need to find out why, for my own sake. So does everyone of us here this afternoon. Might we ourselves be the enemy?" I asked.

"What the hell are you talking about? I am getting the fuck out of here before I do something I will end up regretting later," said Nathan as he left the room.

"Me too, man. I don't want to hear this shit," said another as he left the room after Nathan.

That was the end of the meeting. Everyone left after my last comment. I went immediately down the hall to talk with Leticia Sayers and the director about my concerns regarding the behavior of Nathan Abrasive because he worked for them. I also submitted the new statement of charge for the Committee on Cultural Diversity and a short report on some recommended new processes and procedures for cosponsoring diversity-related programs at the Greenwood Association. They were not the least surprised. In fact, they went on for an hour detailing all the attitude and performance problems they had with him. They had been trying to deal with some of the attitude problems as well.

"But Nathan Abrasive allowed no criticism," said Leticia Sayers. "Any criticism of his behavior—no matter how carefully you say it—is a criticism of all black men and racist. We can't wait for him to find another job."

About a month later, I heard Nathan had started working at the Social Work Institute as their "chief diversity officer." I ran into him at the Institute when I was over there a number of occasions in order to conduct training seminars they sponsored at their facilities. He appeared friendly and less uptight than he was before, but he did not attend any of the seminars. I assumed he felt sensitivity training was only for whites.

6

The Cabal

In October 1989, I saw an advertisement for the position vacancy for associate vice president for personnel services and diversity at Eastern State University (ESU). I knew nothing about ESU and never even heard of it. However, the job sounded great, and the university was in warmer weather, which made the opportunity more attractive. As I read the position announcement aloud to my wife, she reminded me I had expressed frustration about diversity-related jobs and a yearning for something new. I told her I might just throw my hat in the ring and wait to see what happens. I had one major concern though. The affirmative action affairs office reported to the associate vice president. I had very little experience with affirmative action issues. This would soon change because working at ESU was one big lesson in EEO and AA violations!

The interview at ESU went very well. I met several key people in the university administration, including the vice president of personnel services and diversity, Maryann Cole, to whom the position reported administratively, and the chair of the search committee, Daniel Marks, who was associate dean in the School of Arts and Sciences (SAS) and formerly the special assistant to the president for minority affairs. I did not get to meet with the new president, Diane Franklin.

My meetings with Maryann Cole went very well. She was infectiously excited about the new position and the potential for transforming the university. She emphasized the need for lots of training for faculty, students, and staff and told me my experience as a diversity trainer and my administrative background made me a highly desirable candidate for the position. She struck me as a warm, friendly, and a genuinely committed person. Her enthusiasm infected me to the point that, by the time I returned to Albion, I could not get the university out of my mind. However, I still had lingering concerns about the supervisory responsibility for the affirmative action office.

My discussions with Maryann Cole had touched upon the concerns I had about combining the AA and diversity functions. I informed her that many universities kept both of these functions separate in the hopes of not "tarnishing" their diversity initiatives with all the political negativity associated with affirmative action. She said the idea of separating the two functions sounded like a good one, particularly in a place like ESU, which had gone through a recent unpleasant experience with the affirmative action office. I suggested she might want to consider separating the two functions. I hastily added I was very interested in the position the way it was advertised. I did not want to leave her with the impression that I was negotiating with her before I had been offered the job.

Soon after my return to Albion, Maryann Cole called to offer me the job. She informed me I would have one executive secretary and a coordinator-level position I could fill as soon as I started to work at ESU. When I went for an informational meeting in April, she mentioned to me that two senior black administrators, Vernon Machiavelli and Alfred Pratt, associate vice president and associate provost respectively, had pressured her to remove Sheryl Swift from the affirmative action office because they did not like her and felt she was incompetent. Maryann further mentioned that, while she did not generally consider "not liking" someone a good reason for reassigning a staff, there were other problems in the affirmative action office that needed resolution. She said she planned to appoint Penny Pierce as the interim director of affirmative action and eventually give her a fair chance to compete for the permanent job, for which I would be conducting a national search when I arrived. Maryann also informed me she had to "borrow" the coordinator-level position for Sheryl Swift and promised to give back the position after the affirmative action director's position was filled.

During the afternoon, I met with Penny Pierce because, as the interim director of affirmative action, she wanted to discuss how she should classify me racially because she could not find my Affirmative Action Data Card. I told her I do not normally return Affirmative Action Data Cards and could not remember if I had returned ESU's data card. She asked me to identify myself so that she could list me in one of the racial and ethnic categories. I told her to list me as "other," but she was not satisfied. She said that, if I had any African ancestry, I should be listed as black and emphasized that what she was doing was common practice. It helps "the numbers," she said. It didn't occur to me at the time to ask who benefited from those numbers.

I started in the new position in the summer of 1990, as associate vice president for personnel and diversity, which put me about three levels from the president at ESU. Anyway you count it, this was by far the most prominent position I had held in my career as a university administrator. I was excited about the prospect of being so high up in the administration. Not so much because of power and prestige, but because I felt like, for the first time, I would be in a position where big egos and contrary agendas would not block my efforts to make some positive and exciting changes. Even at Fiesta College, where I had been assistant to the president, I still had to accommodate many people because my position was one without rank despite its affiliation with the president. I knew I would not be able to use any power or position to coerce people into changing, even if I wanted to, and I didn't want to. But influence is always helped by position. With "Associate Vice President" in front of my name, I knew people would be more likely to return phone calls and at least accept meetings. Add to this the fact this was the closest climate to my homeland of West Africa I had lived in since moving to the United States almost twenty-five years prior. I was really excited about being in warm weather again and being able to grow at least subtropical fruits I loved such as wax jambu, papaya, mango, and guava. I had always wondered how so many Africans could live in a place like New York City or Washington, DC!

My first assignment was to fill the vacant director of affirmative action position and begin developing the new diversity office. A day after my arrival on campus in July, Penny Pierce came to talk to me about the affirmative action director's search. She wanted to know if I was going to conduct a national search or a more limited search within the state university system. She favored the more limited search because she felt a national search reduced her probability for getting the job. I told her I favored a national search because I felt that would broaden the pool of applicants for the position. She was not pleased with my response. She blurted out that Maryann had promised her the job, and she could not understand the need for a search for a position that was already hers. I reiterated she would get serious consideration (although I was beginning to have serious doubts about her based on actions like this), but I wanted a broad base of candidates to ensure the best decision. She also informed me she had sent me the paperwork for a maternity leave via campus mail.

I told Maryann what Penny had said about being promised the job. Maryann told me that Penny had been having problems lately and showed me a couple of memos in which people complained about Penny's personality and interpersonal style of dealing with people. She assured me that she never promised her the position and that Penny had suggested the limited search earlier, but she was noncommittal and told her she would leave it up to me.

I met again the next day with Penny to discuss her request for maternity leave, which I approved. Just before she left, she asked me again if I was still firm on the issue of conducting a national search. I responded affirmatively and watched her turn very angry. And then she accused me of wanting to hire a Hispanic person over her and informed me she had seen the woman's résumé on my desk the other day. (Maria, despite her name, was black, not Hispanic). As she left, she threatened to fight the decision to conduct a national search.

At first, I was perplexed by her comment about a Hispanic woman's résumé, but, when I inspected my desk, I had a good laugh at her foolishness. She had seen Maria Montenegro's résumé on my desk. Maria was not interested in the affirmative action job at ESU. Penny Pierce had seen nothing but the name on the résumé and jumped to paranoid conclusions. Maria Montenegro was an African-American woman from Boston who was married to an acquaintance from the former Portuguese colony of Cape Verde Islands located off the west coast of Africa. The Cape Verde Islands had spent centuries as a Portuguese colony, hence the "Hispanic" name. I had her résumé on my desk because she had applied for a job at another university where I had contacts. She wanted me to put in a good word for her, and I asked to see her résumé since I knew her on a social level rather than professionally. I wanted to be well-informed about her credentials in case I was asked any questions about her previous experiences. What was with Penny Pierce's insinuation that I wanted to hire a Hispanic and had chosen this particular one? Did anybody ever really say, "I'm going to hire a Hispanic. Let me go find one."? At ESU, I would eventually learn that they did.

One afternoon, Sheryl Swift, Penny Pierce's former supervisor who had been reassigned to the vice president's office, came to see me and warned me to be very careful because she said "Penny was a pathological liar" and was responsible for all of the problems in the affirmative action office, which led to her removal from her former position. She told me Penny was stirring things up against me in the BFSA by telling them I had denied being black on the affirmative action reporting data form when she confronted me about it. Sheryl advised me to go public about my racial identity in order to avoid problems with blacks on campus. I told her what I had told everyone else: I really had no racial or ethnic identity. After which, she advised me to expect my identity to become an issue if I did not identify myself soon. She added that identifying myself as an African would not work.

She said, "They want to know whether you are black."

As I walked back to my office, I pictured myself on top of the tallest building on campus with a megaphone proclaiming to the world, "I AM BLACK!" or walking across campus, shaking hands with everyone I came across and saying "Hi, I'm black, nice to meet you." Maybe I could have new business cards made: Samir Dyfan—Black Man. As my mood turned more cynical at the foolishness of all of this, I pictured myself with a cable access television show where I proclaimed daily that I had black African ancestors. Would being black make my judgment clearer or my policies more right? Or would it simply make them think I would be on their side? Sometimes looking back, I wonder, just out of curiosity, how things might have been if I had said I was black but continued everything else exactly the same as I did. I am not sure it would have made a difference when push came to shove, as it often did, but it might have forestalled a lot of hostility.

In August 1990, Alfred Pratt and I went to lunch. Over General Tso's chicken, Alfred said the Diversity Planning Program as well as education and training programs for faculty, staff, and students were what he felt needed to be focused on immediately. Then he turned his attention to another matter, Sheryl Swift. He said he and three other senior black administrators, Johnny Brown, dean of Fine Arts; Daniel Marks, associate dean of Arts and Sciences; and Vernon Machiavelli, associate vice president for academic affairs had pressured Maryann Cole to remove Sheryl from the affirmative action director's position because Sheryl was incompetent, enumerating all her failures as affirmative action director. He praised Penny Pierce as "100 times more competent than Sheryl." After the meeting, we agreed to consult frequently.

Three weeks later, I went to lunch with Vernon Machiavelli, a senior black administrator in the university. After a perfunctory discussion about the problems at ESU, he also turned his attention to Sheryl Swift and repeated the story about her incompetence and how he, Alfred, John, and Daniel had pressured Maryann Cole to remove Sheryl from the EEO office. He also emphasized they were pleased Maryann listened to them because they had some reservations about her. Finally, he praised Penny Pierce as the best choice for the position and also praised Maryann for naming her interim director of affirmative action. At the end of lunch, he also urged me to work closely with him as I developed the new diversity office. I promised to stay in touch.

By September 1990, I had the first draft of the position announcement ready for review by Maryann Cole. The search committee had been constituted, and the first meeting date was scheduled for late October. The director of personnel, Lucy Dalembert, was the chair designate of the search committee. The committee membership included the assistant university general counsel and diverse individuals representing the various minority groups on campus.

The first meeting ended abruptly after Joe Mills, chair of the Presidential Advisory Committee on Blacks (PACB), abruptly asked me, "So, what *is* your racial identity? We are all curious."

I had been explaining how Penny Pierce had accused me of wanting to hire a Hispanic when she had seen Maria Montenegro's résumé on my desk, mistakenly assuming she was applying for the job and she was Hispanic.

"My identity has nothing to do with the search and position," I replied.

"Yes, it does. Now quit dodging the question. Are you black?" he asked.

"I am an African immigrant that is now an American citizen. What does this question have to do with the search?" I asked.

"We want to ensure the person who runs and supervises that office is black. That's why we must know your identity," he responded. "You keep saying you're an African, but that doesn't tell me if you're black. There are many white people who say they're African."

"I don't believe this search should continue until we know your racial identity because you're the person who is going to eventually select and hire the new director of affirmative action. That's why you must answer the question," he continued.

Before I could say anything else, Maryann Cole said, "You know, Joe, Samir is multicultural and has African ancestry. Isn't that enough?"

"I don't want to hear that from you. I want Samir to answer the question," Joe responded.

Sensing an impasse, Maryann Cole called off the meeting. Other members of the committee appeared frustrated while others were alarmed at Joe's "racial attitude." After the meeting, Maryann Cole asked me what I thought about Joe's behavior. I told her what Sheryl Swift had warned me about weeks earlier. Maryann said she would determine the next move regarding the search after a meeting with President Diane Franklin.

A week later, Maryann invited me to lunch, adding we needed to talk about the affirmative action office. During lunch, she told me President Franklin had requested I give up supervision of the affirmative action office. She explained blacks were agitating and pressing the president to take the affirmative action office away from me. She added that it was "no secret they do not trust you." I told her I do not have any choice but to agree to the president's request. I was deeply disappointed President Franklin had caved in (and so quickly and without involving me) to the intimidation and agitations. Maryann thanked me for agreeing to the changes, and she informed me the position would report directly to her until the president decided what she wanted to do with it. We both recognized this was what I had suggested to Maryann during the job interview. Yet, when Maryann had presented it to the president on its own merits (that is, affirmative action and diversity functions should be separated to avoid the appearance of conflict of interest and a bully pulpit), she had snubbed the idea. Add a little self-interested intimidation, she caved. Apparently, reason and principle were no reason to do something except for saving your ass.

In November 1990, I received a memorandum from Maryann Cole that the search for the director of affirmative action had been terminated. The president had decided to appoint a committee to "examine the functions and reporting relationships of that office."

In early February 1991, I heard an urgent meeting of the BFSA had been called to discuss its recommendations for the Affirmative Action Review Committee to be chaired by Lisa Crist, the university's general counsel. During the meeting, one of the leaders of the BFSA, Tom Strung, spoke openly about what he believed "black folks wanted."

He said, "Blacks had told the university administration two years ago that we wanted a black man, Daniel Marks, appointed to the newly created position of vice president for personnel services and diversity [Maryann's job], but they failed to listen. And instead, they went ahead and put a white woman in the position and ignored our demands. If they had done what we had demanded and put a black person like Daniel Marks in that position, they wouldn't be in the mess they are in now. We need to send President Franklin a strong signal we are not going to accept anything short of the removal of Maryann Cole and replacing her with Daniel Marks."

"It is important that a black person supervise that office, and I support what Tom is saying here. We must fight for what we want and demand they put Daniel Marks in that position," Joe Mills added.

"Tell me, Tom," I asked. "If it is so important to have a 'black person' in top positions, why then don't you want Clarence Thomas in the Supreme Court. Is he not black?"

"Why are you always against black people? This is another example of why you should not supervise that office," he responded.

"Look," I said, "what you are doing is wrong and even illegal. Furthermore, it is unprincipled and unfair for you to go through with this plan. Maryann Cole has done nothing wrong to deserve this attempt to push her out of her position." At this point, Baron Brown, the chair of BFSA, interrupted the discussion and abruptly ended the meeting in a very disappointed tone as he admonished them about their attitude. After the meeting, I went up to Baron and made a point of saying, "I hope you remember what just happened here because I will never be involved in it."

He responded by promising he had chaired his last BFSA meeting because he disapproved of what Tom and Joe were doing in the name of BFSA in general and their move to oust Maryann in particular.

The next day, I told Maryann about the discussions at the BFSA meeting. She said Tanya, her secretary, was at the meeting and had informed her about it. I told her Tanya had spoken against what the BFSA were planning to do and that Tanya's exact words were, "I know Maryann and have worked with her for fifteen years. She is a good person. I can't go along with anything that will hurt her." Maryann was saddened by what was happening and deeply disappointed that others did not speak out against what they were planning to do.

The next week, I heard that several black administrators had started to put pressure on President Franklin to remove Maryann Cole and install Daniel Marks as vice president for personnel and diversity. I also heard that Penny Pierce and several black administrators (all in interim positions) were working politically with Tom Strung and others to ensure they were the permanent appointments for their jobs and for the removal of Maryann Cole from her vice presidential position on Daniel Marks' behalf. I had developed a close relationship with one of the conspirators, Delma Sheets, so I naturally went to talk with her about what I had heard. She confirmed everything and added that one of the other conspirators, Tina Lickton, was closely related to Virginia Sulfer, the associate chancellor of equal opportunity at the State University System's Board of Regents. Delma said Penny Pierce and Tina were working with Virginia at the University Board to pressure President Franklin to remove Maryann Cole from her position. Delma appeared very nervous as she talked with me.

Delma went on to tell me how Al Richards, vice president for student services, and Sheryl Hendrix, his associate vice president, were mistreating her. She was close to having a nervous breakdown. Sheryl and Al were both senior black administrators. I offered to help if she needed my assistance. She promised to keep in touch with me for support because she said I was one of the people she trusted and respected in the university.

After my meeting with Delma Sheets, I went straight to the president's office to speak with her about my concerns regarding efforts to push Maryann out of her position. She saw me for a few minutes and assured me she would talk to me again before any decisions were made about Maryann Cole's situation. But she never talked with me.

One morning in March 1991, Maryann came into my office in tears and told me "they" had destroyed her career and everything she worked for all her life. I was stunned when she told me President Franklin had given her a week to find another job. And then she showed me a memorandum from Virginia Sulfer accusing her of numerous failures in her supervision of the affirmative action office. I could not believe it. Diane Franklin had done one of the most unprincipled things I had ever seen in my entire career as a diversity officer. I was determined to talk with her about it, but she would not meet with me. So, I went to her speechwriter, Ted Lemons, and asked him to please tell President Franklin that I was very disappointed and angry because of the way Maryann Cole had been treated. I wanted her to know that many on campus were deeply disappointed with her unprincipled leadership.

A week later, Maryann was given the choice of a reassignment if she could find another position elsewhere in the university. She talked with Al Richards in the student services office, but he dragged her on for weeks and then disappointed her in the end. Maryann was eventually reassigned to the Medical Sciences Center as assistant vice president for faculty affairs—with a significant salary cut.

The president had miscalculated the effect of her decision; everyone was talking about how "blacks had pushed Maryann out of her job for Daniel Marks." Ted Lemons told me he had heard about it and had relayed the information to the president.

A group of directors from several administrative departments demanded a meeting with the president to talk about their displeasure with her decision to reassign Maryann Cole to the Medical Sciences Center. A few days before the meeting, the vice president for administration sent his directors a memorandum cautioning them about getting too deeply involved in the matter and reminding them Maryann "served at the pleasure of the president." Many of the directors who received the memo were outraged that it appeared to be condoning what the president had done to Maryann.

The memorandum was perceived as an implied threat by some of his directors, and many heeded it. Just before the meeting started in a meeting room in the School of Business, the president walked up to me.

She asked, "Who is in charge here?"

"You," I responded.

"I am in charge?" she asked.

"Yes, you are the president. Aren't you? You make all of the tough political decisions," I replied.

"Yes, I am the president, and I am in charge. Don't you ever forget that," she said aloud as she poked me in the shoulder and walked away toward the podium.

During the meeting, she talked about all of the changes that were occurring on campus and promised a lot more in the near future. There was silence when she finished. Maryann Cole was not discussed, and the meeting ended. Most of the people I talked with afterwards felt "bullied" by the way the president had blown off their concerns. Racial tension on campus remained very high for several months.

In April 1991, I received a copy of a report authored by Lisa Crist containing recommendations from the Affirmative Action Review Committee. The key recommendations were to upgrade the position to assistant vice president for affirmative action from the director's level with one of three possible reporting relationships: to the president, to the provost, or to the new vice president of personnel and information. The president chose the last option, exactly as I had recommended months earlier. Maryann Cole was gone by late March, and Lucy Dalembert was appointed interim vice president until President Franklin completed the reorganization.

Sometime in early April 1991, Vernon Machiavelli invited me to lunch with the some senior black administrators (SBA) at ESU. The lunch meeting was scheduled for the following week at the Big Trees Country Club. He informed me they were a group of administrators above the rank of assistant dean that met once a month to discuss issues relevant to black interests.

I attended the meeting and met many of the SBA members. The meeting itself was uneventful, but the ride home from the meeting was memorable. I hitched a ride back to campus from the country club with Daniel Marks. On the way back, we talked about what had happened to Maryann Cole. I mentioned to him that Tom Strung and Joe Mills had said in a BFSA meeting they were demanding Maryann Cole be removed from her position so that a black person could be appointed to the job. I mentioned they had named him, Daniel Marks, as the person that should replace her in the vice presidential position.

"How do you feel about it?" I asked him.

"Well, Diane Franklin had telephoned me the other day and offered me the job, but I am no longer interested in that position as I was last year before you came," he said.

"What do you mean?" I asked.

"My interest has changed since I have been over in the School of Arts and Sciences. My interest is now in the dean's position in the School of Arts and Sciences. It is a natural progression from where I am now located as associate dean," he replied.

"Daniel, I hope you turned down the offer because I feel it will be wrong for you to accept that position given everything that has transpired on campus in the past few weeks," I responded.

"Well, as I said, I am now interested in the Arts and Sciences job. The current dean will soon be leaving ESU," he assured me.

He did not look pleased with my comments. After the lunch meeting with them, I became very curious about the role of the SBA in Maryann Cole's removal from her job. Daniel seems to have been in lock-step with the idea until he recently set his sights higher.

During the early parts of June 1991, President Franklin pulled me aside at a meeting in the Student Union to inform me she was reassigning me to report directly to the provost's office as soon as the new provost, Ron Liste, arrived in June. I wanted to talk about the resources and space Maryann had promised me before she was removed, but the president said she was in a hurry and promised to talk with me at a later date. All my efforts to schedule a follow-up conversation were rebuked.

I continued to attend the SBA meetings because I was curious about how they operated. I mentioned my interest to study the workings of the SBA to a couple of people on campus as future witnesses about my reasons for attending SBA meetings. I also kept them regularly informed about my discoveries. I felt that, in order to do my job, I needed to know what they were up to. But I also knew they might go so far that I would need to be protected from association with them. And finally, I felt like it was my responsibility, as chief diversity officer, to protect the university from illegal actions by its employees, especially senior administrators. Among those I kept informed were a vice president, a director, and a lawyer in the general counsel's office.

By mid-fall 1991, almost three months after my transfer to the provost office, the associate provost approached me about "a serious problem in the office between Vernon Machiavelli and the white female administrative assistants in the office." She mentioned that the problem had deteriorated because everyone was afraid to deal with Vernon's abusive behavior toward the women that worked for him. She added that, over the years, the women in the provost's office had encountered one of his assistants crying in the women's restroom. She said Vernon had not been able to keep a secretary for more than six months lately. Most of the women in the provost's office (even those that didn't work for him) were afraid of him because of his emotional tirades. She indicated that people were afraid to deal with him because he was a senior black administrator. Although it was ostensibly appropriate to assign this task to me, it was clear that, as a white woman, she was politically and physically frightened to handle it herself.

I mentioned to her that someone had told me the previous provost had discussed Vernon's behavior and possible disciplinary actions with the former vice president of personnel services. However, the provost had decided that he and his SBA friends were too powerful and well organized. He did not want to risk antagonizing them. He decided to leave it up to the next provost.

A few weeks later, the issue of Vernon's temperament and relationship with his staff appeared on the agenda of the provost's staff meeting. As it turned out, the support staff in Vernon's office had complained to the new provost about problems with Vernon's behavior. Most of the discussions focused on his nasty temper and abusive behavior toward the women in the office. It showed up on the agenda because of the provost's discussions with several people among the senior staff. Even though the provost did not attend the meetings, he felt we should be able to discuss and resolve the problems.

But Vernon would have none of it. He became very angry and defensive. As a result, a decision was made to table the issue until the next staff meeting. But Vernon did not show up for that meeting, so we decided to try again during the next meeting. That attempt also failed to get anywhere because of Vernon's refusal to take any responsibility for the problems. He insisted the women were incompetent and deserved the treatment they got and that we all "hold our staffs to the same rigorous standards."

One week later, the assistant provost asked me to intervene and explore the possibility of mediation between Vernon and the support staff. I agreed to try and went to talk with Vernon about it.

His response to the idea was typical. "I don't see how the hell these fucking allegations relate to diversity," he said.

"In many ways," I said.

"Well, stay the hell away from me if you know what's good for you," he responded.

"You are a man. They are all women. You are black, and most of them are white. So you can see the potential here for a diversity-related problem," I replied.

"I am not the problem here. All I have done is uphold high standards of performance for my staff. When they cannot cut the mustard, I fire them. If others would do the same with their incompetent staff, we would not have this problem in the office. Would we?" he asked.

"Now, the problem used to be Mona Barry organizing the women against me. But we took care of her; she is gone. Now *that* incompetent bitch has gone to the new Hispanic Studies Department, Janet Inkster is the one behind organizing problems. Go talk to her and stay the hell away from me—if you know what's good for you," he threatened again as he walked away.

I went back, reported his response to everyone, and did not try again. Needless to say, everyone was disappointed because they felt the problem had gone unaddressed for so long that it had affected morale among the support staff. As I talked with senior staff in the office and others who were familiar with the problems associated with Vernon's behavior, everyone ended their comments with the same phrase, "It continues because 'they' are black and too powerful."

The problem continued unaddressed, and everyone went back to behaving as if there wasn't a problem until the next victim was found in the women's restroom. In fact, the problem was dealt with some years later. Two women filed a formal complaint against Vernon, and the university hired an independent counsel to investigate. The independent counsel provided a 160-page report that detailed twenty years of systematic emotional abuse and intimidation and failed attempts to address the problem by the university (not to mention an affair with a white undergraduate student that worked at a popular strip club and a 3:00 AM DUI arrest). The new provost at the time, Daniel Marks, an SBA member and buddy of his, "disciplined" him by reassigning him to a nearby regional campus with his title and salary intact.

Someone in the president's office told me the president had ordered the new provost, Ron Liste, to deal with the "Vernon Machiavelli problem" in his office before an official complaint was filed in the affirmative action office. But there was one big problem: Ron had the same problem with his temper. Within the first three months of his arrival on campus, his reputation as a "raging maniac" was well-established in the administration office complex. Now we had to deal with two raging maniacs in the provost office.

By late fall 1991, I had firsthand experience with Ron Liste's abusive temper. In a brief encounter in the secretarial lobby in front of his office, he stopped me one afternoon and started yelling at me in front of everyone, including the guests in his office about my consultancy with the regional water management agency.

"Any damned consulting fee you make belongs in full to this fucking office," he announced. "I own all of your time seven days a week, twenty-four hours a day. So, any money you make consulting belongs to this office."

"First," I said, "I would like you to know I am not a slave. Second, the university officially permits limited, outside activity. Third, I do not appreciate the way you are talking to me. I treat you respectfully and expect to be treated the same way. If it happens again, I will take appropriate action." After this incident, he stopped meeting with me and never again met with me until he left office.

As morale problems in the provost's office worsened, another problem was emerging in the student services office. Al Richards and Sheryl Hendrix, both

SBA members, had developed a reputation for "mean-spiritedness." By spring 1996, they had, by some estimates, fired or demoted as many as twelve people—mostly blacks and Hispanics. As I talked with student services professional and support staff, I began to realize they were living and working in a state of fear. Even people with a reputation for calmness and discipline were "running scared."

As I studied the situations in the provost's office and student services office, I began to realize that, unlike the situation in the academic affairs office, which involved yelling, swearing, and cursing in angry outbursts, the problem in the student services area was created by a set of different behaviors. Al Richards and Sheryl Hendrix were quiet, reserved, short, and abrupt in conversations with their staff, and many of the directors told me they had never received annual performance evaluations, which put them "on edge" because they did not know how they were doing.

As one director put it, "When you add all the wanton firing and demotion of competent people to their arrogance and mean-spirited behaviors, you have a state of fear in the student services office. Everyone is wondering who is next."

Al Richards and Sheryl Hendrix had, by late spring, after Delma Sheets had a nervous breakdown and more firings, became the most feared and despised individuals on campus. Rumors started circulating that Al and Sheryl were having a sexual affair, that Sheryl had been given ten to fifteen percent annual raises (which I confirmed by consulting public documents), and that they were both incompetent. Word about Al and Sheryl's abuse of fellow blacks spread in the community; they had become pariahs. Some of it was a result of their mistreatment of Delma Sheets, who, in addition to being the daughter of the president of the local NAACP, was married to a prominent local doctor who himself was the son of a county commissioner and provost of a nearby community college. Things were getting uglier.

I had heard enough. I decided to talk with Al about what I was hearing and my own perceptions. After many attempts to get an appointment with him failed, I unexpectedly ran into him in the staircase in front of the president's office. He pulled me aside and said, "I heard you want to talk."

"Yes, very urgently," I responded.

"That urgently?"

"Can we talk now?" he asked as he pulled my arm back up the stairs to the lobby.

I told him that his and Sheryl's reputation in the student services office, elsewhere on campus, and even in the community was one of "mean-spiritedness." I told him that both blacks and Hispanics were expressing unhappiness with their leadership. The consequences of which is low morale among his staff.

He pulled up his lips, furrowed his forehead, pointed at me in close range, and said, "I have done nothing wrong. The incompetent and unproductive ones are being let go. Among them have been many whites, blacks, and Hispanics. No group can claim discrimination. As for the black ones, I am blacker than they are." He then pointed at the very dark skin on the back of his hand. "I can't see how they can claim discrimination." He jabbed his finger at me in rhythm with his words.

By the time he finished his first statement, he was very angry. Something tempted me to tell him that maybe that was the reason why someone recommended the two of them for the "equal opportunity abusers awards." I reminded myself this conversation was for the sake of those affected and not so I could amuse myself with an arrogant bastard's reaction.

I then asked, "You are not angry with me. Are you, Al?"

"No, I'm angry at those who don't understand you have to do your job dispassionately, but they bring up all that emotional crap. I don't have anything personal against any of them. The decisions are made on merit, not whether or not we like the individual."

"Well, I hope you're not angry with me because I cannot deal with other people's anger. I have enough of my own. But I believe it is my obligation to inform you about serious problems with immense implications for diversity at ESU," I said as I walked away.

I realized, weeks later, that he was indeed angry with me because he refused to acknowledge my presence or to make eye contact with me for a long time. As I talked with colleagues about the problems in academic affairs office and student services office, I realized the magnitude of the problems had begun to worry some people in the provost's office. People began to refer to the executives of the SBA as the "Gang of Four" (Vernon Machiavelli, Alfred Pratt, Daniel Marks, and Al Richards). But what could people do? Diane Franklin refused to deal with the Gang of Four "because they were *too* powerful and organized." To some, that was understandable." But what was keeping President Franklin from dealing with Ron Liste? He was new, not "networked" like the others, and could not pull the "race card" either. People felt powerless to do anything when the president was refusing to do anything. The problems persisted, as did the rapid slide of morale.

By late spring 1992, the searches for vice provost and the dean of Arts and Sciences positions had wound down. Rumors started circulating that two SBA members—Alfred Pratt and Daniel Marks—were going to get those respective positions. People were saying things like "Diane wouldn't dare pass them over for those positions. They are too highly organized and powerful."

Rumors began to circulate that Ron Liste was in a dilemma in the two job searches. Word had it that Daniel Marks was Diane's choice, and Ron had to go along with it. But, in the vice provost search, Ron was under heavy pressure from other blacks to hire Alfred over his first choice, Phyllis Autry. Alfred had threatened to resign if Ron did not select him because, as associate provost, he was the next in line for the job. It would be discriminatory not to give him the job he told anyone who would listen. He spread rumors he would file an EEO complaint if he were passed over for the vice provost job. Did Diane and Ron hear these rumors and take heed? I could not say for sure, but, if they didn't, they are the only ones who didn't.

In response to Alfred's threats, Ron decided to split the position and hired two vice provosts instead of one. I went to talk with Ron about the rumors and if he thought any response was needed. But he arrived fifty-five minutes late for our scheduled one-hour meeting. The next day, he announced his choices for the vice provost's search.

By early summer 1992, Ron Liste had managed to alienate almost everyone in the provost's office to the point where he stopped attending provost's staff meetings—despite being the provost! The two vice provosts cochaired the meetings. One morning, as I walked to my office through the parking lot, a colleague mentioned to me that Ron had reassigned me to report to the new vice provost, Alfred. I told her I had not heard anything about it, but I would look into the rumor. Within days, four others mentioned the same thing to me. So I decided to talk with Ron about it.

He confirmed that I had been reassigned to Alfred, but I had been too busy to tell me himself. He said the decision to reassign me to report to Alfred Pratt had come from recommendations made by President Franklin, Daniel Marks, Alfred Pratt, and Vernon Machievelli because they argued diversity is really a human resources-related function and should report to the vice provost that is responsible for faculty human resources. I expressed my disappointment at his discourtesy and protested the decision on my reassignment. I mentioned he should know that, since my arrival two years ago, I had had four different supervisors and been located in two vice presidential areas. In each case, I was not consulted or informed about the changes. He said Alfred would explain everything to me and that I would find him a great advocate for my office.

Three of the Gang of Four recommended I be moved to Alfred's supervision. I was beginning to realize they felt threatened by my challenges to their methods and wanted to keep a closer eye on me. Why had Ron not been suspicious? Didn't Ron wonder why they had even been *thinking* about where my position should report?

I continued to attend SBA meetings, but they were uneventful except for the fact the senior executive members of the SBA expressed great frustration they could not get everyone at the meetings. It appeared to me that some of them, namely Vernon Machiavelli and Johnny Brown, wanted to talk about something but needed everyone present in order to discuss whatever they had in mind. I became curious about the need to have everyone present before we could talk. I talked with Vernon about it, but he brushed me off with "I would rather wait until we have everyone together in the same room."

In early fall 1992, I heard from Cynthia Peters, the new director of Black Community Advancement, that Jack Okun, an engineering faculty member from West Africa, and Jim Aaron, associate dean for diversity initiatives in the School of Medicine, were attempting to revive the mothballed BFSA. Jack told me Alfred had told him it would take a man of his charisma to revive the BFSA and had asked him to work with Jim on the task. He mentioned the time, place, and date of the next meeting. I showed up on the date of the first organized meeting to express my deep concerns and reservations about reviving the BFSA. I told them, at the beginning of the meeting, that I was opposed to the revival of the organization because "the BFSA leadership had in the past behaved very reprehensibly. Some of the things they had done like targeting Maryann Cole because of her race were illegal and had caused a lot of racial problems on campus."

"Who exactly are you talking about when you say the leadership?" demanded Tom Strung, director of multicultural recruitment in the admissions office.

"I don't want to get personal," I responded.

"No, please tell us who exactly you are talking about," he repeated.

"Tom, I don't want to get personal. I am talking about behaviors, not persons," I replied.

As we talked, he jumped out of his chair, pushed it back, and raised his voice. "No, tell us exactly who the hell you mean."

"Well, Tom, as you have obviously already assumed, sometimes *your* behavior is reprehensible. I wish you would do something about it because it has become a serious problem," I finished.

"What are you doing here?" asked Lynette Fallers, coordinator of diversity in the School of Education. "This is a meeting for black people, and you ain't one of us—so please get the hell out of here." She pushed back her chair and pounded her fist on the conference table.

I stayed until the end of the meeting and went to see Alfred to inform him about the BFSA meeting. He was not pleased to say the least. He said we were working at counter purposes, and that means I must consult with him before taking major actions like that. He asked me to reflect on the consequences if I continued to antagonize BFSA members. Besides, he said it was the SBA that was trying to revive the BFSA because they could be handy as leverage from time to time. I told him my concerns were with the behaviors of some of the leaders, who claim to speak on behalf of BFSA and blacks in general.

In September 1992, I received an invitation from the president's office to attend a Black Awards Luncheon downtown. The secretary informed me I would ride along in the president's car as she wanted to speak with me. During the twenty-minute trip on the day of the event, she told me she wanted me to know how deeply disappointed she was with certain black administrators who misled her about the Penny Pierce affair. She wanted me to know she had learned a lesson from it all. On our way back, she wanted me to tell her about my life, particularly my childhood experiences, and joked this may help explain "why you are the way you are." As we approached the campus, she mentioned again that some people (in whom she had placed a lot of trust) had misled her. As she pulled into her reserved parking space, she said, "And some of those who deceived me are in important position in this university. But it won't happen again."

In October 1992, my secretary and I moved out of the provost's office and the Administration Building into our new office located in one of the annex buildings that contained many of the student service functions. I was provided a modest budget for furniture and new equipment. I was given a $10,000 operating budget and was told to forget about the other staff position I had been promised. "It's a new ballgame now."

By early spring 1993, Vernon began to speak openly about his frustrations with failed efforts to get everyone together to talk during SBA meetings. One afternoon in late November, he hinted he might be handing me the task of planning future SBA meetings. He said Alfred wanted to make sure I attended the next SBA meeting to discuss the details of my new assignment. But I missed that meeting even though I received a telephone reminder from Vernon's secretary. The next day, I received an e-mail from Alfred Pratt, informing me I owed him $13.50 for confirming but not showing up for lunch at the Big Trees Country Club. He explained he was not aware of the "no-show policy" and had to pay the charge for me. He wanted cash only. When I went to pay him in cash, I mentioned it sounded like a fine for missing the SBA meeting. In the future, I asked if we could plan the meeting elsewhere without a "no-show policy." He agreed.

As I walked out of Alfred's office, Vernon approached me with a manila folder marked SBA. He said Alfred wanted me to include planning SBA meetings as part of my new assignments. And he strongly encouraged me not to miss any future meetings.

I attended the March meeting at the Big Trees Country Club. Toward the end of the meeting, Vernon and Alfred asked me to plan an urgent retreat at my home for a Saturday in April. They suggested I would be doing the SBA a big favor. Daniel Marks also encouraged me to do it, and he even volunteered to host the next weekend retreat in the fall at his home. Daniel suggested that SBA meetings alternate between retreats and regular weekday meetings. "I like the idea of meeting where it is really safe to talk one Saturday every two months." Everyone was excited and enthusiastic about it. They settled for Saturday, April 5, 1993, at my home. I saw this retreat as a real opportunity to find out more about the modus operandi of the SBA. I also thought the leadership felt comfortable that I was securely under Alfred's control to the point they might spill the beans. I mentioned the retreat to a couple of individuals I was reporting my SBA findings to, for the record. On Saturday, April 5, nine of the twelve SBA members showed up for the retreat:

1.   Alfred Pratt: Vice Provost

2.   Daniel Marks: Dean of Arts and Sciences

3.   Vernon Machiavelli: Associate Vice President for Academic Affairs

4.   Dottie Marks: Professor, School of Business

5.   Sheryl Hendrix: Associate Vice President for Student Services

6.   Johnny Brown: Dean of Fine Arts

7.   Jinney Brown: Director, Institute for Blacks

8.   Anthony Day: Assistant Vice President for Equal Employment Opportunity

9.   Erica Bolton: Assistant Vice President for Student Services

10. Jim Aaron: Associate Dean, School of Medicine

Absent were Al Richards, vice president of student services, and Donna Green, associate dean of the College of Education.

After the meeting started, Vernon suggested we talk first before "we" social-ized because "we have something very important and urgent to talk about." Everyone agreed. He opened the meeting with words of encouragement about the need for people to attend SBA meetings and his frustrations with low atten-dance at some of the meetings.

Vernon emphasized the need for strong black organizations on campus because he said their interests and everything they had fought for were increas-ingly at stake at ESU. He thanked me for organizing and hosting the retreat and added my "good" work would eventually benefit diversity and "black folks" in general.

Daniel Marks added the ESU administration was taking blacks for granted because of "apathy" among blacks over the past few years. He strongly encour-aged the revival of black organizations on campus because, in his words, "Latinos are out organizing blacks. They are more united behind a common agenda, and they are going to get what they want. Just look at how they organized the internal and external communities in order to get the Hispanic Studies Department."

Johnny Brown said that all the progress blacks had made at ESU was currently threatened by "complacency and apathy among blacks, not only in the BFSA, but, indeed, even among members of the SBA." He continued by strongly emphasizing that everything he was going to say about how the SBA works must stay within the group and must never be repeated under any circumstances. He informed the group he first had the idea for the group many years ago in a small town in the Midwest. As the story went, he had run into a black professional that lived in a small, white town with only a few black professionals. He explained the black professionals in the town were able to accomplish a lot because they spoke with one voice. They met regularly, spoke about mutual concerns and interests, and decided on who would take the lead.

"It's simple. We, the SBA members, discuss important issues or problems con-fronting blacks on campus, decide on a unified course of action, and select the appropriate point persons to take the lead. We all then support that person or persons and the agenda."

"Believe me, it's the only thing that works. That is the way we did everything in the past when it was just the four of us—me, Vernon, Alfred, and Johnny," said Daniel Marks.

"In fact, that's the way we have achieved most of the changes that has occurred in this university. And let me say this, whether we like it or not, that is the way we have all gotten to where we are today," continued Daniel.

"In the beginning, it was just the four of us. Now we are more than ten senior black administrators. Imagine what that means and how powerful that sounds?" exclaimed Alfred.

Vernon and John alternately emphasized we never reveal the meaning of SBA to anyone because "it would cause problems if people found out about the group's existence." Vernon suggested we tell those who ask about it that SBA stands for "Small Business Administration."

"What if someone already knows what it means?" I asked.

"My secretary, for example, knows what SBA means. What should I do in that case?" I asked.

A couple of others indicated their secretaries already knew as well. Johnny Brown added, "Even if people found out about the group's existence, we can always say it's a social group of black administrators who just have lunch together once in a while. There's nothing wrong with that, is there?"

"What about all those times that white administrators go to lunch together? We can make that an issue," added Johnny.

"What if one feels very strongly that one cannot, in good conscience, go along with the consensus regarding a particular course of action? What happens in a scenario like that?" I asked.

"Once the group has discussed an issues and a consensus has been reached, everyone will be expected to put aside their personal reservations and support the decision," Johnny responded.

"We can't be divided. We must stand united," Daniel Marks declared.

It was funny how no one else said anything about it or questioned how those positions would be arrived at. There was silence for about three minutes. Breaking the silence, as people pondered the meaning of what had just been said, Vernon asked, "Who's that artist, and what song is that?"

"It's Michael Frank's *The Eggplant Song*," I replied.

"I like that. Let's relax now and have something to drink and eat," answered Vernon.

"What did you cook, Samir?" asked Erica Bolton.

"I cooked West African okra stew with smoked, dried barracuda fish and beef in a palm oil sauce and shrimp gumbo," I replied.

The meeting ended around 6:00 PM with the understanding the May meeting would occur on a weekday that was to be announced.

After the retreat, I talked with Anthony Day, the new assistant vice president for affirmative action, who is originally from Martinique, about his thoughts regarding the SBA agenda. He had often struck me as a fair-minded and independent person, and I thought he, if any, might share my misgivings. I asked him about whether he thought, given our official responsibilities for diversity and equality, we should continue to attend SBA meetings.

I asked, "What if you face a conflict of interest in one of your investigations? What would you do?"

Anthony did not feel they could pressure him to do anything against his will. "They have not been able to do that so far. I have no problems with that. We should keep attending because that is the only way we are going to find out what they are up to," he added.

"I am going to mention this to a number of people in the ESU administration, especially Judy Krup," I informed him.

A week later, I went to talk with Judy Krup, vice president for personnel, about the SBA and its secretive agenda. She mentioned that Anthony Day (Tony) had also told her about the SBA and encouraged me to continue attending SBA meetings. She advised me to talk about it with Tony. The next day, Tony came to see me and informed me Judy had also encouraged him to continue attending SBA meetings. I agreed to continue attending the meetings because of my interest in finding out how they operated in real situations, for instance, how issues surfaced, how decisions were made, and how the point person and the group collectively operated to carry out their agenda. Tony said Judy had encouraged him to find out more about what they were up to.

For the record, I continually reported my findings about the SBA to several individuals I had entrusted with the information from the beginning of my involvement with that group.

The conversations regarding the SBA as a unified and politically oriented organization continued during the following SBA retreat at the country club. Organizational questions were discussed at the beginning of the meeting. Daniel Marks promised to host the August retreat.

Vernon asked the group, "What if Tom Strung has a personal issue? Could he bring it to the SBA for support? Do we take up the issue on his behalf?"

"You can believe he would be the first one here," said Alfred.

"No, we cannot deal with personal matters," responded Sheryl Hendrix.

"Issues may come from the BFSA or the advisory committees that we support or pursue on our own. But they cannot be personal issues," emphasized Alfred.

"Well, let me give one example. As president of the BFSA, I have been asked to bring the issue of funding Black History Month and MLK celebrations before this group for your support. They are asking for a doubling of both budgets from $2,000 each to $4,000," said Jim Aaron.

"That's an easy one. One of us should talk with the president, and that should take care of it," said Daniel Marks.

"Those budgets used to be $4,000 each before I left the president's office. What happened during your watch, Samir?" he asked.

"The budgets were cut back a year ago because the president wanted to put some of those auxiliary funds into scholarships for minorities. I supported the cuts because scholarship monies help the university in its recruitment efforts," I responded.

"The only way the university got away with that is because of black complacency and apathy. They have taken us for granted. That's all the more reason why we need to become more active," emphasized Daniel.

"We have scheduled a meeting with the president for May 17. Can someone else from this group join us?" asked Jim.

"I'll be there," announced Alfred.

"I hope you'll be there, Samir," he added.

"I will do my best," I promised.

Several individuals, including the president of student government (who was black); Alfred Pratt; Jim Aaron; Tom Strung; and Jenny Davies, director of a scholarship program, attended the May 17 meeting with President Franklin. Everyone supported increasing the budget except for me. The president turned to me and asked why I had been uncharacteristically quiet throughout the discussion. She asked my opinion about the budget increases and perhaps hiring someone to coordinate all the celebrations.

"I am not in support of increasing the budget of the celebrations because there are strong indications the money goes to support programs and structures of avoidance and segregation on campus," I responded.

"I am also not in support of hiring someone to coordinate the celebrations because the search process would further fuel black/Hispanic competition on campus. The only way out is to hire two coordinators, one black and the other Latino. Anything else will leave someone aggrieved. And after that, we should be ready to hire an Asian coordinator as well. Eventually, we will need five new positions to solve this problem," I suggested.

"Oh no, we are not going to have that here. No sir. Not here and not in this university," said the president.

"I think I have to say something here. What you are saying here, Samir, is very dangerous. Even just talking like that is genocidal," said Tom Strung.

"Can someone explain to me what Samir Dyfan and that diversity office do in this university? Because I don't know!" interrupted Jenny Davies.

"I am glad you asked, Jenny. I want to invite you to visit the diversity office. We have brochures and other publications that answer your question. But I am sure that's not your point. Because you and I know that, if you really wanted to know what my office does, this is not the place to ask that question," I responded.

"Well, I will have to think about this, and let you all know what I think later," the president announced as she left the conference room very annoyed. Alfred was not the least pleased either. He warned me during our next biweekly meetings that, if I continued to do things that blacks perceived as "hostile to their interests," they would "isolate and ostracize" me. I told him I was not "hostile to their interests." I just have a different perspective regarding the issues. "I cannot support programs that contribute to segregation on campus. It goes against the mission of the diversity office and everything I believe."

A few weeks later, I was invited to attend the next meeting of the Human Resources Task Force. They requested my participation in the discussions about changes to the university's recruitment and hiring guidelines. They were concerned that Anthony Day's inflexibility regarding EEO/AA requirements was increasingly frustrating members of the committee and wanted me to ask Tony to "lighten up a bit" and allow the committee to decentralize the process in the emerging guidelines.

Vernon also approached and invited me to the next meeting scheduled for November 4, 1993. His reasons were to have my input in the discussions because he said Tony was being rigid and inflexible against the wishes of everyone in the committee. He wanted my input to counter Tony's unreasonable rejection of their recommendations to change the hiring procedures. Vernon clearly wanted me, the only other officer of the university with "diversity" credentials, to gang up with them against Tony. I carefully promised to help to facilitate the discussions to a resolution. Vernon continued to sputter on about how angry he was and how Tony was being deliberately difficult because he wanted too much control over the recruitment and hiring processes.

I attended both the November 4 and 8 meetings and tried to facilitate the discussions when they got stuck, but to no avail. Tony insisted the changes the committee wanted to make would put the institution in jeopardy in the event of a Department of Labor audit. And, as the chief compliance officer, he refused to support the proposed changes to decentralize the hiring process. Both were emotionally intense meetings because Vernon repeatedly became visibly angry, huffing and puffing. At times, he stormed out of the meeting to cool down. Tony was adamant and refused to approve the proposed changes by the end of the November 8 meeting. But the group decided to try again after the Christmas holidays.

After the second meeting, I had a long conversation with Tony about the concerns of some committee members and Vernon's frustration and behavior toward him. He mentioned he recognized Vernon's anger and was concerned about it, but he wasn't going to allow it to affect his decisions. He went on to tell me he believed Vernon was capable of physical violence because he had been present before when he almost got into a fistfight with one of his staff. Ron was a complaint investigator whom Tony had hired on Alfred Pratt's highest recommendation. Alfred and Ron were old college buddies. Ron was eventually dismissed from his job after he got into an altercation with Vernon during an EEO investigation regarding a sexual harassment complaint. Tony was present when one thing led to another until Ron reached across the table in an attempt to grab Vernon's necktie. Vernon then told Ron he carried a switchblade for self-protection and he would find him on a dark evening in the parking lot. Tony believed that, had it not been for his intervention to separate them that day, someone would have been killed at that meeting. Vernon was armed and angry and had his switchblade pulled. Ron was extremely athletic, muscular, and angry. It was a recipe for disaster. Ron was dismissed a few months later because of his "quarrelsome tendencies." Alfred supported the decision to not renew Ron's contract, abandoning him for Vernon, apparently because Vernon was an SBA member and had an ability to help him.

Tony recognized Vernon's emotional bullying behaviors and was determined to be assertive but cautious with him. But I was concerned to the point of talking with some of the psychologists in the Counseling Center about concerns Ron would return to harm Vernon because of comments made during a BFSA meeting. Ron was quoted as saying he was going to confront Vernon one evening after work "to kick his switchblade up his light-skinned ass." Tony didn't believe Ron would follow through on his threats to hurt Vernon, but he was confident Ron would file a federal EEOC complaint over his termination.

A few days after the December SBA meeting (which I didn't attend), Vernon and Alfred approached me in Alfred's office to discuss SBA plans to pressure Judy Krup to fire Tony. Alfred said he was building a folder on Tony Day by putting in writing all of his transactions with him. He asked if I had any problems working with Tony because he said Vernon had many problems with him and they were building a case against him. He encouraged me to put any problems in writing to him and to encourage others to do the same. Vernon indicated he had many problems with Tony, whom he frequently referred to as incompetent. When I asked how he was incompetent, Vernon could only repeat that he was incompetent.

Alfred said he had already talked with Tony's boss, Judy Krup, but Lisa Crist was protecting Tony.

He said, "They can't protect him forever. One day, the axe will fall whether Judy likes it or not." He reiterated his earlier statement that both Vernon and some other SBA members, namely Daniel Marks and Johnny Brown, had had enough with Tony and wanted to know about my experiences with him, preferably in writing. He mentioned again that he and Vernon were documenting all the difficulties they've had with Tony and the Affirmative Action Office. This was *déjà vu* all over again to me. It reminded me of the way Alfred had described their efforts to push Sherly Swift out of the affirmative action office in 1990. This was their trademark modus operandi.

I informed both of them that I had not had any problems with Tony and that he and I had worked very well together. I added that, even though we saw things differently at times, we've done so with respect and trust. I mentioned that, when it comes to affirmative action matters, I usually defer to him because he is the one with the expertise and responsibility for those issues. That doesn't mean he and I don't have significant philosophical differences about issues pertaining to diversity in higher education. But that's what diversity is all about, and I don't consider mere differences as problematic. Vernon did not seem pleased with my response and announced his departure with a comment that he had more than just a philosophical problem with Tony. He promised Alfred that he would put it in writing as he left the office.

Alfred did not appear pleased with my response either and encouraged me to think hard about it and put my overall assessment of Tony's performance in writing. As he and I walked toward the Student Center, he encouraged me again to put anything I had on Tony in writing and send it to him as soon as possible. Hadn't I made myself clear to this man? I honestly thought he believed I was confused by the difference between reality—that Tony did his job well and was an honorable person and "the SBA agenda" of character assassination. Didn't this man get that I was not going to support any SBA agenda that I did not think was right? What kind of lock-step cronyism did they expect?

That afternoon, I talked with Tony about my discussions with Vernon and Alfred and warned him to be careful in his dealings with them. He said he realized Alfred had started putting all of his inquiries to him in writing and knew what he was up to. He said he had experienced some problems with Alfred over requests for hiring waivers and some other issues, but he did not consider them personal. But he was wrong because, with these guys, everything was personal. They tolerated no disagreement I also talked with Judy Krup, Tony's boss, about my concerns that Vernon, Alfred, and the SBA had targeted Tony for removal from office, using the same method they used against Sheryl Smith and Maryann Cole. She assured me they would not succeed in getting her to push Tony out of his position. She encouraged me to do whatever I could to help resolve the immediate problem with the hiring guidelines. I encouraged Tony to meet them halfway without giving up the monitoring responsibility of his office. He said he realized they were angry and promised to find a compromise—as long as he was on record opposing the changes the provost's office wanted to make. He was painfully aware that, as the chief compliance officer, he would be held accountable by a Department of Labor audit unless he was forced by a superior to give up performing the duties of his office.

With Tony's assurance he would eventually work out some compromise with them to help defuse some of the tension, I decided not to attend future committee meetings, but I promised to return if and when they saw the need for that. From all the reports I received, a compromise was worked out and everyone, except Vernon and Alfred, was pleased.

7

The Head of the Beast

By spring 1994, I could sense Alfred and Vernon were angry with me. Alfred had become more authoritarian and micromanaging in his dealings with me. Vernon became increasingly short and abrupt, refusing to make eye contact with me. I could sense their attitude toward me had changed. By the end of January, I had decided I could no longer participate in the SBA and decided to give up all planning and scheduling responsibilities for their meetings.

I returned the SBA folder to Vernon at his office one morning in January, informing him about my decision regarding SBA meetings. He refused to accept the folder when I handed it to him—in the same way he had handed it to me a year earlier. He told me to return the folder to Alfred because he was my supervisor and the one who had assigned me the task of planning and scheduling SBA meetings.

During my next biweekly meeting with Alfred, he looked me straight in the eye and asked me in a stern, authoritarian voice why I had refused the SBA assignment he had given me. He ordered me to reconsider my decision regarding the assignment and my attendance at future meetings. I told him my decision was final and I would not be attending future SBA meetings because I couldn't go along with some of the things they were doing and the way they operated. I added that, because of this, I didn't intend to continue attending or scheduling SBA meetings. He looked at me intensely (with one eyebrow raised in disbelief) that I would have the nerve to disobey his orders, but he said nothing.

Before I left his office, he again stressed the importance of attending and scheduling SBA meetings. I informed him I had already returned the folder to Vernon, who was now in charge of scheduling the meetings. Within days of our meeting, Vernon had scheduled the next SBA meeting for late February. In early March, Alfred confronted and questioned me about my reasons for missing the February SBA meeting and continued to urge me for several months thereafter to reconsider my withdrawal from the SBA. But I never again attended any of their meetings, even with Alfred's repeated attempts to intimidate me during my biweekly meetings with him. I made it a point of informing Anthony Day each time Alfred questioned me about missing SBA meetings because I had become increasingly concerned about retaliation by SBA.

In early March 1994, Cynthia Peters, director of black community advancement and interim chair of the Presidential Advisory Committee on Blacks (PACB), informed me she was going to be calling an urgent PACB meeting to discuss the committee's annual report to the president. I was surprised because the committee had not been able to achieve a quorum or discussed anything of substance in fifteen months. I wondered what the PACB's members were up to. What's there to report? Most of the presidential advisory committees were unproductive, and the PACB was particularly dysfunctional. The president had lost interest in her own advisory committees and refused to meet with them, expect for the Annual Reporting Meeting in April. PACB, in particular, had many earlier run-ins with the president when they went from being a presidential advisory committee that was supposed to make "recommendations" to the president to a political interest group that made "demands" on the president.

So it was within this context that the committee met to discuss the content of an annual report. Sensing there wasn't really much to report, the interim chair for the past eighteen months asked if there was anything urgent enough to report or something the PACB could investigate quickly to include in the April report to the president. That's when all hell broke loose. Some of the students wanted the committee to recommend the president immediately ensure that minorities were getting their fair share of merit scholarships at ESU. Alice Pratt, the wife of the vice provost, wanted the committee to do something about allegations of discrimination at Southern Mental Health Center (SMHC). She also strongly endorsed the student's suggestion by emphasizing that "Merit scholarships were a very critical area that is seldom scrutinized." She also said she and her husband, Alfred, had to deal with that very issue when their daughter was a university student.

As the committee got excited about the report and started to formulate the wording of each recommendation, I reminded them of two things. First, we needed to ensure we were addressing real problems and not imaginary ones. One way to ascertain that is to get demographic data about merit scholarships. The data would tell us if there was a problem or not. I would have hated to see us make recommendations about a problem that did not really exist. We would lose credibility with the president. Second, the PACB had no authority to investigate complaints or allegations of discrimination; we were supposed to refer such matters to the affirmative action office.

"Talk about investigating the investigator. That's an office that should be investigated. But they are not the only ones. There are many others doing nothing about the problems black people face in this university. Others are in critical positions to do something, but they are instead doing nothing about racism on this campus. In fact, I know them so well. I even sleep with one of them every night, and I can't believe that I am even associated with a person like that," said Alice.

"Thank God for Mr. Strung in the admissions office. If he was not for him I don't think ESU would have a single black student. They are so racist down there," said one of the students in the committee.

"How do you know they are racist in the admissions office?" I asked.

"I do because I've been working for Tom Strung for three years, and I know what's going on down there," she replied.

"It's not just the admissions office, honey. The whole institution is that way," added Alice.

"I don't understand how you can give all the credit for black student recruitment to Tom Strung without giving credit to the department and university that hired him and funds student recruitment. If the university was racist, why would they go to the extent to do all of that? Do you know that, since 1990, ESU has doubled its black student enrollment to nearly 3,600?" I asked.

"Why do you always have to invalidate black people's experiences? Goddamn it!" shouted Alice. "Who the hell appointed you guru of diversity? And what makes you think you can tell black people what to do? Who the hell are you? You see, I can say that to you. You can't touch me or do anything about it because I am the vice provost's wife and he is your boss. Tell me who appointed Samir Dyfan the diversity guru and validator of what is legitimate in black people's experiences."

"Alice, please let's not get personal here, let's focus on the issues." I responded.

"No, let's get personal. You guys don't want to hear the truth when you get that high up in the administration. I know, I told you all before. I sleep with one everyday," she replied.

At that point, the interim chair ended the meeting. As soon as I left the meeting room, I ran into Alfred in the hallway. He could sense I was frustrated about something. So he invited me into his office. After I explained to him what had happened at the PACB meeting, he became angry and asked me not to give his wife any special treatment.

"Don't give her special treatment just because she is my wife. I want you to treat her as you would anybody else," he suggested.

"But she isn't anybody else. She is my boss' wife," I replied.

"Well, I can't help you then. That's your problem," he concluded.

"Every time I have had to deal with problems associated with her, I've had serious conflicts of interest because she is your wife," I replied.

"Well, go talk with Vernon and my other direct reports. They've had to deal with her, and they feel no conflict and report to me as well," he replied.

"How do you really know they feel no conflict?" I asked.

"Because they've said nothing to me about it," he replied.

"Well, I do have problems with it," I said as I walked out of his office.

By May 1994, I had missed five SBA meetings, and Alfred seemed to be getting angrier with me each time. I knew he was going to do something. That's his style. But I could not figure out what he would do and when. And then, in late May, Alfred urgently summoned me to his office for a meeting about a complaint against me. At the meeting, he gave me a copy of a memorandum dated a few weeks earlier from Daniel Marks and addressed to Vice Provost Alfred Pratt. In it, Daniel Marks, who was then the dean of the School of Arts and Sciences, made several allegations against me claiming I had failed to provide diversity assistance to his school during the past four years. Alfred informed me that he was not prepared to discuss the memo until a June 5 meeting with Daniel Marks and Sarah Steinberg, his associate dean.

At the June meeting, Daniel Marks and Sarah Steinberg took turns expressing disappointments in my "failure to be actively involved in their school's diversity initiatives." They accused me of "gross negligence and failure" to assist them with diversity problems in the hard sciences and social work programs and charged I had continually refused to meet with their school's diversity committee. They recommended that Alfred appoint a task force to study the failures of the diversity office. Daniel added that I had failed to do the job in the way he originally envisioned the position when he wrote the job description in the 1989 as special assistant to the president for minority affairs and chair of the search committee that hired me for the position.

When it was my turn to speak, I informed both of them I had the most extensive involvement in their school than any in the university. I mentioned I had been teaching African history in the department of African studies at no financial cost to the school since 1991. I also mentioned that, a week earlier, I had facilitated a retreat with the faculty in the Social Work program. I also mentioned my extensive involvement in collaborative projects in the department of communication and much more. I suggested they talk with their department chairs before they made assumptions about the extent of my involvement. I also informed them I had to reschedule only one meeting with their school's diversity committee, not as many as they had alleged. I mentioned the other academic and administrative areas in their school I had been working with and the extent of my involvement in those areas. I also added I had asked the deans, vice presidents, and directors of the various areas in the university I had been involved with to evaluate (in writing) the extent and quality of my involvement in their respective areas.

Finally, I reminded Alfred my job description had changed in the fall of 1991 because of my reassignment to the provost's office and he had approved the changes. Daniel said he was unaware of the changes and wished he had been consulted at the time the changes were made. He also said he was not aware of my work in other areas of the university and expressed a desire to see me more involved in the efforts to diversify the students and faculty in the sciences. Sarah Steinberg asked me to develop or identify an experiential sensitivity workshop for faculty in the sciences.

Daniel added, "I don't see any need for you to be so defensive about what we had to say. Your defensiveness makes me wonder whether you have something to hide."

"Daniel, I promise to send you copies of all the letters regarding the extent and quality of my work so that you don't have to wonder very much," I added.

"Well, you have been defensive this morning when all we wanted was your help with our school's diversity initiatives. We've been waiting for five years, but you refused to help," he charged.

"I am amazed by your method. Every other dean or vice president that requested my assistance has done so by asking for it. But you chose personal attack and professional assassination in an accusatory letter to the vice provost, and you have the nerve to accuse me of defensiveness when I respond to inaccuracies in your accusations?" I replied.

"Why are you so thin-skinned and defensive?" he responded. "I have said we need your help."

I am willing to help as much as I can, but you, as the dean, must be involved in the process," I emphasized.

"That's all we are asking. Stop being defensive," he reiterated.

"I find your approach to soliciting my assistance very problematic, if not outright malicious," I responded. "But I know what this is all really about. It is not what it seems on the surface. So you can't fool me. The next time you write a letter regarding me or the diversity office without checking your facts, I will go public with it and use it as an example of the kind of foolish games that senior officers play that create problems in the university. And let me add that this is a poorly written letter with lots of grammatical errors, not befitting of academic administrators."

At the conclusion of the meeting, Alfred accused me of being defensive. He claimed, "Daniel did not really know about changes in my job description nor was he aware of the extent of my work throughout ESU. The reason for this is because you failed to publicize both."

He then ordered me to prepare and distribute biannual reports of the accomplishments of the diversity office programs. And he demanded the report clearly state the office's mission and responsibilities.

After the meeting, I strongly protested to Alfred his lack of evenhandedness in the way he handled the matter. I told him I was not pleased with what had happened and felt the whole thing was an attempt to intimidate and control me. I demanded it be stopped. But I became even more concerned they might try something else in the future, and I wanted to put a stop to it.

That afternoon, I talked with Vernon about my concerns that Daniel was trying to intimidate me on behalf of the SBA. I made it clear that I would never again attend SBA meetings and no amount of intimidation would make me go along with their political agenda. I asked him to tell Daniel and Alfred that I knew they were the point persons for SBA's retaliation against me. I wanted it made clear that, if it continued, I might take the matter to the president or go public.

My concerns were serious enough that, on Monday, May 8, 1994, I talked about my concerns with Judy Krup. I asked her to intercede to stop the SBA from trying to push me out of my job because of my refusal to go along with its political agenda. I reminded her that I had, on several occasions, talked with her about my concerns regarding the SBA and its activities on campus. She told me to relax and promised to talk with Daniel about it. A week later, she informed me she had sent Daniel an e-mail explaining the extent of my involvement in her vice presidential area. She said Daniel was surprised and sounded pleased She assured me I had the support of most vice presidents, including the Medical Sciences Center. She encouraged me to stop worrying because she was concerned I might start thinking about leaving ESU. And she added that, if that happened, they would have succeeded in intimidating me into leaving.

I mentioned to her that I had talked with Jane Musik and Derick Bantam, department chairs of the social work and communication departments, respectively, and they were surprised that Daniel Marks, as dean of the School of Arts and Sciences, had failed to consult with the department chairs in the school before raising this matter in the provost's office. Both promised to inform Daniel about the extent and quality of my involvement in their respective departments. Derick thought they perhaps felt threatened by some of my ideas about diversity. He explained it was no secret that I had questioned some of the central tenets of multiculturalism. That might have threatened them. Judy Krup mentioned that, from talking with Daniel Marks, she suspected Daniel and Sarah felt threatened by something I might have said or done. She agreed with Derick's assessment of the situation and assured me my job was safe.

That very Monday evening, I received a telephone call from Alfred telling me to drop the matter with Daniel Marks, or everyone will suffer. He said Daniel did not really know the extent of my work, and the biannual report would provide additional information and clear the air. He said Daniel was not really at fault. The idea for the memo had really come from Sarah Steinberg, and it was she who even composed the letter for Daniel's signature. I asked if his intent for calling was to threaten me. To which, he said he was just letting me know what would happen if I pursued the matter any further, particularly if I talked with the provost or president.

I agreed to drop the matter on the condition they stop trying to intimidate and control me. He assured me that Daniel had dropped the matter, and it was not an issue with him any longer. He also assured me I did not have to include the letters regarding my work throughout the university in my annual report and self-evaluation. He pleaded with me not to send them to the provost or the president because of the problems that would create. But I was certain the president already knew about it. The provost told me years later that he never really knew about it, even though he had instructed all of his deans to take such matters directly to him. He mused about why Daniel had gone to Alfred instead. But I knew why. They didn't want the provost to know about the letter. They knew very well the provost would not believe their accusations, would clearly see through their political agenda, and would not appreciate it one bit.

On separate occasions, during the course of that week, I ran separately into Alfred and Vernon who warned me against going outside of academic affairs or SBA with future problems, or there would be consequences. Both emphasized they "weren't threatening me—just clarifying consequences."

As time went by, Alfred became more authoritarian in his role as my supervisor. He ordered me to start submitting detailed quarterly reports with appendices and self-evaluations of my performance. My graduate assistant and secretary began to spend a significant percentage of their time preparing these reports. In addition to the annual report and self-evaluation, he also wanted me to increase the number of open enrollment workshops I offered. I asked if he would consider a summary instead of detailed quarterly report. He said he wanted both: "a summary within a detailed report." When I commented to my graduate assistant that I was spending too much time preparing reports on my activities to have any activities, he suggested I include a section on "preparing quarterly reports" in my reports. I became so frustrated that I listed in each quarterly report that I spent twenty-five percent of my time preparing each report for each quarter. Alfred never commented on their inclusion in my reports about how the resources of the office were committed. It was clear to everyone that Alfred was using the reports to punish me. When I mentioned it to Judy Krup, she said detailed quarterly reports and self-evaluations were excessive. She only required "summary reports with lots of bullet points" from her staff.

To make matters worse, Alfred started treating the review of the reports as quarterly performance evaluation sessions. I felt he was always trying to intimidate and control me. He made it clear I was not to take any major initiative without first seeking his clearance. In addition, he started treating me as if I were his administrative assistant. He ordered me to compile a comprehensive list of minority faculty, staff, and student organizations on campus for him. He ordered me to review and edit a section of the faculty handbook. He ordered me to prepare detailed demographic reports for him. On several occasions, he encouraged me to return to the SBA, but I refused. Even when I felt he was implying he might be more lenient with me if I returned to the SBA, I listened without saying anything.

By September 1994, leaders of the Latino Association on campus began to openly discuss their disappointment with the almost complete absence of Latinos in ESU administration, particularly in academic administration. Some felt aggrieved that black gains had been achieved at the expense of Latinos. Many felt the administration's real commitment was to black issues and not to a wider definition of diversity. Many were demanding parity with blacks because they felt "the city is primarily Latino." In reality, they were right. While there were now thirteen senior black administrators, there were only two Latinos. The same was true for faculty. There were ninety-four black and twenty-eight Latino faculty members in the university. There were other disparities as well, including (but not limited to) the total amount of scholarships monies spent for each group. Although it was an overstatement to say it was a Latino city, the city did have a rich and extensive Latino history.

In late October 1994, the provost received a letter from the Latino Presidential Advisory Committee expressing concerns regarding Latino concerns at ESU. Many of the Latino Presidential Advisory Committee members expressed deep disappointment that, after several searches to fill a total of ten vice presidential and deans' positions in the past two years, there was still no Latino in academic positions in the university. Deeply frustrated that ESU was ignoring Latino concerns, especially because there were Latino candidates among the applicants, the Latino Presidential Advisory Committee requested a meeting with the provost. Dissatisfied with that meeting, attended by Provost Liste, Alfred Pratt, Jose Nievo, president of a local bank, and myself, they asked for a meeting with the president. To help focus the discussion, Alfred asked me to compile comparative data on minority representation in the faculty, student body and staff, student scholarships, and retention figures for the provost. The data confirmed Latino concerns and further fueled resentment towards blacks and speculation that blacks had hijacked ESU's diversity agenda.

It all came to a head on November 10, 1994, at the Latino Presidential Advisory Committee breakfast meeting with the president held in the president's on-campus residence. The meeting started with the traditional pleasantries, amid a palpably tense environment in which everyone knew what laid ahead. The president was very formal, which was an indication she was very angry about the pressure she felt from the Latino Presidential Advisory Committee to address Latino concerns. After breakfast, the committee's chair did a short presentation about their successes in raising scholarship monies for Latino students and promised to do much more in the future. Then he went over a list of concerns about faculty representation and the need to diversify the administration of the university. When he was finished with his presentation, President Franklin was invited to make her remarks. That was when she dropped a bombshell that left Latinos deeply disappointed with her administration's commitment to them.

She walked over to the podium with her eyebrows raised in anger. She started with words of appreciation for their commitment and successes for all of their assistance in a number of projects, especially the fund-raising for Latino scholarships. Then, in a stern voice, she warned them against excessive rhetoric and political demands on her administration. She explained the university was doing its best to address their concerns, but she stated emphatically she would not tolerate demands and ultimatums from anyone. There was complete silence in the room when she finished her remarks. Things stayed quiet until everyone left.

That afternoon, I heard from several Latinos about their anger with President Franklin's arrogance and demeanor. Some promised to fight back; others threatened to file federal EEOC complaints against ESU. A few resigned from the Latino Presidential Advisory Committee to show their displeasure with the "president's disrespectful behavior" in response to their concerns. Many expressed anger not only with the president but also with Al Richards for mistreating Latinos in his administrative area and for his failure to address long-standing Latino student grievances regarding the lack of adequate student support services for Latino students.

Indeed, Al Richards had become the most hated man in the Latino community. They accused him of "Latino ethnic cleansing" in the student affairs office. Since his arrival in 1994, he was believed to have fired most of the Latino administrators in his area. Indeed, since his arrival, he had fired three Latinos in significant positions: an assistant vice president, an assistant dean, and the director of the Student Center. All of this was within a student services area in which the vice president was black, the associate and assistant vice presidents were black, along with six of the nine directors in that area. While it was probably true that Richards' firings were motivated by emotional issues and mean-spiritedness (and not racism), the appearance was strong to those complaining.

To his credit, he pointed out he had hired two Latinas as his special assistants and had appointed one Hispanic male as interim assistant vice president (an appointment he never formalized). But they were not pleased. What he failed to accept was that he and his associate vice president were universally viewed as incompetent and mean-spirited. Even those he still had working for him were reportedly abused and were looking for opportunities to leave. Those who had left had told stories of abusive treatment of Latinos and others in the student services central office.

As Latino grievances focused on Al Richards, they increasingly translated into resentment against blacks on campus. This inevitably led to multiple interpersonal conflicts between many Latinos and blacks, which, in turn, fueled mutual resentment and mistrust on campus. It was a state of affairs that got worse a year later after another Latina was demoted and pushed out of the student services office.

In April 1995, Alfred mentioned to me he had heard I had written an article for a publication on diversity in higher education and requested a copy for his review. A few days later, in his characteristic authoritarian style, he summoned me to his office to discuss the article.

First, he asked, "Why would you want to publish such a provocative article like this? And what do you mean by the statement that you have no racial or ethnic identity?"

"Christina Diaz, director of Latino affairs, invited me to write 'a very provocative article' for publication, and that is what I have done," I responded.

"And how did you arrive at the decision to write this particular story?" he asked.

"As I read the other published articles in the series, I realized they were all meant to be provocative to whites. So I decided, in the interest of balance, that an article that was provocative to minorities might be 'very provocative' as Christina had requested," I responded. "Perhaps I should have asked her who she wanted me to provoke."

"Well, make sure the reader knows the article is an opinion piece and does not represent ESU's policy," Alfred ordered.

"These articles are usually opinion pieces, but I will discuss the matter with the public relations office," I offered.

By late spring 1995, Latinos were still angry with Al Richards and Sheryl Hendrix. Latino faculty, staff, and students were openly and frequently alleging there was "Latino ethnic cleansing" occurring in the student services office. A number of individuals asked me to intercede before the problem got worse, particularly because there was a rumor that Latino students were planning a large "takeover" protest in Al's office by the end of the school year in May.

I approached Al one afternoon to talk about the matter, remembering how he behaved the first time I approached him about problems with the perception by other blacks they were "uncaring and mean-spirited." That was a time when blacks alleged he had fired and demoted over seven blacks in the student affairs office. I mentioned the problem and the fact that over twenty-five individuals in the student affairs office who were concerned about those and other problems had approached me. He denied everything and said he was simply pushing out the unproductive staff. He said they were just complaining because they had been let go. If he was against Latinos, as they had alleged, why then would he have three Latinos in his immediate staff? He expressed concern about the rumors regarding student "takeover" demonstration in his office. He believed his old nemesis, Juan Molina, a graduate student of Puerto Rican descent, must be behind the demonstration plans.

I refrained from telling him that one of them, Marina Rodriguez, his special assistant, was viewed by other Latinos as a "lapdog and traitor" because she was always supportive of Al's actions against Latinos and was suspected of engineering firings of other Latinos. I also wanted to tell him people believed it would not be long before one of his "Latinos on his staff" was pushed out of the student services office by Marina. I wanted to tell him that people throughout the university viewed Sheryl Hendrix as incompetent. The word was that the only reason she was still around was because she was alleged to be his mistress. I also wanted to tell him the word around was that he had directly fired thirty people since he became vice president for student services in 1990. Many, if not two-thirds, were alleged to be minorities. Indeed, many of the individuals that spoke with me about their concerns were minorities. I wanted to tell him many things, but I did not because, like before, he became angry. I wanted to be cautious because several people had warned me to be careful in my dealings with him because, aside from being an SBA member, he and my boss, Alfred Pratt, were best of friends and golfing buddies.

As I left his office, he asked me to find out more information about the demonstration for him. He also suggested I try to get close to Juan Molina as a way of getting information about Latino student plans. I told him I knew Juan and talked with him frequently, but I told him that I did not believe he was fermenting discontent where one did not already exist. I promised to do my best to help the students handle their grievances in a constructive way through dialogue with him.

By summer 1995, rumors had it that President Franklin might be leaving her position at ESU because the Republicans, who now controlled the Board of Regents, both houses of the legislature, and the governor's office, were pushing her out because she was a Democrat. As with most situations involving the departure of a university president or provost, there was nervousness amongst the vice president and the deans about their fate in a new administration. It was within this context of anxiety and uncertainty that I approached Daniel Marks to discuss a faculty diversity issue that had been brought to my attention a week earlier by several people on campus, including faculty in his school.

I met Daniel one afternoon in the waiting area of the provost's office and quietly mentioned to him that concerns had been expressed to me that the School of Arts and Sciences had lost sixteen women and minority faculty during the previous academic year. I also mentioned to him that some of the concerned faculty members were very angry that most of the women faculty members were leaving because of problems in the dean's office.

He turned to Ben Maden, one of the associate deans in the School of Arts and Sciences, and asked him if he had heard they had lost sixteen female faculty members. Mark was not aware of it, but he promised to look into the matter. Daniel started to count the departing women and minority faculty he was aware of, but he stopped when he got to eleven and promised to monitor the numbers. He then informed me that, even if the numbers were correct, his school had just completed a very successful recruiting year. He then informed me he intended to discuss the matter with the provost when they met that afternoon.

The next day, a Thursday, I received a voice mail message from Alfred, which sounded very urgent. The tone of his voice indicated he was angry. He asked that I immediately return his call. By the time I received the message, he had left the office for the day. On Friday, I called his secretary and left a message for him with my telephone numbers. By the end of the day on Friday, I called him at home and left a message for him to call me back at home over the weekend, but he did not return my calls. By Monday, I called his office again in desperation. His secretary told me he had called to take the next two days off and would not be in the office again until Wednesday. He said Alfred wanted to see me as soon as he returned from annual leave.

On Wednesday, I received a telephone call from him, summoning me immediately to his office. When I arrived, he asked, "Did you have a conversation with Daniel Marks about faculty diversity issues?"

"Yes, I did."

"Why didn't you talk with me first before you said anything to him?" he asked.

"I intended to discuss the issues with you during our biweekly meeting next week," I responded.

"You should have talked with me first before you said anything to Daniel. Now, do you know what has happened? Daniel talked to the provost about the rumors, and the provost talked with me soon after he left the provost's office that very afternoon, but I was in complete darkness about it because you failed to communicate with me in a timely manner. And now, it has been a whole week since the provost talked to me about the issue, and I still don't know much about it. I am the last person to know about it. How do you think that looks?" he lectured me.

"I regret not talking with you before mentioning anything to Daniel, but I have also been trying to reach you by telephone since Thursday of last week. I even tried to reach you at home on Saturday, but you were not there. In the future, I will talk with you first before I say anything to anyone about faculty diversity matters," I promised.

"Well, I have to meet with the provost this afternoon, and he has already hit the ceiling about this. So I am not sure how he is going to react when he finds out how long you have been sitting on this information. So tell me what you know about it," he ordered.

"Everything you know," he added.

"There are two issues. The first deals with the number of female faculty leaving the School of Arts and Science."

"How many?" he asked.

"Well, I have heard that sixteen are leaving this year," I replied.

"Who said that?" he asked.

"I have heard the same number from three different people during the past week." I replied.

"From whom?" he asked.

"I would rather leave out the names of the individuals and focus on the issue," I replied.

"The hell you will. I need to know the names of the individuals who spoke with you about this because they may be disgruntled individuals in the School of Arts and Sciences who are out to get Daniel Marks," he said.

"I would rather focus on the issues. In fact, several faculty members in the School of Arts and Sciences talked with me about their disappointment that Daniel had not been able to make a significant dent in diversifying the faculty. One in particular was disappointed because he said, 'Daniel was black and was formerly special assistant to the president for minority affairs.' He expected more of Daniel. He even said that, if Daniel was a white dean, he would have been called a racist if he were in the same situation," I replied.

"Oh, that is nonsense. Everyone knows how difficult it is to recruit and retain women and minority faculty," he replied.

"I bet I know who has been talking with you. It is Joe Waters and his wife. Old Joe is just angry because Daniel would not let his prima donna wife charge the cost of her round-trip visits to Washington to the university when she goes on leave to the National Science Foundation. Daniel would not permit it, so they have been very angry with Daniel and are the ones spreading the rumors about sixteen faculty members. Aren't they? Tell me now because the provost wants to know," he demanded.

"I can't tell you that," I replied.

"You know also that Joe has an axe to grind with the provost and this office. So, if the provost believes you are withholding information from him, do you know what he would do?" he threatened. "I know it's Joe Waters because he has brought that kind of fucking shit to me before in an encounter in the staircase going down from the Administration Building. I let him have it then. He started cussing and swearing as he started to say something So I cussed and swore right back at him. I can cuss and fucking swear too, and I am not going to take that shit from a white boy."

"Alfred, I face serious conflicts of interest when you try to pressure me to reveal information that was given in confidence," I replied.

"Well then, I will tell the provost to talk directly with you. Maybe, after he's jumped all over you, you will remember which side of this conflict your interest lies," he threatened.

As I left his office, he advised me to start attending future SBA meetings again because he said "that is the place to work out a lot of things." I thanked him for the suggestion and walked out of his office. I went straight to the affirmative action office to discuss my concern that Alfred's continued pressure on me to attend SBA meetings was tantamount to racial harassment. Anthony Day agreed that, if he kept pressuring me to attend SBA meetings after I told him I did not want to attend their meetings and did not consider myself black, a case could be made for racial or skin color harassment. He wondered why Alfred was so insistent on forcing me to attend SBA meetings and indicated he had missed several meetings lately and, therefore, was not aware of the latest SBA developments. He promised to keep me informed about what they were up to after the next SBA meeting in the beginning of the fall semester of 1995.

By late summer, Latinos were on the warpath again against Al Richards. This time, he was alleged to have demoted Olga Mendoza, a Latina and one of his special assistants, to the level of coordinator of Greek Life as a "reward" for completing her doctorate while having promoted a black administrator, Tom Strung, from director of multicultural recruitment to associate dean of student services. The decision angered many Latinos. Word of Olga's demotion spread like wildfire on campus. More than a dozen individuals contacted my office about what they saw as a cynical move by Al to ingratiate himself with the BFSA and other blacks on campus by promoting Tom Strung. Some saw Tom Strung's promotion as a sign that Al was worried his black critics in the BFSA would make trouble for him at a time when he was vulnerable. They also alleged he had already promised Erica Bolton's assistant vice presidential position to another one of his BFSA critics after Erica's retirement in a couple years. Latinos saw the alleged promise as another "buyout" at the expense of Latinos. Erica Bolton, assistant vice president for academic support services, had recently announced her interest to retire in a few years and had fueled speculations and rumors that Al intended to use that position to buyout another black critic.

There were also rumors that one of the vice provosts, Phyllis Autry, had complained about Al's treatment of both Ricardo Alvarez and Olga to Provost Liste. Many non-Latinos were concerned because both Ricardo and Olga were very highly competent and liked individuals on campus. My discussion with Olga confirmed that Al had demoted her and given her two years to find another job after she talked with Al about advancement opportunities soon after she completed her doctorate in higher education administration.

Everyone I talked with was puzzled about how Al could justify demoting Olga, but they were even more amazed that he could use Tom Strung's completion of his doctorate to justify promoting someone as Tom who was perceived as openly intolerant and a bigot. The only explanation for the promotion of someone who had frequently referred to Al Richards and all of the senior black administrators as "sellouts and traitors" was the one in the rumor mills on campus. Many became convinced that Al had bought out Tom Strung because, soon after his promotion to associate dean, Tom changed his tune from criticism to praise for Al everywhere he went on and off campus. Many asked, "Why the sudden change?"

My curiosity led me to talk with the director of admissions about Tom's promotion because she was his former boss. She said she had grown so tired of Tom's divisive, destructive behavior that she requested his transfer out of the admissions office or she would fire him. She added she had strongly opposed the decision to promote Tom, not only because he had not earned it, but, more importantly, because he was the wrong person for the position of student advocate. When I talked with the associate vice president for enrollment management about my disappointment with the decision to promote Tom, he informed me he had nothing whatsoever to do with it. He made it clear that, if it were up to him, he would not have done it, but Al made the decision all on his own and referred me to him.

It was clear that many faculty and staff were not pleased with the decisions involving Olga and Tom, but Latinos were particularly angry and very vocal about it. Many among them started calling for Al and Sheryl's removal from their leadership positions in the student services office as the only solution to the problems in that area. My efforts to talk with Al about the problems I had about Tom Strung's promotion and Olga Mendoza's demotion got nowhere because he became immediately defensive as soon as I mentioned Tom's name. He cut me off and told me he had heard about my concerns. He then walked away angry. The problem continued to simmer among the Latinos on campus.

During the spring of 1996, I was approached by a number of individuals who were concerned about problems associated with Alice Pratt's behavior at the Southern Mental Health Center (SMHC). Some of them wanted advice on "how to deal with her." Others wanted me to do something about her "angry behavior." Some were her colleagues; others were from different levels of the SMHC administration. Alice, Alfred Pratt's wife, was quoted as having said that, because she was the wife of the vice provost, nobody in the SMHC administration could touch her. I was told that Alice's behaviors had led to a number of formal grievances and complaints. I told all of them that I could not get involved in anything that related to Alice Pratt because of conflicting interests. She was my boss's wife, and even I had experienced her angry temperament. I referred them to the provost.

By the early fall of 1996, I continued to conduct the series of educational programs I had started in late spring at SMHC. The associate dean had asked me to conduct the series of workshops in late spring on "Emotional Intelligence." Participation was great with more than sixty-five people present for the workshops. As the series continued, Debra Lewis, associate dean at SMHI, became increasingly disappointed that Alice Pratt had refused to attend any of the workshops, particularly those that dealt with issues related to fear, anger, conflict, and respect in the workplace. After the last workshop, I went to talk with Debra in her office about my concerns regarding complaints I had received about Alice Pratt's uncontrolled, angry behavior. I mentioned to her that, in the prior week, two individuals in the ESU administration had talked with me about what they had heard about Alice's behavior. These were non-SMHC employees who knew someone at the institute that was very angry about the perception the dean's office was indeed afraid to deal with "Alice's outrageous behavior" because she was the wife of the vice provost.

But, before I could finish telling her how many times people over at SMHC had talked with me about Alice's behavior, she put her head on her palm and said Alice was continually creating problems and was out of control. She expressed deep frustration about her concerns that her efforts to deal with Alice's behavior might create problems for her with the provost's office. She felt only the vice provost himself could resolve the problems. However, she said, "Alfred does not want to deal with his wife." I mentioned my experience with Alice in the spring of 1994 and Alfred's response when I told him about his wife's angry behavior in a public meeting.

"I've about had it with Alice. She is always saying we couldn't touch her because she is the wife of the vice provost. And the truth is that, even when we have tried to take disciplinary actions against her, we have run into problems with the provost's office. She is right. She has been untouchable so far," she said in frustration. "You won't believe what she did the other day. I was in my office working on a project when she waltzed into my office to tell me how disappointed she and other blacks at SMHC were in my leadership as a black administrator. My response was simple. I said, 'Alice, in case you didn't know, I am not the associate dean for black affairs. I am the associate dean for everyone at SMHC. I hope you understand that.'"

"What did she say?" I asked.

"Nothing. I tell you. I am just concerned that, if she does not change her behavior, we will have to do something in the future, and that might create problems between Alfred and myself," she added.

"Well," I said, "Alice has been that way since she was a social work student in the master's program in the early 1990s. She managed to alienate most of the other graduate students and faculty, which eventually led her to file official complaints of discrimination against both groups," I added.

"My personal experience with her has been very unpleasant and difficult for me because she is my boss's wife. The last time, I tried to deal with her angry outburst directed at me in a committee meeting. Alfred got angry with me and has been ever since," I explained.

"Well, I am going to be having lunch with Alfred in the next few days. I may raise the issue with him," she concluded.

"Debra," I added just before leaving the meeting, "nowadays I don't touch anything that has to do with Alice Pratt. I tell everyone that speaks to me about her behavior that she is my boss's wife and I face a conflict of interest in dealing with her."

"I know Alfred doesn't see the conflict of interest because he has told me to treat her as I would anyone else in the same situation. But it's not that easy. If you raise the issue with him, I bet that's the same response you will get from him," I added.

"Well, we will see," she responded.

As I walked back to my office, I could feel her frustration and the potential for problems with the provost office and with Alfred. But I could not help her because I was already in trouble with the SBA and, particularly, Alfred.

I knew it was going to be a matter of time before he pushed me out. And I certainly could not afford to upset the princess of the SBA. Even though I could not do anything directly, I decided to discuss the matter with Judy Krup about my concerns.

Judy advised me to intervene between Debra and Alice to help them resolve the problems before things worsened. I told her I faced a conflict of interest because Alice was Alfred's wife. I believed he was already angry with me because of my last encounter with his wife. I suggested the administration perhaps consider reassigning me to report directly to the president. That might allow me to deal with a lot of academic affairs problems associated with Ron Liste and Vernon Machiavelli's behaviors, as well as those associated with Alfred and his wife. I explained that anything directly associated with problems in the provost's central office posed a serious conflict of interest for me. She advised this was not the right time to talk about the reassignment of my office. But she promised to think about my suggestion and to talk with Lucy Dalembert about Alice Pratt's situation.

As I left, she reached out and touched my arm in a gesture of support and assurance. She said, "You worry too much. Stop worrying. You are doing well and have the support of most of the vice presidents. Alfred or the SBA can't do anything without discussions at the senior staff level."

The next day, I talked with Lucy Dalembert about my discussions with Judy Krup regarding Alice Pratt's behavior and my concerns about conflict of interest. She mentioned to me that her office was familiar with and involved in some parts of the problem over at SMHC. She said even they were frustrated with Alice's attitude, and the only person who could fix this problem was Alfred. She added she would have advised Alfred to discourage his wife from seeking employment at ESU because of her temperament and his administrative position in the university.

With regard to the conflict of interest issues, she said, "Alfred believes that, as long as he himself is not directly involved in any of the decisions, then there should not be any conflict of interest. But, what he doesn't realize is the conflict extends to his subordinates when he refers Alice's problems to you guys. You guys report directly to him."

"Well, I am already in trouble with him for precisely that reason," I responded. "And I know he is going to find a way to push me out of my position."

Lucy's response was that Judy Krup would have a better read on my concerns about Alfred because she was close with the president. She said her assessment of the situation was that I was fine for now because I had the support of the vice president.

Nonetheless, she did say, "And I have to be honest with you, there are no guarantees because the administration could change at any time. And then everyone becomes vulnerable."

Sometime in late September 1996, I received a telephone call from the football coach requesting I conduct a team building and sensitivity training for his team. On the day of the training, approximately forty student-athletes and coaching staff were present. The focus of the training was on the disciplines of emotional intelligence and team success. Among the disciplines presented were shared vision and core values, as well as personal accountability and flexibility. Strategies for dealing with personal prejudice were discussed, as well as behaviors that undermine trust and the consequences of mistrust on team coherence and performance.

At about two-thirds through the workshop, I noticed two African-American students in the team were carrying on with a private conversation that had become disruptive. So I decided to invite them to share with the rest of the team the insights of their conversation. This was my way of letting them know their conversation had become disruptive. But, as soon as I said that, one of them jumped up and walked out of the training room. The other student mentioned they were talking about something I had said regarding hate. They were concerned about the idea that people project negative stuff about themselves at others. For example, I suggested that deeply racist individuals were very quick to label others as racist. Similarly, I said that deeply selfish individuals were very quick to label others as selfish. He indicated his friend who had just left the room did not appreciate my comment.

At the end of the workshop, I was introduced to Jack Screen, the assistant director of athletics. He was the one who had investigated the complaints of discrimination and racial prejudice against the football coach. He also informed me that my workshop had met the desired expectations he had set for the training and mentioned the student that had "stormed out" of the training was the one who had filed the complaints against the coach. He continued to talk with me for an hour after everyone had left, for example, about how many of the ideas I had expressed in the workshop applied to his personal life. He promised to attend some of the other workshops I conducted in the future.

I now realized this student had accused the coach of racism. Thus, he assumed that, when I said "deeply racist people accuse other people of racism," I meant him. While I wished someone had informed me of the details of the situation (or even there was a "situation"), I realized my comments had hit the mark.

Sometime in late November 1996, Alfred summoned me to his office to tell me he had a proposal from the School of Education for the creation of a Diversity Institute. He instructed me to review the proposal with the assistant vice provost with an eye to rejecting it as nonviable. This was his way of saying he did not like the idea.

"Why do we need a Diversity Institute?" he asked. "We already have your office and the Center for Excellence in Teaching. Why? Besides, I can smell that goddamned black bitch, Maryann Waller, all over the proposal. This is simply an attempt to promote her and give her $80,000 a year. For what? I won't approve it. But review it with the assistant provost, and provide me with feedback."

I did not ask why he seemed so angry with Maryann Waller, who had recently become president of BFSA. We reviewed the proposal and identified several areas that needed clarification and further development because the proposal did not adhere to the university's guidelines for the creation of centers and institutes.

I provided this information to Alfred. After which, he instructed me to provide the feedback to the dean of the School of Education. I met with the Diversity Committee that had written the proposal, including Maryann Waller, and did exactly as the vice provost had instructed. He appeared pleased with the outcome of the matter when I met with him a week later. He asked me about Maryann's reaction to the feedback. I told him she was very quiet in the meeting and appeared to be considering the changes. He felt the revision would take at least six months and that should delay them. But he vowed to never approve the proposal.

As soon as he saw "Urban Education in the proposal" written, he said, "I knew immediately it was intended for that black bitch, and that just turned me off to the whole thing."

In December 1996, I was asked by Provost Liste to chair the Diversity Strategic Planning Task Force and to recommend to him a list of names of potential task force members, including a faculty cochair. I accepted the appointment to chair the task force and submitted a list of names, along with the name of the recommended cochair, Jack Okun, by the end of December. The provost approved the list of task force members and the cochair a few days after he received my recommendations.

By late February 1997, the Strategic Planning Diversity Task Force had begun to meet regularly to discuss the charge of recommending "three to five key strategies and priority actions." Some issues were easier than others to get consensus on. But, when we began to tackle issues related to the multicultural celebrations and the five separate Presidential Advisory Committees on Affirmative Action, the discussions became intense and difficult. Of the two issues, the Presidential Advisory Committees proved to be the most contentious. Some members recommended consolidating the five advisory committees into one inclusive Presidential Advisory Committee on Diversity Issues. Their reasons were not just logistical, but they were based on hard experience that many of the advisory committees were unproductive. In fact, two in particular had become outright dysfunctional.

The Presidential Advisory Committees on Blacks (PACB), the Presidential Advisory Committees on Women (PACW), and Title IX had histories of confrontations with President Franklin. PACB in particular had fallen on hard times because of attendance problems. In fact, the PACB was unable to achieve quorum and was chaired by an interim, Jack Okun, for several years because attendance at meetings had been so poor that he was not able to hold elections for officers. Of course, this was not the first time this issue regarding reforming the advisory committees had been discussed. We had dealt with this same issue before on four different occasions since 1991. But, every time we tried, we abandoned the idea as soon as the BFSA raised complaints of "racist attacks" against the advisory committees.

On the other side of this issue were those committee members who acknowledged that, even though PACB had not been productive since spring 1997, any attempts to reform it would be perceived as racist by BFSA members, particularly Tom Strung. Those who were against reforming the advisory committees for political reasons wanted the advisory committees left alone. The most forceful proponent of this position was Jim Aaron, former president of BFSA and associate dean for diversity initiatives in the School of Medicine. He warned the task force of impending turmoil if they tampered with any of the advisory committees, particularly PACB.

In March 1997, the task force decided to suspend action on the advisory committees until fall 1997 to see if renewed efforts to revive PACB worked. Judy Krup was leading the renewed efforts. She had asked Anthony Day to lead a small workgroup, of which I was a member, to work with the BFSA to develop strategies for improving attendance at PACB meetings. Since the initial recommendation to consolidate the advisory committees was already in the written draft report, I decided to leave that item in the draft document until it was reviewed again in the fall. I explained this to members of the task force, and there were no objections. The issue did not come up again until the August 1997 meeting of the task force. We continued to meet in the summer with an eye to October 1 as the deadline for submitting the recommendations to the provost.

In June 1997, I received a memorandum from Alfred Pratt, asking me to convene a workgroup to recommend some strategies for enhancing the recruitment and retention of Latino faculty and staff at ESU. I informed him the Diversity Strategic Planning Task Force intended to address those issues as part of its overall charge. But he refused to accept that and wanted a separate workgroup.

Then he turned toward me and said, "The reason for a separate committee is that I have that Cuban bitch, Christina Diaz, climbing up my black ass. So, you see, I have to cover my fucking ass. Let's go with separate committees."

"Do you mind if I use the same individuals who are in the Diversity Task Force to write a separate set of recommendations?" I asked.

"No, but add a few others as well so that both committees don't have exactly the same members," he explained.

"You see, Christina is up to her old shit again and has told a Cuban faculty member who resigned from ESU to talk with me about that Latino crap she believes. That nobody cares about them. I can't stand these goddamned Cubans. They think they own everything in this fucking town," he added. "I was on the telephone when the faculty arrived for the meeting. He refused to wait, got angry, and left after waiting for only about twenty minutes. Now Christina is trying to make a fucking federal case out of it, trying to exploit the situation to make a political point."

"I will convene a workgroup composed of faculty and staff in early August. Is that okay with you?" I asked.

"Yes, go ahead. It shouldn't take long to do. I don't want a detailed plan. I am looking for only a few recommendations—less than five if you can do that. Nothing prescriptive. Just something to get that bitch off my ass," he added.

July 1997 was notable because that was the month the provost's "retirement" was announced. But it was not until a few weeks later that we learned the president had appointed Daniel Marks as interim provost. That was when all my alarm bells went off, signaling danger ahead for me. All the stars were aligned against me. Daniel Marks was now going to become provost with Alfred Pratt as vice provost and Vernon Machiavelli as associate vice president—all in the same academic affairs office in which I worked. To make matters worse, President Franklin, who was hip to the workings of this cabal thanks in part to me, had left a few months earlier. The new president was unfamiliar with the nature of "cabalistic race politics" on the campus. They had the perfect scenario for pushing me out of my job. Knowing, as I did, how they operated in the SBA, I was certain it was not a matter of if, but when, they would do it. This unsettled me.

Soon after the new president, Debby Judge, arrived on campus that summer, allegations of racial discrimination and prejudice in the athletic department hit the front page of the local newspapers. The story involved allegations of cover-up in the investigation of racial discrimination in the athletic department. The story remained on the front page for several months as former players and assistant coaches, including a white program secretary, joined in the allegations of racism within the football program. At one point, the total number of complainants reached nine. All of whom filed federal EEOC complaints and several lawsuits in federal courts. As the scandal spiraled out of control with daily front-page coverage, the new president became more desperate for countermeasures that would diffuse the bad publicity.

8

The Beast Strikes Again

It was within this context of spiraling racial scandal in the athletic department that the new president appointed Daniel Marks to the position of interim provost. Many saw the appointment as "window dressing" and a public relations gimmick aimed at pacifying the black community and intending to undermine the allegations of discrimination in the athletic department. But the problems associated with the allegations worsened each month as former players and staff joined in the EEOC complaint and lawsuits. The scandal led the new president to retain the services of Martin Job, a black, former state supreme court justice to review ESU's EEO investigative procedures, particularly the policy that allowed the athletic department to investigate itself. At about the same time, the EEO office began a new investigation into allegations of retaliation filed by the original black complainant after she was dismissed as a player from the women's basketball team. This was the same student who had stormed out of my session with the team.

By late fall 1997, the EEO investigation had led to the determination the coach had lied during the investigation, which led to his firing. This development just made matters worse because it kept the story alive in the local press and led to several national news stories about the scandal in the national press and media.

One early indicator of SBA power, soon after Daniel Marks was appointed as interim provost, was Jim Aaron's newfound aggressiveness with regard to "black issues" in the Diversity Task Force. I had always watched Jim's demeanor and behavior as indicators of how the SBA "Big Five" felt about an issue. This is because, as Vernon's childhood friend in Jacksonville, Florida, Jim had been close to Vernon. From time to time, he had allowed Vernon to manipulate him into becoming the SBA point man on "black issues."

As such, I immediately became concerned when he came to the August 11 meeting and asked in an angry tone of voice, "Why is this damned issue regarding the advisory committees still in the draft report? I thought we had resolved this matter by agreeing to table it as efforts were being made to revive the PACB. Listen, y'all, I can't support an effort or recommendations to change any of these advisory committees. It will create a lot of problems if we touch them."

"I understand your concerns, but, if you remember, this item was on the list of three subcommittee recommendations from the initial brainstorming sessions. I decided to leave it in the draft document until August or September when we intended to revisit the issue again," I replied.

"Well, it can't remain in the report, whether we revisit the issue again or not. If it does, I will not sign off on the report. I can't put my signature of approval to such a report," he replied.

"Jim, we can't just summarily remove from the draft report a recommendation someone else has made. We must first discuss the merits of the issue and, if need be, put it to a vote. I would like us to discuss this item before we do anything. It is in the report because someone recommended it. But before we discuss the draft recommendation, we need a brief report about the BFSA's attempts to revive the PACB," I remarked.

"Okay then, let's have it. Can Anthony Day give us an update on how well the BSFA efforts to revive the PACB is going?" asked Jim.

"Well, I was unable to attend the joint BFSA/PCB meeting on March 16, so I can't really say. Maybe Jack Okun can update us?" he suggested.

"Oh, I couldn't make that meeting as well, so I can't say either. But I heard that Samir was there. Maybe he can give us an update on how the meeting went," Jack suggested.

"Well, I was deeply disappointed I was the only PACB member present for the meeting. Alfred attended the meeting to urge the two groups to work closely to come up with a common 'black agenda.' He focused mostly on the changes in the administration on campus. He said, 'It's a new ballgame, and we now have a new Republican president. We'd better come up with an African-American agenda soon, or we will be left behind.' But, to his disappointment, only three BFSA members were in attendance," I reported.

"Has attendance at PACB meetings improved over the past five months since we last talked about this issue?" asked Jim.

"It's the same as before. Attendance has not improved one bit. And I have attended every meeting since March. The only people in attendance are as always the chair, Jack Okun, Anthony Day, and me. Tony and I are ex-officio members of PACB and all of the other advisory committees," I responded.

"Even with the attendance problem, I still think we should leave the committees alone.

"I agree with Jim on this one," added Anthony Day.

"I am willing to leave this issue alone until our next meeting in August when, hopefully, we will have everyone present," I replied.

Everyone agreed to continue the discussions during the next meeting in August. My job now was to get everyone in attendance for the last meeting before we submitted the draft report to the provost. After the meeting, the task force cochair, Jack Okun, privately expressed to me his concerns that the issue regarding the advisory committee might become divisive. He suggested we seek a compromise position during the August meeting because he did not want to get caught in the middle of a political fight. I assured him I would do my best to compromise, but others in the committee believed the advisory committees needed reform, and it was up to those individuals as well.

The Diversity Task Force met in late August 1997 to discuss the final issues and draft report to the provost. As far as I can remember, everyone was present for this meeting. The last item on the agenda was the issue of the advisory committees. But, when we got to that item, Jim Aaron expressed deep concerns about signing off on any report that recommended changes to the advisory committees.

"As a black man on this campus, I cannot put my name next to a report that is going to be perceived by other blacks as an attack on their interest and everything they have worked for over the years," he said.

"How about creating a Presidential Equal Opportunity Advisory Committee with the existing five advisory committees reconstituted as subcommittees," a committee member suggested, striking a note of compromise.

"That's a great idea. Create one advisory committee that preserves all the current committees as subcommittees. This way, you can avoid problems and make the subcommittees more accountable," said another.

"That's like creating a sixth advisory committee. Do we really need anymore advisory committees? Why do we think that, if people are currently refusing to attend meetings of the five existing advisory committees, creating a sixth, by whatever name, will improve attendance?" I asked.

"It will because people will have to be accountable to the super committee," added cochair, Jack Okun.

"That is if you have an effective functional 'super committee.' My concern is that we end up creating one more committee that ends up similarly dysfunctional because of attendance. It's easier for you guys to come up with these optimistic recommendations, but, for those of us who are ex-officio members, it's a nightmare," I replied.

"But, if the super committee is what the task force wants to recommend, I am willing to defer to your collective wisdom," I quickly added.

"I think that's the best we are going to get, and I think it will work," intoned Jann, the faculty graybeard in the task force.

The matter was put to a vote, and the majority voted to recommend the super committee concept as a way to strengthen the advisory committees. Jim Aaron had no objections. Anthony Day was enthusiastic, and Jack Okun was relieved. Needless to say, I was disappointed that some individuals had allowed themselves to be intimidated by Jim Aaron's comments and implied threats. I promised to make all of the approved changes in the draft and share the final draft with everyone again before sending the report to the provost. After the revised draft was ready, everyone signed off on it except for Jim Aaron. We sent him three e-mails requesting his approval or disapproval of the report. It was to no avail He didn't even acknowledge any of the e-mails we sent him over a seven-day period.

Jim Aaron stayed back after the August Diversity Task Force meeting to talk with me about his feelings regarding the discussions about advisory committees. Jann Meier joined us as we entered the elevator on the fourth floor going down. Jann was one of the bright spots on the committee—an old-fashioned, gray-bearded, corduroy-jacketed intellectual who was genuinely committed to the cause of diversity and equality.

After he left, Jim turned toward me and said, "Look here, man. I don't really give a fucking goddamned what you do with all of these goddamned advisory committees. You can abolish all of them tomorrow, and it won't bother me one bit. It's those goddamned niggers I am concerned about. Those goddamned niggers like Tom Strung, Jenny Davies, and others in the BFSA who will throw a fit if you touch the PACB."

"Jim, I have to tell you that I find your choice of terms to describe Tom Strung's behavior unacceptable. Disapproving of his behavior is one thing but using racial epithets is unacceptable," I reminded him.

"You will have to excuse me, but they are goddamned niggers. Excuse me, again. But I can't believe Al Richards promoted that goddamned nigger to associate dean of students. I don't know what he was thinking. Maybe Sheryl's pussy has gone to his goddamned head," he added.

"Jim, please stop using racial epithets. I mean it," I warned, realizing I sounded angry and condemning.

"I really don't care what you think. I can call them anything I want. I am black and can do it. That political correctness shit is for white folks. What can you really do? Report me to the provost? The vice provost? They are goddamned niggers," he added.

Just at that very moment, Daniel Marks drove by in his black Mercedes-Benz and stopped to chat with Jim. As I walked away, I wondered what Jim was up to. I had never seen him that aggressive before.

A few days later, I received a memorandum from Daniel Marks. The memorandum was short and had the following cryptic note, "Samir, Alfred Pratt shared with me your annual report and self-evaluation. This is just a note to say I was extremely impressed with the thoroughness of the report. You are to be congratulated."

The memo was copied to Alfred Pratt I found the whole exercise interesting and the memo itself telling. At first, I wondered what would be the purpose of congratulating me for writing a thorough report. He did not congratulate me for my achievements or accomplishments that were thoroughly reported. It merely congratulated me for a thorough accounting that quantitatively and qualitatively measures the accomplishments of the office against a set of goals and objectives established at the beginning of the academic year. The question I had to answer was: What did this memo represent and mean? Was it looking for meaning within the context of my experience with both of these SBA members?

I figured the purpose of the memo was to deceive me into feeling a false sense of security, that is, to buy them more time until Daniel had consolidated power and had time to present to the new president some justification and pretext for pushing me out of my job. But I didn't buy it. I could see through the memo for what it really was. And, each time I interacted with Daniel or Alfred, I became even more convinced they were going to retaliate against me because I had refused to go along with their racial-political agenda.

It was within these developments that I was copied an e-mail (dated August 31, 1997 from Alfred to his secretary, instructing her to schedule a meeting with me "as soon as possible" to discuss the Multicultural Engineering Program (MEP).

There were two items on the agenda during the meeting with Alfred: the recruitment and retention of underrepresented faculty and staff and the Minority Engineering Program (MEP). He started the meeting by reprimanding me for having done nothing about the first item since June when he first asked me to constitute the workgroup. I explained to him that I was working with most of the same group of faculty and staff in the Strategic Planning Diversity Task Force and that the group had requested we suspend meeting in July and meet again in late August on both projects. I added that significant progress had been made on both tasks and that we first intended to complete the Diversity Strategic Plan from which we would extrapolate recommendations for the second report addressed to him.

By the time he got to the second agenda item, the MEP, he had already become annoyed and authoritarian in his attitude and tone of voice. He abruptly cut me off in mid-sentence as I explained the reasons for not meeting in July.

He said, "Now let's move to something else more pressing. I don't want to hear any excuses."

"I wanted to explain that even I was on annual leave for two weeks in July. Most of the faculty in the task force were not in town in July," I responded.

"Stop it now. I have told you I don't want to hear excuses! I want to talk about the Minority Engineering Program or, as they now call it, the Multicultural Engineering Program, particularly Darla Carter's behavior. I am sick and fed up with this problem. The provost and I have been dealing with it since Darla wrote to him in July. We have met with her several times, but we got nowhere. I want you to take it over and use whatever method or approach you believe will work. But there are three things the provost wants you to ensure. First, in the transition from the old to the new MEP, the numbers of African-American students in the program do not decline. Second, there is no diminution of program services to black students. Third, Darla Carter does her job," he emphasized.

"I don't know what I can do to help. I will look into the matter and let you know how I might be able to help. It depends on how messy things have become since the problem began. I prefer to get involved earlier rather than later with these kinds of problems," I responded.

"Okay, just keep me informed about your progress so that I can do the same for Daniel," he replied before I left his office.

He handed me a thick folder containing several letters addressed to the president and provost from concerned alumni, members of the community, and corporate sponsors. The folder also contained several memos between Darla Carter, Del Alexander, and Armando Segundo, the associate dean. Even though on the surface of things the problems appeared to be complex, there were two major issues: Darla Carter's allegations of insensitivity, unfairness, and racial discrimination and the perception held by Daniel Marks, Alfred Pratt, and Vernon Machiavelli of Armando Segundo as being insensitive to black issues.

An hour or two after my meeting with Alfred, I met with Del Alexander, interim dean of the School of Engineering, to discuss the MEP problem. After he was through explaining the chronology of events, I asked him to identify the most immediate problem he wanted me to focus on. He asked me to focus on getting Darla Carter to cooperate with the new MEP director, Evelyn Hernandez, and do her job. He said Darla had been refusing to do certain parts of her job and had vowed "not to work for" Evelyn because she felt better-qualified. But she promised to "work with" her only if she, Darla, was reclassified as a coordinator of MEP.

"What was the nature of Darla's relationship with the previous director, Becky Barr?" I asked.

"Not very good. In fact, twice in the past five years or so, we've had to call Darla into the dean's office and order her to cease spreading nasty rumors about Becky. In the first incident, Darla was spreading rumors that Becky was having a romantic affair outside of her marriage. We called her in and ordered her to stop spreading false rumors," he replied.

"And what was the second?" I asked.

"Similar to the first. Darla was called in again after we received complaints she was spreading rumors that Becky Barr was having an affair with Jack Okun. She was again ordered to stop spreading false rumors," he replied.

"What about the quality of her work during Becky's tenure as director?" I asked.

"Becky was not satisfied with her performance either. But she felt stuck with her and just hoped for the best with her behavior and job performance," he responded.

"How was Becky's relationship with Armando Segundo?" I asked.

"Well, he was not impressed with Becky's performance and the way the old MEP was administered by her. And that may have created tensions between them and forced Becky to leave for Billard University. Armando was just beginning to address some of the problems in the MEP when Becky resigned from the program. So, after Becky left, we decided to reorganize the program and broaden the scope and responsibilities of the director. We required an engineering degree for the position and changed the position title to director of student services, which includes the new MEP as well as other student services," he answered.

"I will try to help and do what I can to facilitate a resolution of the problem between Darla and Evelyn. But success depends on their willingness to resolve the problems," I offered.

I met with Darla in September for ninety minutes. During which, she made allegations of racial discrimination against her by Armando Segundo because he hired Evelyn, who she viewed as "less qualified" than her for the position of director of student services. She believed the decision to pass over her and hire Evelyn amounted to racial discrimination. I reminded her the position required a bachelor's degree in engineering, which I knew she didn't have. She responded she had three bachelor's degrees and Evelyn had only one. She then threatened to go off campus to seek help for her case because she claimed all of her efforts to resolve the matter had not worked. She said that talking to Daniel Marks and Alfred Pratt had led nowhere. She assured me the MEP and the students were doing fine. All of which, she took credit for and saw as proof of her capability. She concluded by saying, "The students are becoming impatient with the unfairness and discrimination they are seeing and with Evelyn's mistreatment of me and them. Many of them see her as unqualified for her job because she has been unprofessional with some of them," she threatened.

"Darla, I cannot deal with the allegation of discrimination except to advise you to file an official complaint at the EEO office. My advice is to file your complaints as soon as possible before you run out of time," I advised. It didn't sound like she had anything to go on, but that part was out of my hands. There were official channels, and her case would fail or succeed on its merits.

"Secondly, I want you to tell me what exactly you want. What do you want the school to do that will resolve this problem? Tell me, please, because it is still not clear to me," I added.

"Well, I want three things, or I am going outside of ESU. One, I want to be promoted to coordinator of the MEP. Two, I want Evelyn to stop ordering me around like a slave. Three, I want Evelyn to clarify my job responsibilities in the MEP. This is because they want to demote me to a receptionist, and I don't want to do that. If anything, they should be promoting me, not demoting me. I have worked and run the MEP for nine years. Even when Becky was here, I was the one running that program. I know in my heart that I can do it. All I want is to be treated fairly," she ended her response.

"Have you been refusing to do your job or things Evelyn has asked you to do?" I asked.

"All I have done since they made me a receptionist is what I am supposed to do. I will do coordinator work when they make me coordinator," she replied.

"What does that mean? Tell me. Has your job title or description changed since Becky's departure?" I asked.

"Well, I am not going by that. I am going by what they have told me. They have told me to do the job of a receptionist, and that's what I am doing," she replied.

"Darla, stay with me for a minute here. Has your job title or description on paper changed since Becky left? Because it is what is on paper, black and white, that counts. And that's what they are going to hold you accountable for and, indeed, what you are accountable for. I will recommend that, if there have been no changes since Becky left, that you continue to do everything you did when Becky was here because, if you don't, you will face corrective and disciplinary actions," I added.

"No, my job title and description have not changed, but what they want me to do has changed. That's what I am talking about. As I have said in my letter to Dr. Segundo, again, I don't foresee any problems working with the new director of student services. But I have a major problem working for her. It's not right to ask me again, with ten years of experience in the MEP office, to work for and share my experience in MEP as the boss. If she is going to be director, why should I train her?" she responded.

"Does that mean you will continue to pick and choose which part of your job you want to do? Does that mean you will continue to refuse to do what Evelyn asks you to do? Tell me because, if you do, you will most certainly get into trouble for insubordination. Do you know what that means?" I asked.

"Yes. Really I have not technically refused to do anything she has asked me to do. I have just not completed the tasks as yet. Since she never gave me any exact dates, I am still working on things. But, I tell you that I will never give her the list of corporate sponsors of the MEP that I personally cultivated for the program. That's like stealing my job and my blood, sweat, and tears…hook, line, and sinker," she responded.

"Everything she has asked me to do that she claims has not been done are things that take a long, long time to do. You see, as a receptionist, I am too busy answering the telephones all day long. When I find time from my receptionist job, I will complete those tasks," she responded.

"Have you talked with Evelyn or Armando about your desire for a promotion to coordinator?" I asked.

"Yes, they told me in two to three years that they might consider it, depending on how well I do my current job. They want to learn from me everything I know about the program. And then, when they don't need me anymore, they will push me out like a slave. But I don't buy it. I know what they are up to. I want to be promoted now, not tomorrow. No, sir!" she demanded. "Mr. Dyfan. Samir, I hope you are successful in solving this problem. I really do. From the bottom of my heart. I wish you luck because I have given up. If you fail, I'm going outside of ESU. I can't take this unfairness anymore," she added.

"I am sure of one thing. This problem will be solved if you and Evelyn really want it. Only you and Evelyn can solve this problem. I'm just a facilitator," I clarified for her.

I promised to talk with Evelyn to get her perspective on the problem. I hoped to eventually get both of them in the same room. But, for now, I wanted to meet with both of them separately to get each person's side of the story, uninterrupted. She thanked me for my help, wished me luck, and left.

A few days later, I met with Evelyn Hernandez to discuss the problems in the MEP. She expressed deep frustrations with Darla's behavior and performance. She emphasized that all she wanted was for Darla to do her job. She said this had always been a performance problem. Because of this, she had sought advice from the personnel office. She informed me she had already begun corrective action procedures with Darla's performance, particularly her refusal to do certain parts of her job. She refused to bargain about anything with Darla when I mentioned Darla's three demands to her. She was specific about Darla's first demand. She would not discuss anything to do with promoting Darla when she said she was having problems with her performance in her current position.

"What would be the basis of her promotion?" she asked.

"Well, she said she had served the program with distinction during the past nine years; therefore, she has the knowledge and experience to coordinate the MEP."

"I have not seen it. Since I arrived several weeks ago, I've had nothing but problems trying to get her to do the job she claims she has done with distinction when Becky was here as the director," she responded.

"Have you looked at her past performance evaluations? Maybe you will learn something about her performance—even why Becky never promoted her during the past nine years," I advised.

"What about items two and three among Darla's demands?" I asked her.

"Well, I am willing to talk about them with her. In fact, I have already done that several times. But I am willing to try again. Let me tell you what she is talking about. I have been giving Darla written directives and timelines because I am trying to avoid confusion over what and when I want things done in the office. This is part of the corrective action procedures I am following," she responded.

We agreed to meet again with Darla within a week to discuss the issues and seek a satisfactory resolution to the problems. I cautioned her against losing her cool because I could see how frustrated she had become in the weeks since she became director. Before she left, I gave her my business card with all my telephone numbers where I could be reached if she needed to talk. That very evening, I received a telephone call from Evelyn, expressing concerns about her safety. She said that, when she was leaving the MEP after work that evening, she had an encounter with one of the black male students, Clinton Davidson. During which, he made implied threats against her. She said the incident began when she asked Clinton to turn over the key to the lab after she learned he had a key. She said students are not allowed to have keys to university offices and labs. But Clinton refused to turn over the key and got very angry instead. She wanted to seek advice if she should report the matter to the University Police and seek protection. I advised her to do it only if she genuinely felt threatened. She shouldn't do it to get even or intimidate them.

The next day, I went to the provost office around 11:30 AM to talk with Alfred about Evelyn's concerns for her safety and her encounter with Clinton. But, as soon as I arrived in the Provost office, Alfred ordered me into the president's conference room, where he was having an impromptu meeting with thirteen minority students (twelve black and one Latino) regarding the MEP. My first response was to ask Alfred if the students had spoken yet with the dean of the School of Engineering. His response was that he was dealing with the students because they walked into his office and requested an urgent meeting with him.

"And since you are the diversity officer, you should be in the meeting," he said.

"Alfred, maybe we should not rush into this meeting. We should find out first if they have talked with the dean. Is that not the protocol?" I asked.

"I am dealing with what is now. I want you there," he ordered.

"I am," I replied.

In the president's conference room, about ten students were already waiting for Alfred. Others came in streams during the meeting. He sat at the head of the conference table, and I sat on the first seat to his left. Alfred called the meeting to order and asked if Clinton was their leader because he had initially requested the meeting. Everyone seemed to accept Clinton as the spokesperson. Then he asked Clinton about the purpose of the meeting.

"To talk about Ms. Hernandez's unprofessional behavior and lack of services and space for black students in the MEP," Clinton responded.

During the course of the meeting, the students took separate turns accusing Evelyn of being unqualified to be the new director and praising Darla as better-qualified. They even alleged that discrimination was involved in the hiring process that led to Evelyn's hiring. They also accused her of being aggressive, loud, and abusive toward Darla and everyone, including students in the MEP. They accused Evelyn of treating Darla unprofessionally and unfairly. In short, they blamed Evelyn for all the problems in the program. I remained quiet throughout the discussion between Alfred and the students. But, at about forty-five minutes into the meeting, I asked if I could say something because I had a comment and a question.

When Alfred gave me the nod to go ahead, I asked, "What can you tell us about Darla's behavior that might be contributing to the problem?"

"Nothing, absolutely nothing," one of them said.

"I have always believed that, when two or more people are having a problem, the chances are that each one of them may be contributing to the problem. The key is for each person to be accountable for what he or she is contributing to the problems. I believe the only ones who can resolve this problem are Evelyn and Darla. But the key to solving problems between people is respect, truth, and fairness. All I have heard from you today suggests to me that you believe Evelyn alone has created all of the problems in the MEP. Is that right?"

"I must admit that Darla told us some of the things we are talking about. But she is just reporting what they told her," said one of the students.

"Look, I am the only one in this room who has talked with all of the individuals involved. And I don't agree with the premise that Evelyn alone is creating all of the problems in the MEP. I, on the other hand, believe some of the problems predate Evelyn. In addition, some of you said you believed Darla was better-qualified than Evelyn to be director. How do you know that? Have you seen Evelyn's or, for that matter, Darla's credentials? It is clear to me you are just repeating Darla's allegation without firsthand knowledge," I said.

At some point during my last statement, Alfred began to tap his pen on the conference table as I talked. When I was finished, he told the students that his and my job were in the final analysis about student learning.

"We must recognize we have thankless jobs and accept our jobs for that. We don't need to go around asking people to write letters to the president and provost about how wonderful and fantastic we are. That's what some people fail to realize," he said.

The students appeared baffled about what he was talking about and why. But I knew who and what he was referring to in his comments. At the end of the meeting, he advised the students to take their concerns to the dean in the School of Engineering and promised he would talk with the dean about their concerns. As soon as the students left the conference room, he walked over, closed the door, and turned around.

In an angry voice, he asked, "Where is your tie?"

"I left it in my office. I had taken it off when I was grading students' papers this morning. I didn't put it back on because I'm teaching this afternoon. What does my tie have to do with the MEP problem, which is what I thought we are dealing with here?" I answered.

"I don't want to hear any excuse. You are a vice president and should never be on campus without a tie," he barked.

"Alfred, can we talk about the tie later? I have some questions regarding the MEP and your expectations of me with regard to the students' meeting with the dean," I requested.

"This is a new president. She is strict and formal. She has a stricter dress code for all administrators. In fact, I heard she reprimanded one of the vice presidents for not wearing his gown during graduation ceremonies," he added.

"Alfred, are you saying I am expected to wear a necktie during my three-hour lectures or daylong seminars and training?" I asked.

"Yes, you are a vice president. I expect you to have on a tie whenever and wherever you are on campus," he responded.

"Are you suggesting the new president is mandating this dress code? I can't believe this is what the new president wants," I responded.

"Well, I, or we, in the provost's office, Daniel Marks, have that expectation of you. Now is that good enough for you?" he asked.

"Alfred, I am frustrated and surprised you've chosen this time to deal with the necktie issue after such an important meeting. I assure you I will obey your orders," I replied.

The following Monday, I decided to talk with Judy Krup about my concerns regarding Alfred's handling of the MEP problem and intuition that Daniel Marks might abuse his authority in conspiracy with the SBA to push me out in retaliation for my refusal to support the SBA agenda. I reminded her of my experience with each one of them over the past five years. I asked her what would stop Daniel, as interim provost, from firing me. I asked her to intervene before it was too late. She thought I was overreacting to Alfred's management style. But she advised me to go and talk with Lisa Crist about my situation. She thought Lisa was the only one that could help me because she herself was going to be out of the picture on her way to the regional campus as interim vice president.

That afternoon, I received a message that Alfred, Vernon, and I were scheduled to attend a meeting the next day in the School of Engineering. The meeting was scheduled with Del Alexander, Armando Segundo, and Evelyn Hernandez, beginning at 2:00 PM in the school's conference room. But Del Alexander, the interim dean, did not attend the meeting. Alfred and Vernon were not pleased with that. They made a point of it at the beginning of the meeting, and the negative tone of their comments permeated the rest of the meeting. Needless to say, the meeting didn't go well because Alfred and Vernon's attempts to intimidate Armando, the associate dean, didn't work. He would not be intimidated by Alfred's frequent references to the authority of the provost's office or Vernon's use of collective bargaining and human resources jargons. Toward the end of the meeting, Alfred conceded he should not have met with the students before he talked first with the school's dean. He announced that, in the future, he would refer the students to the dean and not meet with them because, as he put it, these things were too messy.

Just before we concluded the meeting, Alfred admitted that, even though Darla Carter was a very good friend of his, he wanted Evelyn to know he did not have any problems with disciplinary actions she may take against Darla for failure to do her job. He expressed that he and Daniel Marks had tried on several occasions to advise Darla against what she was doing but to no avail. He added he had made Darla aware of possible consequences if she continued on the path she had taken. He advised Evelyn to work closely with Vernon dealing with Darla. The meeting ended an hour after it started and left me seriously concerned the MEP problem was increasingly becoming a black/Latino power struggle. Even the way they sat around the conference table was telling. Armando and Evelyn sat on the same side of the table with Alfred and Vernon on the other side. I sat alone at the head of the rectangular conference table.

The next day, I went again to speak with Lisa Crist about my overall concerns regarding potential conflict of interests in my reporting relationship to the provost's office while at the same time dealing with problems directly related to the provost and vice provost. I mentioned again some of the problems I had with Daniel Marks, Alfred, and Vernon. I discussed my experience with the SBA and the MEP and my concerns the MEP problem might worsen already tense black/Latino relations on campus. She informed me she wanted me to meet with her again in the future when she returned from a trip so that we may talk again about the problems and my preference of reporting relationships. I agreed to return, and she promised to have her secretary set up the meeting in a couple of weeks.

During my regular biweekly meeting with Alfred Pratt that afternoon, the only item on the agenda was the MEP. He spoke angrily about Darla Carter and Armando Segundo and declared he "didn't give a shit about what happens to both of them." He was angry with Darla because he and Daniel had failed to convince her to stop making trouble and creating problems for the interim provost. He said Darla had met with him again recently to talk about transferring her to another department. A few days later, Darla had phoned him to threaten she would go outside the university for help if the provost's office did not solve the problem to her satisfaction.

"That's extortion!" he said.

"We will never agree to that," he added.

"We're just gonna have to move her black ass from over there. I am gonna talk with Al Richards to see if he can find something for her in student services. She is my friend. I have said that before, but, if she doesn't straighten up, I can't protect her," he continued.

"Alfred, have you wondered why Becky Barr never promoted Darla during the nine years she worked for her in the MEP? I asked Darla this very same question when she claimed to me that Armando and Evelyn's refusal to promote her to coordinator amounted to discrimination. But she wouldn't respond directly to the question. Her response was, 'I worked for ESU, not Becky Barr or Evelyn Hernandez. It's the university that has refused to promote me,'" I informed him.

Instead of responding to my suspicions that Darla had been coached, Alfred turned his attention to Del Alexander and Armando Segundo. He described Del as ineffectual and guilty of dereliction of responsibility for giving Armando Segundo carte blanche in the reorganization of the MEP. He said he was "sick and tired" of hearing excuses from him every time the subject of the MEP was discussed. He spoke at length about the dean's excuse that he had delegated the reorganization of the MEP to Armando Segundo as a "dumb-ass excuse" that did not sit well with Daniel Marks. And he added that Del's absence from the September meeting in the School of Engineering with Evelyn and Armando was unacceptable to the provost. But he saved his anger for Armando Segundo because he said it was he who pushed Becky Barr out of the MEP.

"Imagine that, the incompetent son of a bitch pushed out a black female director. None of this would have happened if he hadn't done that. And, to add insult to injury, he showed great insensitivity to black students, who are the majority in the MEP, by hiring a 'damned Cuban like himself' and not a black program director to replace her," he said.

"Alfred, I am really concerned this problem is fast becoming a black/Cuban struggle. When you first asked me to try to resolve it, you mentioned Darla was the problem. Now, if I hear you right, it is increasingly becoming an ethnic vendetta against Armando Segundo because he is Cuban. It sounds like a violation of Title VII," I responded.

He ignored my comment and added Becky had "coincidentally" telephoned him one afternoon just when he was meeting with Armando and Mel about the MEP.

He continued, "Becky gave them an earful of how, during her tenure in the program, they had never supported her and how she felt pushed out by Armando Now, with Jack Okun gone from the School of Engineering, the only black person left over there is that fool, Darla."

"Alfred, I am very concerned this problem might intensify black/Latino conflict on campus. I have become even more concerned after my meeting with Armando and Evelyn. Increasingly, as I listen to you, I am beginning to believe you and Vernon feel Armando pushed Becky out because she was black so that he could hire Evelyn because both he and she are Latinos of Cuban descent," I cautioned.

"I am also concerned that separate meetings between you and Darla about the MEP at the same time I am working with Evelyn and her will create confusion and make matters worse," I added.

"Well, we'll see how you feel when we meet with Daniel Marks next week," he said as he abruptly walked out of his office and left me sitting there by myself.

After a few minutes, I felt even more concerned I was heading for a major problem with Daniel Marks and the SBA. As I walked out of Alfred's office, I ran into Vernon, who was heading to the back of the provost's office. I mentioned to him I might withdraw from the MEP problem because of potential conflict of interests and my concern that he, Alfred, and Daniel were blaming Armando Segundo for the problems at the MEP. I added that I believed it would create many problems given long-standing Latino grievances regarding the limited number of Latinos in academic administrative positions in the university. As we approached his administrative assistant's office in the back, he bade me farewell with a short salute as he turned, went into her office, and shut the door behind himself.

The next day, I received a telephone call from Alfred asking me if I was planning to attend the meeting between MEP students, Armando, and Evelyn that was scheduled that afternoon in the School of Engineering. I told him I did not know about it and that I had a scheduling conflict with a history class I taught. He informed me he had planned to be there, but he had decided not to attend. Yet, he wanted me there and expected a report about the meeting the next day. He added just before he hung up, "This is an example of how your teaching is interfering with your responsibilities. This is something I will discuss with you before you are allowed to teach another course next year. It's up to you. You decide whether you should or not attend the MEP meeting this afternoon, but you should know the provost and I are expecting a detailed report from you tomorrow."

I decided to have my students watch a video while I attended the meeting in the School of Engineering a quarter-mile away. Armando Segundo and about ten MEP students, including Clinton Davidson and some of the same students who met with Alfred in September, attended the meeting. Needless to say, the meeting was intense from the beginning when Armando asked the students about their concerns. They responded with all of the same concerns that had been raised with Alfred, including attacks on Evelyn's qualification and claims that Darla was better-qualified than Evelyn to be MEP director. They also demanded that Clinton Davidson be rehired as a tutor in the MEP. But, before Armando could respond, I decided to jump in to facilitate the discussion. First, I told the students it was inappropriate to raise Evelyn's qualifications. Second, I volunteered to talk with Evelyn about Clinton's rehiring in the MEP if it was made as a recommendation rather than a demand. By the end of the meeting, Armando had agreed to respond favorably to most of the students' concerns regarding tutors, space, computers, and the social atmosphere in the MEP.

The following day, I sent Alfred and the provost a detailed memorandum regarding the proceedings of the MEP meeting. That morning, I went over to the EEO office to ask Anthony Day a question about the September SBA meeting. I also mentioned to him some of the problems I was dealing with involving the MEP, Armando Segundo, and SBA members at the provost's office.

I asked, "Did they talk about me during the recent SBA meeting at Italiano's restaurant?"

"Oh yes, yes. They did talk about you quite a lot. It all began when someone asked Alfred if he knew anything about the problems in MEP. He responded that he didn't know much about it, but he informed the group present that he had directed you to work on it. That's when Jim Aaron started to angrily talk about you," he replied.

"What did he say?" I asked

"Well, he started by saying that putting you in charge of looking into minority concerns in the MEP guarantees you would never get to the bottom of things. He said he was convinced of that because you are opposed to affirmative action and everything black people have fought for, including all of the on-campus minority advisory committees, celebrations, and programs," Tony responded.

"What else?" I asked.

"That's when he started to complain that, as chair of the Diversity Task Force, you have been silencing minority voices in the meetings. He complained you've continued to ignore minority wishes during discussion about task force recommendations," he added.

"At some point in the conversation, Alfred said 'leave him to me. I will deal with him. I will schedule a meeting with the provost and we will take care of this problem once and for all.'"

"I simply said I thought the problems in the task force are more philosophical than procedural. I mentioned that you and I have always openly discussed our philosophical differences about diversity issues and that I have no problem with that because that's what diversity is all about," he responded.

"Watch out. They appear serious this time. He emphasized he was going to deal with you once and for all," he added.

"Thank you, Tony. Now I know the purpose of the meeting they have scheduled for Thursday. Was Daniel Marks present during the SBA meeting?" I asked.

"No, he wasn't. Please let me know what happens on Thursday," he requested.

The meeting with Daniel and Alfred was scheduled for 10:00 AM on September 28, but I waited in the lounge almost thirty minutes before I was invited into Daniel's office. Alfred started the meeting by informing Daniel he had two agenda items: the MEP and the Diversity Task Force. Daniel asked Alfred to begin with the MEP. He began the meeting by concluding that Armando Segundo has caused all of the racial problems in the School of Engineering because he lacked sensitivity to black concerns in the MEP. He added the problems would not have occurred had he not pushed out Becky Barr and hired a Cuban woman to head a program that was essentially black. He referred to Armando as arrogant and incompetent. He said he should have never been made associate dean, but President Franklin was under a lot of pressure to increase the representation of Latinos among academic administrators in the university.

He concluded by saying, "Armando is going to continue to be a problem until he is dealt with."

"I agree with you, Alfred. He is a problem over there, and I know how to deal with it. It will be a priority for the new dean we hire in that college. I am hoping to hire a Hispanic dean in the School of Engineering, and that will make it a clean sweep to remove Armando," added Daniel.

"Well, I don't know what to say because I see things very differently. I don't think this is an Armando Segundo problem. It was clear in the beginning that you both thought the problem was with Darla Carter's behavior. But, after the September 19 meeting with Evelyn and Armando, the focus has increasingly shifted to blaming Armando. Now Daniel is even talking about dealing with him. If this is the course you wish to take, then I will withdraw from the MEP problem."

"I agree that part of the problem is with Darla because we've even tried to talk with her, but she has a ghetto nigger mentality," said Daniel.

"Well, I want to talk about the next agenda item before we run out of time," announced Alfred as he changed the subject after realizing what had just happened.

"The next item is the Diversity Task Force. Samir, two African-American members of that group complained to me the other day about the way you are chairing the Diversity Task Force proceedings. They believe you are insensitive to black issues and concerns and are frustrated by your comments against affirmative action and attempts to silence minority voices and wishes. I just want you and Daniel to know what folks are feeling and saying," he concluded.

"Alfred, first of all, the task force cochair is Jack Okun. I am not the only chair, and he is black. You may want to discuss these concerns with him as well. Second, I know you are talking about Jim Aaron, and I am not surprised because Jim has been duplicitous during most of the discussions in the task force. When we are in the meeting, he strongly opposes any changes to the advisory committees. After the meeting, he tells me that he 'doesn't give a shit about those goddamned diversity advisory committees. It's those goddamned niggers, Tom Strung and Jenny Davies, I am worried about.'"

"Well, that's an old issue. But he is right," said Daniel.

"Well, I am troubled by the use of racial epithets by both Jim Aaron and you. I want you, as provost and vice provost, to know that, if you continue to use racial epithets, I will be forced to report the matter to the president. Jim had continued to do so even though I warned him several times. He continues to say, 'Excuse me, but they are goddamned niggers.' Now, just in here in the provost office, you just used the same racial epithets," I responded.

"Well, Samir, that's why you are paid the handsome salary you make. You have to put up with a lot of things you don't like," replied Daniel.

It was clear that, by the time the meeting ended, both were very angry with me. Now, I was really concerned about their next move. I decided to wait until I saw the Lisa Crist again on October 28 before I did anything else.

About a month later, on October 28, 1997, I met again with Lisa Crist to discuss my concerns, including more recent events that had compounded the problems of conflicts of interest I faced. I recounted the problems in the MEP and SBA attempts to blame Armando Segundo for pushing out Becky Barr and for hiring a Cuban woman as her replacement in the MEP. I told her the MEP situation was increasingly becoming a black/Latino power struggle. I also mentioned that I knew Daniel and Alfred were going to try to find a way to push me out of the university because I had already told them I could not go along with what they were doing. In addition, I mentioned to her I had told Daniel Marks that his use of racial epithets against other blacks on campus was unacceptable. I added that Jim Aaron had also used racial epithets at least on five occasions and continued to do so even after I asked him to stop.

I asked her to intervene and have my reporting lines changed before things worsened. Finally, I told her that, if the university administration failed to change my reporting line, I would withdraw from the MEP problem because I could not go along with what the provost and the SBA were trying to do to Armando Segundo. I also mentioned to her that Anthony Day had forewarned me about Alfred's comments during the September 11 SBA meeting at Italiano's restaurant.

"I know you will appreciate the legal implications for the university in all of these developments and concerns, and I sincerely hope Daniel doesn't abuse his authority as interim provost to try to push me out or try to intimidate me into going along with their attempts to fire Armando Segundo."

"Do you get annual evaluations from Alfred and the provost? Have they been good?" she asked.

"Yes. Each year, Alfred asks me to provide him with a detailed annual report and self-evaluation. After which, he gives me his overall evaluation of my performance. In the past five years, Alfred has agreed with my overall self-evaluations of between very good and excellent. Not only that, I have been required to submit detailed quarterly reports and self-evaluations since 1993," I responded.

"Have they done anything else to threaten you or are you going just on intuition?" she asked.

"Well, outside of my experiences with them, I've heard rumors from reliable sources that Daniel Marks has mentioned to several vice presidents that he intends to make some changes in the EEO and diversity offices. Either that is an attempt to intimidate me or they are planning to fire me," I replied.

"Let me think about it, and I'll get back in touch with you," she promised.

"You may want to talk with Judy Krup because she referred me to you. She also knows about everything I have mentioned to you because I have been expressing these concerns to her for the past five years," I replied.

"Thanks, I will talk with her," she promised again.

A month later, on November 28, things went from bad to worse when Daniel Marks, at the close of the provost's staff meeting, announced, "One last item is the MEP. I have heard many complaints about the problems that Armando Segundo has created in the MEP since he pushed out Becky Barr. The problems have resulted from his lack of sensitivity to black issues. Now I am asking those of you who may have information about Armando to bring them forward. I know Samir has been doing excellent, excellent work trying to resolve some of the racial problems over there. So let's spend the next few minutes talking about that this morning. I have also heard that Armando spends forty percent of his time doing private consulting instead of doing his job in the dean's office. What else do you have on him? This is a good time to bring it forward because it looks like we are going to have someone else in the dean's position who can deal with him in a clean way."

"Yes, I suppose I'll be the first to say I've had nothing but problems with him. The most notable is the MEP, but he bungled the salary enhancement program. And that was a big one. I can go on, but I will put it in writing to you," responded Vernon.

"As I have already told you, my experiences are similar to Vernon's. Not just about the MEP, but with other problems as well. The man is arrogant and incompetent. Everything in him points to ineptitude. I don't know how they ever chose him for that job. I know President Franklin and Mitch Solovitch, the former dean, were under a lot of pressure to increase Latino profile in the academic administration of the university. I too will put it in writing for you," said Alfred.

"Anyone else? Samir, I know you have been working with him over there. What can you add?" asked Daniel.

"Nothing. I have nothing to say. Thank you," I responded.

At this point, I finally decided I should withdraw from dealing with the MEP because I was convinced they were going to get Armando Segundo fired and I could not remain quiet about it. That afternoon, I went and informed Alfred I was withdrawing from the MEP because of a conflict of interest. I also went and reported the matter again to Lisa Crist and Anthony Day because I believed that targeting Armando Segundo for removal from his job under the current circumstances would violate Armando's Title VII protection under the law. Lisa promised again to look into the matter. Tony told me he could do nothing about the problem until they actually did something about it. Frustrated about their responses, I went to talk with Judy Krup again about going directly to the president about my concern. She told me I should stop worrying that Lisa Crist would take care of it. But she warned me about bothering the president because she was quite busy about the racial problems in the athletic department and threats from the legislature to break up ESU's regional campus. She warned me that going to the new president with complaints about the interim provost would turn her against me.

At this point, I began to realize I had been wasting my time going to Judy Krup and Lisa Crist about my concerns. I began to suspect they were conspiring with Daniel, Alfred, Vernon, and the SBA. Feeling deeply frustrated that no one wanted to do anything to protect Armando Segundo, I went to Anthony Day and informed him that, if they succeeded in removing Armando from his position, I would report the matter to the EEOC. I also told him that I intended to talk to Armando Segundo directly about what I knew so that he could seek legal protection. He promised to speak with both Lisa and Judy and would get back with me.

In early December, I was approached by one of the administrative assistants in the provost's office to solicit my help regarding Vernon's verbal and emotionally abusive behavior toward his administrative assistant. I was told he had already started yelling at and demeaning his new administrative assistant whom he just hired a month earlier. I recommended the administrative assistant report the matter to the provost office and the EEO/AA office because Vernon's abusive behavior toward his staff constituted a violation of OSHA's rules against hostile work environments. I mentioned that Vernon's abusive behavior had been a long-standing problem the administration had failed to deal with for many years. It would continue to go unaddressed until someone had the guts to file an official complaint against him and the university's failures to deal with the abuse. The individual mentioned that Vernon had had twelve secretaries and administrative assistants in the past ten years. I told her that I had been looking into the matter for several years and I had identified twenty-five in the past twenty years. Some were still working on the campus in other departments. He appeared to be an equal opportunity abuser of the women who had worked for him over the years. Many of them had been black and Latinos, but most of them had lately been blonde, white women. I promised her that I would talk with his supervisor, Alfred Pratt, about it. But I was quick to add that I did not have any faith he would do anything about it because they were close personal friends and highly organized members of the SBA organization, of which the provost, Daniel Marks, was also a member.

The next day, I discussed with Alfred the conversation I had with one of the staff members in the provost's office regarding Vernon's abusive behavior toward his administrative assistant. The conversation went something like this.

"Why are you getting involved in this matter?" he asked.

"Because it is a diversity issue, and I am concerned about it," I responded

"How is this a diversity matter?" he asked.

"Come on, Alfred, this is an issue we've talked about before many times. We have even tried to discuss it during the provost's staff meetings as well as in our meetings every time one of the staff has complained to me about his behavior. The only reason he keeps getting away with his abusive behavior is because he is a close personal friend of yours," I replied.

"Are you accusing me of cronyism? You better watch what you say," he threatened.

"Well, this time, if you and Daniel fail to deal with him, I will take appropriate action. I must also add that I will give testimony about what I know regarding your failure to deal with this problem. I will tell everything I know about his abusive behavior," I responded.

"I don't care what you do. No one will touch him as long as I am vice provost and he continues to report to me," he concluded.

"You should know that I will advise Patricia, his new administrative assistant, to file an official complaint because his behavior is in violation of OSHA laws," I responded as I left his office.

On December 1, Manuel Cardinale, faculty assistant to the president, came to meet with me to talk about draft task force recommendations that the Diversity Task Force had submitted for Daniel Marks' review. But, from the moment he arrived in my office, I suspected he had been sent to try to intimidate me. He began the meeting by telling me how disappointed he was with my leadership and advocacy abilities.

He said, "I've had extensive discussions with the president about what I am going to tell you. I am not only disappointed because you don't know where advocacy begins or ends, but also your diversity plan is skimpy on diversity strategies. It's not comprehensive, and I have some problems with its assumptions. By the way, that diversity statistical report you just completed is useless because it lacked any analysis or recommendations. And those trainings that you do, the president wants the Counseling Center to do them. They seem to be the best people to conduct those types of trainings."

"Is there anything else?" I asked.

"Yes, I am not trying to be cynical because, if I wanted to, it could have been worse because you have failed to be involved in policy matters. I have not seen you at any policy meetings that I have attended since I have been in the president's office," he continued.

"Anything else?" I asked again.

"Yes. Here, read this. This is what I call an excellent diversity plan. It is from Ohio State University. Now, use it as a model, and develop a comprehensive diversity plan for this university. I have talked with President Judge about this, and she agrees with me. Now, why don't you begin with an outline? I'll expect that in about a week," he ordered.

"Now, I want you to listen to me carefully. I don't know who you've been talking to about my office, but I know one thing. You have failed to check out your facts before you formed certain conclusions. I don't appreciate your attitude or tone of voice. We work very hard in this office to make the university into a better place for people, and I will not tolerate foolishness from you. Where do you get the nerve to walk in here and make the kinds of statements you've just made? Secondly, have you talked with the provost about this because this foolishness is becoming a serious problem? Do you know I am writing another diversity plan for Alfred in addition to the one I am writing for the vice provost, Phyllis Autry? Now, without talking with them, you want me to write a third plan? Will you get together with them and iron things out because I don't want to write three different diversity plans," I added.

"No, I haven't talked with them. I will do that immediately. I am sorry. And I have to leave. Thank you," he said as he left my office.

On Monday, December 4, I went to continue my discussions with Manuel Cardinale in the president's office. I wanted to respond to some of the specific comments he had made when he came to talk with me on Friday, particularly the comment about my absence from policy discussions at the senior level of the administration. I arrived early in the morning (before 8:00 AM), so I walked directly into his office to ask for a minute of his time. He agreed to meet and came around from behind his desk. He asked, "What can I do for you?"

"Well, you left so suddenly on Friday that I did not have enough time to respond to some of your comments. So I felt I should try to meet with you again so that you can hear me out," I said.

"Okay. Please go ahead," he said emotionlessly.

"On Friday, you said you've had extensive discussions with the president about the university's diversity initiatives and new policies about accountability. Yet, neither you nor the president felt the need to consult with or involve me. And yet, you accused me of failing to be involved at the senior level about policy matters. The current behavior has continued in the tradition of excluding me from discussions about planning and policy matters. Since I arrived at ESU, I have only attended the president's staff meeting three times. I have been excluded from the president's council and have reported to four different vice presidents in six years. And finally, I have been relegated to reporting to the vice provost. Does that sound like an administration that wants my input? And you know what? The same individuals who were trying to silence me are also involved in doing it now. It has been a deliberate effort to keep me out of those discussions," I began.

"I did not know all of that because I was not here then," he replied.

"Well, if you were really concerned about my absence during those discussions, why didn't you invite me or even suggest I be included? That's why I don't believe that is your true motive for what you did on Friday. I also find your timing very interesting," I added.

"I have not heard anything that has impressed me. You should have said something about it at the time," he retorted.

"I have been doing that for five years, ever since Ron Liste reassigned me to report to Alfred in 1995. I have talked with Judy Krup and Lisa Crist many times in the past five years. I am convinced the same individuals who wanted me isolated then are doing it now and the new administration is permitting this to continue. But I want to say one thing. It's an easy problem to fix. Tell the president that, in the event she ever needed input from me in the future, I will be delighted to join in the conversation," I responded.

"Well, that's up to her and the provost," he responded.

"Yes. Do you know the provost has talked with several people about making changes in the EEO and diversity offices? Yet he has still not talked with me about it. Judy Krup has even talked with Anthony Day about the intended changes. But, as of yet, no one in the provost's office has talked with me about it," I added.

"I didn't know that," he responded.

"Maybe I need to speak with the president myself," I said.

"Don't do that without first talking with the provost because she will just refer you back to him," he responded.

"Well, I don't think I am getting anywhere with you because you are not interested in the truth and fairness. Thank you for your time," I said as I left his office.

On December 6, 1997, Anthony Day mentioned to me that Judy Krup had talked about the proposed changes in my office and his at her senior staff meeting. He wanted to know if Daniel or Alfred had talked with me about it yet. I told him they had not, and I was suspicious about their intents.

By December, I had become deeply discouraged about the serious lack of integrity in the university administration, particularly in the vice presidents for personnel and the general counsel. Even though they were fully aware that many of the "political activities" of the SBA were illegal, they didn't want to get involved because they knew the former president had endorsed and encouraged on-campus SBA political activities. They were also not certain about the new president's expectations and political agenda. In addition, they did not want to get involved because they were afraid she might not want to deal with the SBA because of the racial scandal in the athletic department. As for the interim provost, Daniel Marks, and vice provost, Alfred Pratt, I was so repulsed by their lack of moral integrity that I decided not to attend the provost's December holiday party at the Big Trees Country Club. I was told after the party that Daniel Marks had noted my absence to several of the senior staff and to my secretary, Leticia Stasa. The following Monday, Alfred asked me why I had missed the holiday party. I was honest with him.

"I really did not feel like attending" was my response.

On December 13, I attended the president's holiday party for faculty and staff. There, I ran into Lucy Dalembert and asked her how much she knew about the proposed reorganization of my office. She said Judy had discussed it during their last staff meeting, but she did not give too many details and was surprised Daniel and Alfred had still not talked with me about it. I felt so discouraged with what appeared to be a quiet conspiracy that involved the complicity of university administration to push me out. As a result, I left the party early.

On December 14, Alfred called me into his office to inform me Lucy had talked with him at the president's holiday party about my concerns. He said he had talked with Daniel about the rumors regarding the reorganization of my office. He wanted Alfred to tell me that no decision had yet been made. But he promised to inform me as soon as the decision was made. Alfred was short and abrupt and informed me he "was not at liberty to discuss any details" with me.

I did manage to say the following to him before I left his office, "Alfred, given my experiences with Daniel, Vernon, you, and other members of the SBA over the years and, most recently, the issues involving Armando Segundo in the School of Engineering, I am beginning to feel uneasy about Daniel's intentions with regard to this reorganization."

"Well, I can understand why you feel that way, but I really cannot discuss anything with you at this point. You know you serve at the pleasure or the displeasure of the provost," he responded.

"I realize that, and I hope he is honest about his reasons for the actions he takes because I strongly believe in the old adage that 'what goes around comes around.' Please remind him of that."

9

On the Slippery Road Again

My search for another job began in earnest on January 12, 1998, the day Daniel Marks and Alfred Pratt told me I would not be reappointed to my position when my contract expired in six months. They had chosen January 12 because Alfred knew I had been invited for a job interview at the Pacific Northwest State University. I had informed him the day before that I would be leaving for the interview on Saturday, January 13. This FYI was the precipitant for their choice of timing in issuing me the nonrenewal. They even had the nerve to wish me luck at the interview. Daniel Marks promised to give me "an excellent, excellent, excellent reference." He even offered to put it in writing with a copy for my files. But I politely declined their job reference offer. I couldn't bring myself to use people as reference I perceived as having no integrity. I realized this hurt my ability to find a new job, but I just couldn't stoop to their condescension.

My search for another job continued for several months while I continued to work at ESU under the cloud of termination. I had many job interviews in every region of the nation over a seven-month period. I was constantly on the road to an interview almost every two weeks. The provost and vice provost somehow managed to find out about many of the positions for which I had interviewed after every trip, even though I had not given their names as references. I suspected the institutions were contacting them at any rate, even though they were not on my reference list. I continued to do my job writing reports and conducting educational programs as I actively searched for another job. By summer that year, I became convinced my career as a diversity professional was over because I had become a known entity in the diversity profession as a "paradigm buster of multiculturalism" as one person put it and, most importantly, because of my "racial and ethnic ambiguity" in a world of "racial and ethnic certainty."

Of course, I had considered getting out of the field before. My wife even questioned me on it when I applied for the job at ESU. Did I have a chip on my shoulder? Something to prove? Maybe. Maybe I wanted to prove that I could, in fact, be who I say I am. An individual with no racial, religious, or ethnic identity. (Come on, I identify resoundingly with being a "man." Isn't that enough? One out of four?) Americans find the idea unfavorable, and I may have always taken this as a disaffirmation of me, my self. So it may be that part of my stubbornness centered around my desire to be accepted as who I am. Maybe it was a reason I wrote this book. Clearly, however, I also have always understood and sympathized, perhaps because of my singular inability to relate to the constructs of race and ethnicity with those who are disenfranchised and marked as outsiders and different. So, beyond my desire to be exactly who I am and nothing more or less, I stayed in the profession (and wrote this book) also out of a deep commitment to equality, fairness, and acceptance for all, regardless of race, religion, ethnicity, gender, or relative lack of any of these.

Pacific Northwest State University

The job interview at the Pacific Northwest State University was an interesting experience and a harbinger of things to come in my search for a new job. As I answered some of the questions that members of the search committee asked, I struggled with whether I should be honest with them or respond with political correctness and tell them what they wanted to hear. I decided to be honest and tactful in my responses to their questions. I recognized the futility of trying to please all nineteen people in the search committee. The interview itself was fast-paced because each member of the committee had a preprepared question that had to be asked. I was asked to give short, concise answers. Even with these limitations, the interview went well until the last question was asked at the end of the interview, interrupting the chair's statement:

"Well, Mr. Dyfan, we have come to the end of the interview, and I suppose we should give you a couple of minutes over the allotted time to see if you have any questions for us."

"Now, just a minute, I have one last question of Mr. Dyfan. Is that your name?" asked an elderly member of the search committee who introduced himself as vice president emeritus for minority affairs.

"Well, we have run out of time, and I wanted to give Mr. Dyfan a couple minutes to ask us any questions he might have. You know he is supposed to be interviewing us as well," said the chair.

"I just want to know what he is going to do when the students turn to him for leadership in forcing the administration to do right by them. Because I don't care if you call it coercion or extortion or blackmail. Without threats, we would not have had any minority affairs on this campus. I want to know what you gonna do when the students turn to you for help when they have a demand! Tell me, please," he pleaded.

"I need to ask you a few questions so that I can understand the context and the nature of the demand, as you called it," I said.

"Well, let me tell you what I'd do. I went to the president and said to him, 'We want this and that. You can deal with me or deal with the students. You have a choice.' You see, I am vice president emeritus for minority affairs, and that's how I did it. Are you gonna be able to do that? Tell me. Because that's the only thing that works."

He kept repeating himself over and over again until I said, "I will try to understand the particular needs of the students and will articulate the needs to the university administration with specific recommendations for addressing those needs."

"What about if they say 'Hell, no,' what you gonna do then?" he asked.

"I will relate the needs of the students to the expressed mission, vision, values, and beliefs of the institution and articulate the institutional consequences for failure to address the needs of our students," I replied.

"Remember now, the students are looking to you for leadership. What you gonna do then?" he asked relentlessly.

"I will not be a party to any coercive advocacy activity," I replied. I quickly added, "That being said, I must add that I will similarly try to assist the students to understand the consequences of the various options for responding to the administration. In the end, however, they are independent actors with informed choices. If things get out of hand, I will be there and ready to intervene should my services be required."

"I can see we are not going to get anywhere with your kind of approach, Mr. Dyfan." With that, he ended the interview.

"Sorry, Mr. Dyfan. We've run out of time. Thank you for giving us this opportunity to interview you. We'll let you know if you were chosen for the second round of interviews," said the search chair.

Suffice to say, I was not chosen for the second round. I can only assume that passing on my candidacy was yet another ultimatum delivered by the emeritus vice president for minority affairs.

Alden State University

In early February 1998, I applied for the position of director for the Center for International Cultures at Alden State University. I did not hear from them again until early April after they contacted all of my references. They invited me to a job interview scheduled for April. The advertised position reported "directly to the provost and was responsible for facilitating the mission of the Center, seeking support from foundation and or corporations, meeting regularly with advisory and multicultural committees, and working with the academic areas."

The position vacancy announcement listed the qualifications to "include a master's degree in any area relevant to the Center's work, experience working in diversity education and scholarship, fund-raising, and knowledge of the national initiatives in diversity education and scholarship. Desired qualifications include a doctorate or terminal degree and significant faculty experience with a teaching and scholarship record commensurate with tenured position in one of the academic departments."

The mission of the Center for International Cultures, the position announcement explained, "is to promote a positive climate for diversity. The Center provides leadership for diversity education, faculty development, curriculum development, and scholarship and serves as a resource center."

I arrived for the interview in mid-April and was picked up at the Alden International Airport by Stan Lapue, the chair of the search committee. The drive from the airport lasted about one hour through a winding country road. On the way, Stan and I had a long conversation about the genesis, politics, prospects, and mission of the Center for International Cultures and about expectations of the new director. The conversation turned invariably to my professional experience and (inevitably) to my background. The racial ambiguity of my physical appearance and my accent always seemed to increase the curiosity of search committee members. He was curious about my accent and asked about its origin. When I told him I was an immigrant from West Africa, he then told me one of my references had mentioned I was of Lebanese descent and appeared fascinated about the whole thing. Then he told me he had a good friend who worked at Alden State University for almost twenty years who was of Lebanese descent. He said his friend, Daniel Attar, had left Alden State University for Montoya College, where he now served as vice president of academic affairs.

Before long, we were at Alden State University and headed to dinner with the search committee members at a local restaurant. As it turned out, only three committee members were able to be there that evening. As soon as Stan introduced me to the first committee member, Osman Escargo, who was of Egyptian descent, he mentioned to him that I was of Lebanese descent. And he said that he wished Daniel Attar hadn't left Alden State University because he would have loved to introduce him to me.

To which, Osman asked, "Are you from Lebanon?"

"No, I am originally from West Africa," I replied.

"I thought he, Stan, said you are Lebanese?" he asked again.

"I mentioned to Stan on the way from the airport that I am of partial Lebanese descent, but he has picked up only on the Lebanese part of my heritage. Maybe I should clarify that, even though my father is of Lebanese descent, my mother was part French, English, and Susu African. As for me, I don't have any particular racial or ethnic identity. The government of West Africa has tried to label people like me as Afro-Lebanese," I replied.

"Well, that's fascinating. How much of the Lebanese culture have you retained? Do you speak Arabic?" asked Osman.

"No, but I know a lot of Arabic curse words," I responded.

"Yeah, those are usually the first words you learn in any language," said Osman.

A third member of the search committee joined us for dinner as the conversation changed from a focus on my heritage to food. Nevertheless, it was not long before Osman and I were comparing recipes for preparing Mulokhiya, an Egyptian delicacy made with jute leaves. As we compared the Egyptian and Lebanese recipes for preparing chicken molokhiya, Stan Lapue interrupted us and tried to refocus the conversation away from my heritage to my relative experiences before we ran out of time. We spent the rest of the time discussing the Center and some of the programs the interim directors had been sponsoring. This led to discussions about an upcoming program I was scheduled to attend as part of the interview process.

The next day, I met throughout the day with several groups of faculty, staff, and administration as well as with the provost, Reginald Crutches, a black man, and the search committee.

The next day, I met with gaggle of academic deans, department chairs, atudent affairs staff, and Associate Provost Larry Sax. He was a light-skinned black male who was very informal and open with me about what he felt was the greatest challenge I faced as I searched for another job. Here's what he said to me as I walked into his office for the interview with him:

"Welcome, Samir. Come on in, and have a seat. Relax, I am not interested in going over your experiences and credentials. Others will do that. I just want to chat with you to find out if you have any questions about the renovation of the Center or the budget. But those are not going to take long. All I have to do is give you a number for the budget and explain where we are with the renovation of the building in which the Center will be located."

"Thank you," I said as I sat on a chair next to his desk.

"How is the interview going? You see, Samir, the problem you are gonna have nowadays at job interviews is that these universities want to hire someone that everyone knows what they have as soon as you see them. They want someone, as soon as you see them, you know they are black. You don't have to explain to the world or write about them to let people know they are black. That's the same problem I used to have myself, as you can see. Nowadays, they want to hire someone who looks black, and you've got a problem with that," he added.

"How did you overcome your problem?" I asked.

"Well, at least with me, I am from Cincinnati, born and bred in a black neighborhood to parents who have black relatives in the hood. I can tell you anything you want to know about the black neighborhood in Cincinnati. You saw the incidents that led to the race riots the other day. Not only do I know the neighborhood in which the white cop shot that black criminal, I even know the exact building he ran into in order to trick the cop into vulnerability. I even know the white cop. I coached him in minor league baseball. He ate in my house and played with my kids. I have known him all of my life. He is a boy from this town and went to school with my kid. The black community is now calling him a racist because he shot a black criminal. The black community does not like to admit problems in its own community. Now they are going to lynch that good boy who shot in self-defense when he realized he had been set up and cornered. But you'll see no one wants to admit they have a problem," he mused.

"What do you think will happen now?" I asked.

"Well, they are going to announce a bunch of initiatives like urban renewal and reinvestment, the thing everyone else does after race riots. Blame the racist cops, announce urban revitalization projects, and give away a few federal dollars. But you will see no one will talk about the problems in the black community, and blacks will get away with little accountability and responsibility," he added.

"That's self-defeating isn't it?" I asked.

"Yes, that's the same thing in our colleges. Black students are having trouble coping. They blame institutional racism. Then they want a vice president for minority affairs to fix the problem. They want someone black. Then you and I show up for the job. Who do you think they gonna hire? They want someone black," he replied.

"Is that the case here at Alden?" I asked.

"What have they told you so far? Have you met with Provost Crutches yet? He is the one doing the hiring," he replied.

"I will be meeting with him again before I leave this afternoon," I replied.

"That's good. Ask him. He'll tell you," he advised.

"Thank you for your candor," I said to him as we began to realize we were running out of time.

He quickly gave me the budget figures and informed me the renovations were moving along slowly and would take approximately one year to complete. He showed me the draft plans and went over the occupancy list with me. He also mentioned the director of the Center would be the building superintendent.

My last interview before I left for the airport was with the provost, Reginald Crutches. The one-hour meeting was scheduled for 3:00 PM, but the provost was running late. I had to wait for about fifteen minutes before he could meet with me.

He began the meeting by asking, "Do you know Johnny Brown, former dean of Fine Arts at Eastern State University?"

"Yes, I know him well. He left Eastern State for the presidency at a black university, but I heard he just left that position after two years on the job," I responded.

"I see you were at Traditional Tech University. I was at the Center of Music for a number of years. What's the name of the dean of students at Traditional Tech?" he asked.

"Alice Taylor. She was my boss," I responded

"Tell me, do you mind if I call her to inquire about you?" he asked.

"No, not at all," I responded.

"I want you to know that there are going to be a lot of changes around here. We are changing the names of some of the programs. All of these separate programs for blacks will be gone. Tell me about your management style," he added.

But, as I began to speak, he closed his eyes and dozed off with his head drooping to the side of his shoulder. Realizing he had dozed off, I stopped speaking and waited for him to awake. He continued for about five minutes until someone knocked at his office door to announce his next meeting. When he woke up from his nap, he thanked me for the opportunity to be interviewed and promised to be back in touch with me. A few weeks later, I received a letter from Stan Lapue telling me his provost had decided not to fill the position until the following academic year.

Montoya College

By July 1998, I had been to several job interviews without any job offer and still waiting to hear from a few others. A few had turned me down because I did not meet the degree requirement(s) for the positions or for other reasons. Montoya College was one of those institutions that turned down my application because I did not meet doctoral requirements for the position. I had applied for the position of assistant vice provost for academic affairs and diversity.

But, in early May, I received a letter from the search committee chair indicating, "The search committee wishes to express again appreciation for your interest in and your applications for the position of assistant vice provost for academic affairs and diversity There were many highly qualified applicants for our position, and the choices are difficult. At this time, we do not see a fit between your qualifications and our specific needs. Again, thank you for your interest in Montoya College."

My initial reaction to the "Equal Employment Opportunity Survey" the chair of the search committee had sent me requesting information about my racial identity, ethnicity, gender, and so forth was to not respond immediately. I only mailed back the EEO card to Montoya College the day after I received the letter telling me my application was no longer being considered for the position. But, before I sent it back, I crossed out the word "Black" and inserted the words African-American.

Even though I knew, when I applied for the position, that I did not have the required qualification (a "doctorate or equivalent and academic qualifications for an appointment with academic rank to teach at least one course per year"), I decided to apply anyway because I had the required experience of "demonstrated experience in enhancing diversity and improving climate, preferably in higher education; experience working in a collaborative environment with faculty, deans, students, and staff; and an understanding of and commitment to the Catholic Mission of the College and the role of diversity with that Mission." My intent for applying, even though I realized I might not make the cut, was to let them know there are professionals who have the experience to do the job very well, even though they do not have the doctorate.

Well, as you would have it, almost eleven weeks after I received the letter of rejection from them, I received a voice mail message from Daniel Attar, provost for academic affairs, asking me to please return his call regarding the position I had applied for in March.

To my surprise, when I returned his call that same day, he said, "Samir, this is Daniel Attar at Montoya College. I want to apologize for the flip-flopping here with regard to the assistant provost for diversity position that you applied for several months ago. Are you still interested in it?"

"Sure. Yes, I am," I replied

"Let me tell you what has happened so far with the search to let you know how we got this far. Honestly, we have bungled this search for the start. The people I entrusted with the search insisted on the doctoral requirement for the position even though I had considerable doubts about that from the beginning. They decided to interview two African-American individuals who had the doctorate and other required academic credentials but very little professional experience in diversity work. Because of this lack of experience, I didn't hire either one of them. Which brings me to you. I am so glad you are still interested in the position."

"Yes? How do you want to proceed?" I asked him.

"Well, I'll tell you that I would like for you to provide me with the names and telephone numbers of three or four references, and I'll expedite this process. I will also have to re-advertise the position with a master's degree required instead of the PhD. We are already working on that. I will be back in touch with you in a few hours," he replied to my question.

The next morning, on July 11, I received a telephone call from Daniel Attar.

"I have checked with all your references, and everything looks fine. But, before I do anything else, I just want to take some time to talk with you about this position, the needs of the college, and where we are right now. I think you should know what the expectations are up-front. I should also see if you have any questions. Do you have some time now so that we might talk?" he asked.

"Yes," I responded.

"Let me begin by admitting again that we have bungled this search from the beginning, and we are learning from our mistakes. Or, let me say, I am learning. I am not even sure I can fill this position this year because of the mistakes we've made so far. In fact, I was and am still thinking about filling the position for one year with an interim and reopen the search again next year for a permanent person. But I felt strongly when I saw your résumé that you are the most qualified for the position. And that's why, after sitting on it for a while, I have decided to reopen the search and interview you for the position."

"Thank you," I said.

"Well, it is clear looking at all your experience and accomplishments. But I am not sure how certain people will react to you. I know that certain members of the search committee are already angry with me for not hiring one of the African-

American candidates they had interviewed. Now, they are cynical about my reopening the search and may not participate in the process. But I am moving ahead anyway, either with an interim or a permanent appointment."

"Well, Dr. Attar, I am not interested in an interim position," I replied.

"I know that. I wouldn't interview you for an interim position. I am considering you for the permanent position, even though I know some people are not happy with what I am doing. I know the African-American Faculty, Staff, and Administrators Association fully expect me to hire someone black. As long as that happens, they will be okay. Others, I am not sure if I can do anything at this point to ever please them, but that's their problem, I am doing what I think is the right thing to do. You know, Samir, I have spent the last twenty years building trust with blacks. Now, this search threatens all that, but the majority of them will be all right as long as I hire someone black. What do you say to that?"

"Well, I don't know if I can be of much help regarding that expectation. You see, Dr. Attar, because of the circumstances of my upbringing, I do not have any racial or ethnic identity. Does that create a problem?"

"What is your background, Samir? May I ask?" he asked

"Well, I am all sorts of things. I am primarily of Afro-Lebanese descent and an immigrant from West Africa," I replied.

"Well, that's going to cause another problem for me. You see, I am like you...of Lebanese descent. If I hire you, some would accuse me of cronyism because we are both of Lebanese descent. But I can tell them I didn't even know you were Lebanese until I called you. In fact, you know something. Up to the time we talked on the phone, I was under the impression you were a woman because of your name. I hope that doesn't become a problem for some people who felt you were female," he mused.

"Well, Dr. Attar, are you sure you want to continue pursuing my candidacy given all the problems my background will create for you?" I asked him.

"Sure, that's their problem. *They* will have to deal with it. Samir, I'd like you to come for an interview sometime next week. I will be back in touch with you about the exact date," he said at the end of our conversation.

That very afternoon, I received a telephone call from Dr. Attar's assistant inviting me to a daylong series of job interviews scheduled for mid-July. I was encouraged to arrive a day early so that the search committee could take me to a dinner interview that evening. The day before I left town for the interview in the city, I received an e-mail correspondence from Dr. Attar's assistant asking me to write an essay on how the diversity work I'd be doing would contribute to the Catholic mission of the college. The e-mail apologized for the late notice regarding the essay. Dr. Attar explained to me later that afternoon that he had forgotten to tell me about the essay because it was a new requirement for employment. He recognized that it might be too late for me to write the essay and urged me to not worry about it if I didn't have sufficient time to do it before the interview.

I arrived for the interview and went to dinner with two African-American administrators. One of them was a member of the original search committee. Another member of the search committee (who was supposed to be at the dinner with us) couldn't make it. The dinner itself was uneventful. Part of the conversation focused on my ideas on community building in higher education. They also talked about their respective offices and responsibilities. I began the next full day of interviews early in the morning the next day with Daniel Attar. He picked me up at the Sheraton Hotel at 8:00 AM for a breakfast interview. After the obligatory niceties, he informed me that, because we didn't have a lot of time before my next meeting, he wanted to focus on a number of things. He gave me a brief history of Montoya College's diversity initiatives and his expectations of the person he hired for the job. He went over and briefed me about each group on the day's agenda and what to expect, beginning with the deans who were the first on the list. He scheduled me to meet with him again at the end of the day for a planned dinner.

He lamented the fact that he had not been able to reactivate the original search committee because of the summer and the fact that some of the individuals were upset with him. He wanted me to be aware that some of the members of the original search committee would be dropping in on the interviews during the day. He made a point of mentioning a particular female faculty member whom he said might be at one of the meetings that I should be aware of.

"She may come across as aggressive, and that's the way she is. But she means well. Her style has turned off many people over the years, as she has carried the banner of diversity at Montoya College. One of the things she has been responsible for has been the summer institute for curriculum integration, which she has coordinated for many years. That's one of the responsibilities of the new diversity position, so she may appear protective and brash. But don't let it bother you," he advised.

"What else has she been involved with on campus?" I asked.

"Well, I think she was involved with a workshop that a woman conducted a few years ago…what's her name? I can't remember. She did a workshop on 'White Privilege.' I enjoyed it because I learned I could never feel what an African-American feels in America because I can't walk in their shoes with my white privilege," he said.

"Was the presenter Maggie Tendall from California?" I asked.

"That sounds like her, but I'm not sure. Why?" he inquired.

"Well, she is one of the biggest practitioners of the politics of blame and the psychology of guilt. All of which are packaged in her white privilege workshops," I responded.

"We've also done 'Coalition Building Workshops,' which was also highly received by faculty and staff," he said.

"I am familiar with Arleen Bronze's work, and I am not impressed with what they do at the Coalition Building Center either," I responded.

"Why?" he asked with a quizzical look on his face.

"Well, my first concern is the use of the notion of 'shared oppressor' as the lynchpin of coalition building. It is deeply troubling to me, you see. The solution to the competition of on-campus interest groups is not coalition building, but collaboration. The only discernable results or changes of 'coalition building' or 'building allies,' as they call it, are in the rhetoric of advocacy and the attitudes that inform the rhetoric. The advocacy shifts the rationale for diversity from 'moral and ethical' concerns to 'legal and political' imperatives. The institution becomes a rhetorical world of 'victims and victimizer' of 'oppressors and the oppressed' of '*us* against *them.*' In the words of Martin Buber, such a world is characterized by 'I-It' or subject-object relationships, which is antithetical to Montoya College's Catholic educational mission. That, by the way, is what I emphasized in the preemployment essay you asked me to write," I replied.

"Yes, I saw that. I agree with you. Samir, you don't think white privilege is real? I am a white male. When I go into a store, I don't find myself being followed by store security guards or cameras, like every black person that walks into that same store," he explained.

"Believe me, there are not enough store detectives to do that. All I am saying is to not accept tribal stories and myths uncritically because they are all paths to tribal self-righteousness. Remember what Sigmund Freud once said, 'The hero in every story is his majesty the ego,'" I replied.

"Yeah, yeah, yeah. I see what you mean, and you are right about it. What can we do? I'll have to think about it," he said as he walked towards his office door, leading me out for a short walk to my first group interview.

Most of the discussions during the interviews focused on my professional experiences that were relevant to the perceived needs of the college. The questions focused on faculty, staff, and student diversity, as well as curriculum integration. All of the discussions with the various groups went well, except for a brief moment when the female faculty member, whom Daniel Attar had cautioned me about, decided to warn me against advocating adding anything else beyond cultural diversity to the curriculum.

"I just want to warn you against going around talking about adding *emotional intelligence* to the curriculum. They barely have enough room in the existing curriculum to infuse cultural diversity with little time to do it. So, I want to caution you about what you do and say today because it will cause problems."

"I am not sure I understand what you are talking about," I said.

"Well, I don't think your psychoemotional approach will work," she said as she left the room, followed by others, at the end of that interview session.

"Well, I would like to discuss the matter with you if you have a minute," I said to her as she left the room.

"I can't because of time limitations. Good luck, however," she responded as she hurried away.

At the end of the day, I ended up in Daniel Attar's office for the final one-on-one interview before we left for dinner. It took him about ten minutes to finish what he was doing before he turned his attention to me.

The first thing he said to me was, "Samir, I am still not sure what I want to do here. I am still thinking about filling the position with an interim for a year to give us more time to conduct another search for the permanent person. I haven't made up my mind yet. So how did it go? What do you think about what you've heard so far?"

"Well, it was very informative, and I think the discussions during the interview helped me to better understand your institutional priorities for the next few years," I responded.

"And that's why I need to know how we are going to measure success in this initiative. I need you to give me indicators of success. Can you tell me what specifically will have been changed five years from now if I hired you? I need some sure way to measure your accomplishments if I hired you. Tell me," he asked as he picked up a pen to write down my response.

"Well, it really depends on how you conceptualize or define the role of the person in this office. All I can say to you, Dr. Attar, is that I will do my best in the advocacy of these issues and in the development of appropriate, effective processes for accomplishing the goals of this initiative. Some things can be measured, but others do not lend themselves too easily to quantitative methods of assessment. I would recommend that the initial priority be the development of a job description for the person in this position that is consonant with the goals and objectives of the college's diversity plan," I responded

"What about the goals and objectives of the diversity office?" he asked.

"I will also recommend that an initial set of goals and objectives be developed for the assistant provost for diversity. This will create the opportunity to set some measures of accountability," I responded.

"That makes sense. Samir, I want to ask you something else," he announced.

"Sure," I responded

"Samir, you strike me as the kind of guy who is smart enough to find wrinkles in neatly pressed ideas. Do you find that, when you bring up these contradictions, you are giving comfort to those who are against what we are trying to do?" he asked.

"What do you mean?" I asked him.

"You know, Samir, that there are three groups of people on campus: those who are for and supportive of diversity; those who are indifferent about it; and those who are against it, no matter what you do. Do you think that, when you point out these wrinkles, you are undermining diversity?" he asked again.

"No, not at all. In fact, I have found out that, when we deal with the issues in an honest, respectful, open, fair, and truthful way, we bring more of those in the middle group or even the group that was opposed into the conversation about shared vision. Commitment emanates from this. They will join the conversation because they will trust us," I responded.

"Okay, I have another important question. How do African-Americans perceive you on your campus? Do they see you as an ally? How do they relate to you?" he asked again.

"That is a very vague and general question. It is like asking me how whites view me. I can't answer that question. It depends on the individual. I get along fine with many African-Americans. There are also those I am sure that do not like or support me and my work."

"That's fair," he added.

"If you want me to send you a list of African-American references when I return to my office, I will be delighted to do that. Maybe they can answer your question," I offered.

"I might take you up on that," he promised. "Samir, I want to be honest. I don't think I will be able to fill this positions with a permanent appointment this year, but I am not sure yet. I have to wait and see how people reacted to you in the interviews."

"Well, have you received any feedback yet? What are the responses so far?" I asked him.

"I have received three to four evaluations so far, and they are all excellent. But I will have to wait to talk with some key people who participated in the interviews to decide what I'll do about the position. Let's go to dinner. I'll drop you off at the hotel so that you can freshen up. I will pick you up after I get my wife," he said.

"Thank you," I replied.

Dinner itself was uneventful except for my efforts to ensure the meal I ordered be completely free of MSG. He talked about his family and asked me questions about the Lebanese side of my heritage. On the way back to my hotel, we talked about the notion that people generally cocreate their experiences and the meanings of those experiences. I used the Atlantic slave trade as an example of how its causes and, therefore, the effects were cocreated. I explained to Daniel and his wife that my biggest concerns about curricular integration were its preoccupation with teaching students *what* to think instead of *how* to think. The latter was brainwashing; the former was liberating. We needed to have serious conversations about what it was that we were trying to enable students to do when we were through with curricular integration. Were we trying to teach them personal accountability or blaming? The choice was ours.

When we arrived at the hotel, he jumped out of the car to bid me farewell and good fortune in my search for a new job. Before he returned into his car, he promised to call me in three to five days. He expressed the need to have some time to think about things.

I returned home on Friday morning, deeply concerned that Daniel's discussion about hiring me for the position would be determined by racial and skin color considerations. Both of these criteria were illegal and discriminatory. I suspected that Daniel was involved in the very practice Larry Sax at Alden State University, whom Daniel knew from his days at that institution, described.

"Nowadays," he said, "these institutions wanna hire someone who, when you see him, you know he is black. You don't have to go around telling people you are black. That defeats the purpose in the first place."

On that same day, I telephoned Toni Baxter, Montoya College's EEO officer, to express my concerns about Daniel's illegal use of racial and color criteria in the search process. But she wasn't available. I left her a message that I would like to speak with her urgently regarding my concerns about the search and selection criteria. Around 7:00 PM, I received a voice mail from Toni Baxter, but I decided to call her back on Monday.

On Monday, July 23, 1998, I sent a list of four African-American references to Daniel Attar via e-mail. As far as I know, he never called any of them before he made the decision the following day.

The next day, I received a voice mail message from Daniel Attar telling me he had decided not to fill the position this year. He encouraged me to call him back if I had any questions. I called him back immediately to discuss his decision and was fortunate enough to get him on the other side.

After he thanked me for calling him back after the interview, he said, "Samir, I have to tell you the truth. I don't believe there is fit between your credentials and Montoya College's needs at this time in our development. My gut feelings tell me there is no match. So I have decided not to fill the position this year."

"Daniel, I am sure you are making this decision on more than 'gut feelings.' Please tell me what selection criteria you are using in your decision," I requested.

"I used those criteria that are listed in the position announcement, and there was no consensus on your candidacy. I just don't believe Montoya College is ready for you. You have many good ideas, but you bring up controversial issues. And we are not ready for that. It's not you. Believe me, it's us. We are just not there yet."

"What controversial issues are you referring to?" I asked.

"Well, it's not just that. The PhD is still a requirement for many people, even though I have dropped it to the status of preferred, with the master's degree as required for the position. This is the reason why I think we bungled the search from the beginning of the process when many of the faculty fought for the doctoral requirement. We wouldn't be in this situation if that hadn't happened."

"How much did racial considerations, skin color preference, and national origin play in your decision not to pursue my candidacy? I am curious because those were primary concerns in your discussions with me on several occasions," I asked.

"None. But don't get me wrong, race is a very important factor. This initiative is, to be honest, mainly about African-Americans. You see, the city is predominantly black, and the state has a sizable black population. You know the person in this position would have to work with internal and external black organizations. But that was not a factor in my decision. There was no consensus on your candidacy, and my gut feelings tell me there is not a match here," he concluded.

That afternoon, I decided to telephone the president, whom I had met during the interviews, to express my concerns regarding the search process. But he wasn't in. I left him a message requesting a returned call from him. But he never returned my call. Instead, I finally heard from Toni Baxter.

She said, "Samir, I finally get to talk with you. I am sorry for all the confusion, but I must tell you that I wasn't ignoring your call. I have been working on your concerns. I met with Daniel and the president to discuss your concerns, and we were assured that race, skin color, or national origin played no role in Daniel's decision. He said that he based his decision on the lack of consensus on your candidacy and the lack of the doctorate because that's what people wanted from the beginning."

"Well, I am not as convinced as you that those issues played no role in his decision when those were his expressed concerns during most of the interview process. He told me before the interview that he knows that African-Americans fully expect him to hire someone black. That my Lebanese ancestry would create problems for him because of he is also of Lebanese descent. He said he feared that, if he hired me, he would be accused of cronyism. During the interview, he asked me about how African-Americans perceived me because race was very important. And yesterday, he declared race an important factor in the decision because the state has a significant black population and that the person in this position will have to work closely with internal and external black organizations because primarily Montoya College's diversity initiative is mostly about blacks. This kind of reasoning leaves me with the impression that race and skin color were important criteria in the reflection process," I explained.

"What do you want me to do?" she asked.

"Well, what are your procedures for investigating a complaint of this sort?" I asked.

"All I can do is review the process again, talk to a few people, and review the evaluations to determine if there is any evidence that race, skin color, or national origin played any role in the selection process. If this is okay with you, I will talk with you again on Friday."

The new position announcement was finally re-advertised in the *Chronicle of Higher Education*, almost three days after Daniel Attar's fateful decision. The new position had indeed been slightly modified to accommodate my candidacy. Some of the changes were the very criteria that were now being held against me during the interviews. I heard from Toni Baxter on Friday, as she had promised.

"Samir, I want to tell you that, since we last talked, I have reviewed the search process, talked with additional people, and read the interview evaluations. I am now even more convinced that race, skin color, or ethnicity played no role in the decision that Daniel made not to hire you for the position. I want to assure you that his decision was based on the lack of consensus on your candidacy, not having the PhD, not having any experience with curriculum integration, and the strong disagreement with your psychoemotional approach to diversity issues. Those were the reasons."

"What else?" I asked.

"Well, do you want me to read some of the comments to you over the phone? I'll just read you a few of them," she answered.

"No, that's not necessary," I replied.

"Listen to this," she said. "Candidate failed to answer question regarding what's the most difficult expectation of working with faculty," she read aloud.

"Here's another one that criticizes your psychoemotional approach," she said.

"You see, that's why there was no consensus," she added.

"Did you speak again with Daniel Attar?" I asked.

"Yes. Even though he corroborated everything you reported, he said that neither race nor skin color played a part in his decision," she replied.

"Well, I am not convinced of that," I replied.

"Samir, I hope the next time we meet that it's not at the EEOC or our attorney's office. But I have to go now. Please call again if you have any other concerns," she said before she hung up the telephone.

In October 1998, I called the state's office of the Equal Employment Opportunity Commission (EEOC) to officially file a complaint of discrimination. I completed the relevant forms and officially filed a complaint of race and skin color discrimination against Montoya College. A few months later, I followed up the complaint with a telephone call to the state office of the EEOC and spoke with one of the investigating attorneys about my complaint. At first, I was told they could not locate my file. Then, after a few minutes, another person picked up the phone and informed me the investigating attorney, Susan Petroski, would be with me in a few minutes.

"Mr. Dyfan, I am sorry, but your file was on the director's desk for review. We have reviewed your complaint and are waiting for Montoya College's response to your allegations. Do you know if anyone else was hired for the position?" she asked.

"No. As far as know, they haven't hired anyone. Isn't that part of your investigation? Won't you be looking into this particular issue?" I asked.

"Well, no. Not initially. We wait until we receive and review their responses. We then make a decision if there is sufficient evidence to proceed with an investigation," she replied.

"Is the issue of whether they hired someone relevant and important to the complaint?" I asked.

"Well, yes. It makes your case stronger if they did hire someone else, particularly if the person they hired is darker or black. In fact, that is the key to whether or not we investigate the allegation. If they didn't then, your case is weak," she responded.

"So, why then won't you check to find out if they hired anyone?" I asked.

"That's the district director's call," she replied.

"When will I hear from you again?" I asked.

"As soon as we hear from Montoya College, a decision will be made, and we will notify you of our decision," she promised.

In April 1999, I again contacted the EEOC office to inquire about my complaint. This time again, they could not locate my file. I was really frustrated because, five months after I had spoke with them, I had not heard from them. To add insult to injury, they again had misplaced my file. A few hours later, I received a call from Susan Petroski from the EEOC.

"Mr. Dyfan, you must think we are incompetent here at the EEOC. I have your file here with me, and I don't have good news. We have decided there is not enough evidence of discrimination to proceed with an investigation at this time. Montoya College denied your allegations and claimed you failed to answer many of the questions you were asked during the interviews. And that's why they didn't hire you for the job. They also alleged that some of the comments you made during the interviews indicated you had problems working with blacks. Our director has decided we will not pursue the case, but we are willing to give you the right to sue," she informed me.

"Would your decision have been different if they had hired someone black or darker?" I asked.

"I am sure of that. That's the key in failure to hire cases, even when they go to trial," she informed me.

"Well, thanks. When will I hear from you about the right to sue?" I asked.

"In a few weeks," she responded.

"Am I entitled to a copy of Montoya College's response?" I asked.

"Yes, you will need to call and request a copy," she informed me.

A few weeks later, I received registered mail with a document informing me I had been given the right to sue within ninety days of the date in the letter.

At the end of May 1999, I attended a conference on Race and Ethnicity in Higher Education in New Mexico. One evening, around 7:00 PM in the bar of the Santa Fe Marriott, I encountered an African-American man, who introduced himself as Wayne Hicks, director of ALANA (African-American, Latino, Asian, and Native American) Student Services, formerly the Office of Minority Affairs at Montoya College. Since I did not recognize him initially, he added he was involved in the search for the assistant provost for Diversity at Montoya College, for which I had interviewed the previous year.

"Hey, man. My name is Wayne Hicks. I met you at Montoya College as a member of the search committee when you interviewed for the diversity position last year. I was very disappointed that you didn't get hired for the position because you were obviously the most qualified applicant and candidate for the position," he said. "I had pushed for your hiring because of your knowledge, experience, and expertise in the field. I felt that you could have made greater contributions than the person they hired for the position, who is really less qualified."

"If that was the case, why wasn't I hired for the position?" I asked.

"The problem with the search was Dr. Attar's assumption that all blacks wanted him to hire a black person for the position. I wanted greater diversity beyond just black and white at Montoya College. But Dr. Attar was hell-bent on hiring a black person for the job. That's why he quietly hired a black woman from Buck State University who did not have the level and scope of experience required for the job. It was obvious to me and to others in the committee that you were the most qualified for the job in the entire pool of applicants," he responded.

I was shocked because the EEOC had told me Dr. Attar had not hired anyone for the position.

"What's the name of the woman hired for the position?" I asked.

"Her name is Paulette Jackson," he said.

"Why didn't Dr. Attar hire one of the two black candidates that was interviewed earlier during the search if he wanted to hire a black person for the position?" I asked.

"The problem with those candidates that we interviewed was with their level of experience to lead the college's institution-wide diversity initiatives. That was precisely what was appealing about your candidacy, experience, and knowledge. You had successfully led several university-wide diversity initiatives, and you are really considered a national expert on the subject," he emphasized.

"Dr. Attar had argued he was concerned that my ideas regarding diversity would be offensive to blacks. Do you know what he was referring to?" I asked.

"The only person that was opposed to your candidacy because of your ideas was Annie, the woman who ran the on-campus curriculum integration program," he responded.

"Dr. Attar had spoken of Annie in very disparaging terms, describing her as abrasive and someone who was doing more harm than good to the diversity project," I mentioned.

"That perception is correct and on the mark," he responded.

"Is it true the BFSA was pressuring Dr. Attar to hire a black person for the position?" I asked.

"That was what he [Dr. Attar] felt because there were a few who felt that way, but it was not true of all blacks on campus," he responded emphatically.

I thanked him for his candor regarding the search and left. He was friendly and open throughout the conversation.

On Monday, June 3, 1999, I called Montoya College to confirm Wayne Hicks' name and title. I left him a voice mail massage to call me back with my telephone number.

On Tuesday, June 4, he returned my telephone call and left me the following voice mail message:

"Hey, Samir, this is Wayne Hicks. We spoke at the Diversity Conference, and I heard you have been trying to catch up with me. I am going to be in and out of my office most of the day. And I am a little bit concerned. We've had a conversation about what transpired on campus, and I didn't realize that you were still in suit with Montoya College. That really puts me in an awkward situation. You can call me back so that we can talk about what your intentions are, and we can kind of go from there. Talk to you later."

I decided to audiotape the voice mail message into a microcassette for future reference in the event that I filed a discrimination lawsuit in federal court. At this point, I had only a few weeks left to officially file a federal suit under the permission to sue given to me by the EEOC. As a result, I contacted a labor attorney, Ed Einstein, regarding my intent to file a federal race and color discrimination lawsuit against Montoya College. He agreed to take the case, even though there wasn't much time left in which to file the lawsuit. He felt we had a good case, but the key was whether Wayne Hicks would admit the details of our conversation in New Mexico. I also decided to file an appeal to the EEOC decision not to investigate the allegations against Montoya College, given the new information from Wayne and the audio voice mail I had copied onto a cassette. The appeal letter was addressed to the district director of the EEOC. It read as follows:

James Lewis
District Director
U.S. Equal Employment Opportunity Commission
Dear Mr. Lewis:

I am writing to request a reconsideration of the finding regarding charges brought against Montoya College based on new evidence that has been brought to my attention by an African-American employee of Montoya College. I believe this new information provides clear evidence in support of my charge of discrimination against Montoya College.

On May 29, 1999, at the National Conference on Race and Ethnicity in Higher Education in New Mexico, I had a brief discussion regarding the position and search for an assistant provost for Diversity, for which I was an applicant last year, with Wayne Hicks, director of ALANA Student Services at Montoya College. Wayne mentioned to me that the problem with the search was that Dr. Attar, provost for academic affairs, who was the hiring official, had assumed all blacks on the campus wanted him to hire someone "pigmentationally" black, but that was not the case. He said that, he for one, wanted greater diversity reflected in the search, but Dr. Attar was bent on hiring a black individual for the position. He believed that was the problem I encountered during the search. He also informed me that, because of this, Dr. Attar had quietly hired a black woman, Paulette Jackson from Buck State University, with less experience in December 1998.

During my discussions with Susan Petroski over the months she was involved in processing of my complaint, she continually informed me the biggest obstacle in my case in her view was the fact that Montoya College had not hired anyone for the position. She informed me continually that, if Montoya hired a black person who was darker for the position after the fact that Dr. Attar had extensively raised concerns about my racial background, my charge of discrimination would have been stronger and much easier to investigate. Now that this new information has surfaced, I am requesting that your office promptly conduct a thorough investigation of the original charge of discrimination. In this regard, I would like you to be mindful of the fact that the ninety-day "right to sue" clock is running.

I hope this new information and evidence is sufficient enough for a reopening of the case and a new finding. If you need additional information, please contact me as soon as possible. Thank you.

Sincerely,

Samir Dyfan

Needless to say, it was a waste of time. For whatever reasons, they had made up their minds that they did not want to investigate the allegations or get involved in the case. My appeal was rejected, and the letter reminded me I had only a few weeks left of the ninety-day right to sue. By the time I received the EEOC's letter of refusal, my attorney had already contacted Montoya College to notify them of my intent to sue for race and color discrimination in its refusal to hire me as the assistant provost for diversity. He had also prepared the necessary paperwork and was ready to file suit with federal courts. Montoya College's response referred my attorney to theirs, a high-powered law firm just around the corner from mine. As was expected, their initial response was the typical posturing. They rejected the allegations and repeated Montoya College's claims that they did not hire me for the position because I had failed to garner enough support in the search committee because of my failure to answer several questions during the interviews. They also repeated the allegations that my positions on several issues that came up during the interviews were controversial, particularly my "psychoemotional approach to diversity."

As my attorney went ahead with filing the suit in federal court, I decided to do some research on Paulette Jackson's academic and administrative experiences background by contacting a close colleague at Buck State University. I found out she left the faculty where she taught women's studies because she was denied tenure a year earlier. I also found out that the main reasons for the tenure denial was failure to publish. I was told she had problems getting any of her writings published. Part of the research also involved getting copies of Montoya College's written response to my EEOC charge, including information about the search and interview processes that included the curriculum vitae of all the candidates interviewed for the position. In the packet of information from the EEOC was a copy of Paulette Jackson's curriculum vitae. This gave me additional information about her previous experience in higher education administration. As I reviewed Montoya College's responses to the allegations, I realized that, included in the responses, was a passing comment that contained Paulette Jackson's name and references to her as the person they had interviewed and hired several months after my interview in July. This discovery left me wondering if the EEOC had even read the responses from Montoya College in the first place. I was very annoyed because, in all of my conversations with Susan Petroski, she had no idea that Montoya College had interviewed and hired somebody in October, soon after I interviewed in July. In fact, she asked me on several occasions if Montoya College had hired someone else for the position when it was clearly mentioned in Montoya College's written response in their possession. At this point, I was annoyed and convinced the staff at the EEOC was either incompetent or biased against my case because it did not fit within their political agenda, or both.

I decided to make one last call to the EEOC and speak with Susan Petroski about my discovery of the information that Montoya College had indeed hired a dark-skinned black woman for the position in an attempt to appeal to its sense of fairness now that we had the evidence she had mentioned as critical to my case.

The conversation went something like this:

"Susan, this is Samir again. I hope the new information I have will help in your deliberations regarding my request to reopen my case."

"Well, it depends on what you have. But I must tell you. Our district director is not inclined to reopen this case. Once we issue a right to sue, we seldom ever go back and reopen a case unless you have a smoking gun, like a letter in which Dr. Attar said clearly he was looking for someone black for the position," she emphasized.

"Well, you had said to me months ago that my case would be stronger if Montoya College had hired someone darker and black for the position. That was what determined whether you pursued an investigation of the charges. Do you realize that, in their written response to the charges, that Montoya College had stated clearly that they had hired someone for the position in October of that year, just three months after I was interviewed. I have checked with someone I know at Buck State University and was told that she is black and ebony in complexion. Isn't that the information that you need to reopen the case?" I asked with excitement.

"Well, I don't know what Mr. Lewis will say, but I don't think it looks good. He probably will advise you to take whatever new information and evidence you have to court and adjudicate it there. But, I believe he feels he is through with this case. Don't think the new information will make any difference to him. You see, Mr. Samir, we are understaffed. As a result, we cannot investigate every case that comes before us. That's why we gave you the right to sue. If you have a strong case, then you will prevail in court," she responded.

"Ms. Petroski, I am really frustrated with the EEOC's position regarding my case. You either have no sense of fairness, are inept, or are corrupt. I must admit that I feel strongly the system put in place to protect people is a miserable failure. But you have not heard the end of this case, and I intend to go public about my experiences with the EEOC," I said before I hung up on her in frustration.

That afternoon, I contacted my attorney at his office to discuss the EEOC's response. He wasn't surprised with their response because many of his clients had the same experience with them. "It's their standard operating procedure. The only reason people have any dealings with them is because you cannot a file a lawsuit without written permission from them. They are useless other than that," he said.

"When are you going to file the suit in federal court?" I asked.

"Next week. I am waiting to hear back from Montoya College's attorneys regarding my offer to settle before we take the case to court. Their attorneys have contacted their president, Father Lamb, for a response. If they decide not to settle then, I will file the case early next week," he responded.

"What are the chances they will agree to settle?" I asked.

"Well, you never know. It depends on how much bad publicity they want to endure because they are aware that, once we file the case, the press will have a field day with it because of the twist this case offers. But, then again, they may choose to fight it at all cost. One can never say what they will do," he responded.

He called the next day to inform me he had filed the case after Montoya College turned down the offer to settle. A few days later, I began receiving requests for newspaper and radio interviews. The first interview was from a columnist for the *Sun Newspaper*. The next day, the headline read, "Montoya College Told Job Applicant He Is Not Black Enough." The piece was a scathing attack on Montoya College for practicing skin color discrimination among minority applicants. The article was true to my story. That was a relief because I had been warned by some friends that journalists could not be trusted to tell the story as it was intended by the interviewee. Two days later, a radio talk show host called to conduct an hour-long interview.

Several weeks later, Larry Elders, a Libertarian radio talk show host on ABC Radio, called for a half-hour interview with my attorney and me. A week later, the *Chronicle of Higher Education* called for a detailed interview that appeared in the next weekly edition of the paper. By this time, things were spiraling out of control. I had to make a decision on how many more interviews to give. My concern was that the interviews would appear as publicity-seeking stunts by me. But what if Bill O'Reilly of FOX News, *60 Minutes*, or one of the other big guns called? I decided I would carefully consider any requests before agreeing to any more interviews.

In October, my attorney called to inform me we had been given a trial date in mid-February 2000. He wanted to schedule a deposition in November 1999 to depose Wayne Hicks, but he wanted me to know that I would also be deposed by Montoya College's attorneys. He also asked me before he hung up to transcribe the content of the audiotape of Wayne's voice mail for the deposition in November. I sent him the transcript and an audio copy of the voice mail message for his reference. A few weeks later, I received a call from him to discuss the content and significance of the voice mail message. While the information that Wayne had shared with me in New Mexico was a significant piece of the puzzle, it was still not a smoking gun. Everything he told me during that conversation corroborated what I had alleged in my complaint to the EEOC. The key questions were: Would he admit to the facts as I related them? If he did, would he willingly say where, how, and when Dr. Attar made the comments that he wanted someone visibly black for the position? Who else was present when he made these statements or comments? Is there anything in writing (committee minutes, notes, memoranda, and so forth) to this fact? The concern here was to ensure that we were not dealing with Wayne's opinions, interpretations, or assumptions, but facts that would corroborate my allegations of race and color discrimination.

The date for the deposition approached very fast, and, before I realized it, I was at the law office of Val Golden for the deposition. The day itself began with indications that Montoya College might be willing to negotiate a settlement sometime that day. But we decided to go ahead with the deposition of Wayne in the morning. My deposition was scheduled for the afternoon—if we got to it before Montoya College made a settlement offer. I suspected they were waiting to see how Wayne did in the deposition before they decided how to proceed and what the settlement offer would be. His testimony did not last long. I estimated it lasted less than ninety minutes. To my chagrin and my attorney's amazement, he denied everything, including the parts of the recorded voice mail message of his own voice.

The dialogue between my attorney and Wayne Hicks went something like this:

"Mr. Hicks, do you remember meeting Mr. Samir at the Santa Fe Marriott Hotel around 7:00 PM?"

"Yes, if you could call it that," Wayne responded.

"What was the nature of your conversation?" Ed asked.

"There wasn't much of a conversation," responded Wayne.

"Please describe what happened and what you said to him," requested Ed.

"Well, I was sitting at the bar having something to eat when this person whom I did not recognize rudely interrupted me and asked me why he wasn't hired for the diversity position at Montoya College," he responded.

"What did you say in response to his question?" Ed asked.

"Well, I told him the truth. I told him he wasn't qualified for the job and asked him to leave me alone so that I could eat my meal," he responded.

"Did you remember Mr. Samir from the interviews?" asked Ed.

"No," he responded.

"Do you mean to tell me that you did not recognize him, but he recognized you after meeting you for one hour during an interview almost a year ago?" asked Ed in amazement.

"Yes. He recognized and approached me. I did not even want to talk to him, but he interrupted me. He was very persistent and rude with the way he asked the questions," he responded again.

"Did you say anything to Mr. Dyfan about Dr. Attar's decision to hire someone black for the job?" asked Ed.

"No. I did not," he responded.

"Then Mr. Hicks, what were you so concerned about in the voice mail message a few days after you and he met and talked in New Mexico if you did not discuss anything sensitive about the search with Mr. Samir? That's really puzzling to me. You even said, 'I am a little bit concerned…we've had a conversation about what transpired on campus, and I didn't realized you were still in suit with Montoya College. That really puts me in an awkward situation.' Why were you concerned if you said nothing sensitive? Why were you concerned that Mr. Samir was still in suit if you said nothing sensitive that would put you in 'an awkward situation' to use your own words?" Ed asked him.

"Well, I wouldn't believe everything I hear on that doctored tape. It has clearly been doctored. I did not say any of those things you are now quoting. I want that tape examined. It has been doctored. It's getting very hot in here. Can we take a break for a few minutes?"

At this point, he appeared very confused, nervous, and stammering as well as sweating profusely. It was obvious he was lying and did not want to continue with the deposition.

"Before we take a short break, I would like to remind you that your testimony is under oath and subject to perjury if you lie," Ed reminded him.

"Okay, let's take a break. Ed, let's talk please, if you don't mind," asked Val Golden, Montoya College's attorney.

During the break, my attorney asked to speak with me in private. He informed me that Wayne would not be testifying anymore because he was perceived as being determined to deny everything to protect himself, but he said it was obvious he was lying through his teeth. He also informed me we were going to break for lunch and I would be next in the hot seat after lunch. In addition, Val Golden was attempting, as we talked, to get Montoya to settle out of court. But he also wanted to let me know that he did not think we had a strong case without Wayne's candid admission of what he knew and said to me in New Mexico. He said that it was not worth trying to get Wayne charged with perjury for lying under oath. I agreed not to pursue any charges against him As angry as I was, I felt sorry for him and felt the experience was punishment enough for him.

After lunch, we started with my deposition while we waited from Montoya College's president to call back after consulting with the board chairman about a settlement offer. The focus of my deposition was on the reasons for my termination at ESU. My responses, according to my attorney, should have been short and not as long-winded as they were. His efforts to get me to give short, concise answers were not successful because I felt the need to give complete answers to the questions for the record. He was frustrated with me, and I knew it, but there was no stopping. I felt I had nothing to hide and answered the questions fully. I felt compelled to give detailed answers instead of short "no" or "yes" answers as he had advised. In frustration, he asked for a break to speak with me about my responses. He looked disappointed during his admonition of me to stick to the plan of not giving them more information than they needed. He felt I was giving impulsive answers and suggested I slow down my responses and reflect before I answered the questions. I tried to do just that when I returned to the deposition. But, about an hour into my deposition, Montoya's attorney asked for another break. That's when he made a settlement offer with a proviso of a commitment in writing that I would never use the actual name of the college in conversations and in writing and I would not write or talk about the events that related to the case for eighteen months after the date of the signed agreement. I agreed to the terms of the offer. A few weeks later, I signed the agreement. Case closed.

10

What Goes Around Comes Around

In July 1997, after Daniel Marks was appointed interim provost and vice president for academic affairs, I began to search the *Chronicle of Higher Education* for a new job. The writing was on the wall that my days were numbered. I became more convinced of this when the new provost began to act uncharacteristically friendly toward me during provost's staff meetings. He made extra efforts to mention my name and "the excellent job the diversity office was doing" during every meetings, no matter how far-fetched the references of my office was to the subject of discussion. He always sounded superficial and pretentious in his pronouncements and praises of my work and the diversity office. It was uncharacteristic because, before his appointment to the position of interim provost, he had made it known to several individuals that he did not like me and strongly disapproved of my philosophy of diversity.

His attitude towards me became clear in his 1995 letter to the vice provost regarding alleged "failures" in the diversity office. Since that letter and the follow-up meeting with the vice provost, he had made it clear that he and his associate dean were hostile toward me. Indeed, during the meeting, he described the job I had done as the university's "chief diversity officer" as a "total failure" and demanded the provost's office appoint a committee to investigate the failures of the diversity office. So, you can understand when I say that all of my alarm bells went off when he began heaping praises on the work of the diversity office the moment he became interim provost.

To be honest, I had begun looking for another job the moment the new president announced Daniel Marks' appointment in March. I knew my days were numbered, but I wasn't certain whether he would find a way to fire me while he was in the interim position or would wait until he was permanently appointed to the position. Previous provosts had been reluctant to make major decisions about terminations while they were in interim positions. I decided that, to be safe, I would start looking for another job while things took their course. I knew it was only a matter of time. Indeed, as I suspected, he couldn't wait. Less than six months after he assumed the interim provost position, he fired me under the pretext of budget cuts. I decided I would continue to do my job to the best of my ability and as honestly and fairly as possible and not try to appease him and the SBA by doing their biddings.

Indeed, it had occurred to me, as I looked back at my involvement with the problems in the MEP, that the assignment to mediate the conflict was a setup to test my loyalty and determine if I was willing to play ball with them under new conditions. I suspect that, if I been willing to go along with their agenda to fire Armando Segundo from his position as associate dean of the School of Engineering, I would not have been fired. Had I only regretted my refusal to attend SBA meetings and rejection of the SBA agenda and shown contrition by supporting their efforts to remove Armando Segundo, I would have remained in my job. But I could not. Instead, I continued to take the principled position on issues with which I was involved. I could not do otherwise. It was not in me to go along with their agenda of harming and ruining others.

In the end, I received an e-mail from Alfred Pratt informing me of an important meeting with him and the provost scheduled for January 12, 1998. The meeting was short and to the point. As I walked into the office, I felt a powerful surge of energy rushing through my body. I literally shook in nervous anticipation of what was to come. I knew this was it. They were going to fire me. I was very nervous and shaking. When I reached the chair they had pulled out for me, indicating where they wanted me to sit, I began to breathe deeply in order to calm down the nervous shaking. As I calmed down, I felt a sense of sadness that they were about to do to me what they had done to so many others, and they were about to get away with it again. As I sat down, they could see I was shaking with fear.

Daniel said, "This is not going to take long. Samir, there is no need for you to be nervous. Please relax. We have a few issues we would like to discuss with you. You know we are in a budget crunch and some tough decisions will have to be made. I believe you make too much money for the job you do at this university, and I have made a decision to eliminate your position and combine the office with the affirmative action office. I fully intend to make it a director-level position with a very reduced salary. You are free to apply for the new position if the salary is suitable to you, but there is no guarantee you will get the new job. I intend to cut the salary by fifty percent because I believe that is the appropriate salary for the job."

"What does that mean?" I asked.

"Well, it means you will be out of a job in exactly six months from today. So you better start looking for another job," he responded.

"You know that you have a six month nonrenewal period in your contract, and we are not obligated to give you any reasons. But we are being fair with you by telling you the reason for the nonrenewal," added Alfred.

"I am not convinced you are being honest with me about your real motives. I believe the decision to fire me is politically motivated and has to do with the fact that I have refused to go along with the political agenda of the SBA over the years. More recently, I know you have not been happy with my decision to withdraw from the MEP problem because I could not go along with your attempts to fire Armando Segundo," I responded.

"Honestly, it has nothing to do with that. You have done an excellent, excellent, excellent job, and I am willing to give you an excellent, excellent, excellent reference letter for your job search. I will even put it in your personnel folder," Daniel offered.

"No, thanks. I don't need a reference from you or Alfred. I don't ask for references from unprincipled people," I responded.

"Let me give you a piece of advice. You are better off looking at black colleges for a job. Believe me, they are desperately looking for good and experienced administrators like you. Try it. I am willing to serve as a reference, and, as I said, I will give you an excellent, excellent, excellent reference," he repeated the offer as if he did not hear my initial response.

"I don't need it," I said in disgust as walked out of the room.

"You will receive a formal letter of nonrenewal by registered mail in the next few days," said Alfred as I left the room.

A few hours after the meeting with Alfred and Daniel, I went to schedule a meeting with the new president of the university, but my attempt was rebuffed by her secretary because she said the president did not get involved in personnel matters. She referred me back to the provost's office. In frustration, I went again to talk with Judy Krup about my intent to take legal action if the decision was not reversed. She listened to me intently and advised me to talk with Lisa Crist.

She said, "I am about to leave my current position for the regional campus and cannot get involved in personnel matters any longer. But I am confident Lisa would be interested in what you have to say."

"Well Judy, I understand you will soon have a new assignment, but you are a witness to everything that has happened over the past six years. All of my efforts to get the administration to address these issues have gone nowhere because of political reasons. You, Anthony Day, and Lisa have been reluctant to get involved even though these issues were within your respective areas of responsibility. To be honest, I have very little confidence she will do anything," I responded.

"I will try to call her myself and talk with her about your concerns," she promised.

All of this was happening at a time when the local and national media was focused on the engineered racial scandals involving the university. The president had appointed a black provost and black athletic director as a political move to show her administration's commitment to diversity. Therefore, I could not understand why the administration was indifferent to what I perceived as another potential scandal involving the SBA. Didn't they realize that, if I went public with the political activities of the SBA and the BFSA, all hell would break loose in the campus and in the state? Maybe the new president and the executive vice president did not realize the potentially explosive nature of this story if it were to go public.

Since it was clear to me the university administration was not interested in what I had to say, I decided my next move was to inform Armando Segundo about the SBA conspiracy to fire him from his position because of prejudice. I also wanted to share with him all of the evidence he might need to protect himself. I assured him I was willing to serve as a witness in the event they moved against him. I advised him to seek legal advice as to how he may best protect himself against the SBA.

A few weeks after my last conversation with the university administration, Lisa Crist contacted me to discuss her findings. She told me she had discussed my concerns and allegations with the president and wanted to speak with me in person.

When I arrived in her office, she said, "Samir, I am sorry to say it doesn't look very good. I spoke with the president about your concerns and suggestions, but she decided not to intervene after she spoke with Daniel Marks. In fact, I was present when she spoke with the provost. She told him I had made some allegations against him and other members of the SBA. She asked him if his decision not to renew your appointment was influenced in any way by your refusal to attend SBA meetings or the problems in the MEP. He was adamant that those issues had nothing to do with his decision. He assured the president that his decision was made on the merits of the vice provost's recommendations that the affirmative action office and diversity offices be consolidated into one. The president appeared satisfied with his explanation and decided not to get involved any further in the matter."

"Well, I am disappointed to say the least. I would recommend the president or a trusted adviser, such as Frank Hazan, the executive vice president, do a limited investigation to determine if there is any evidence to corroborate the allegations. He may check with the staff who were present during the provost's staff meeting when Daniel spoke openly about firing Armando Segundo and with Anthony Day about SBA efforts to get him fired. He may also want to look into their discussions during their last meeting at Italiano's restaurant when Alfred spoke openly about getting with Daniel to 'deal with' me because I refused to go along with their political agenda," I recommended.

"Samir, let me be frank with you. She is not going to agree to do anything else unless you provide incontrovertible evidence the provost or vice provost has violated the law. Take my advice. You are one person going against several senior black administrators during a time when the university is under scrutiny by the press because of allegations of racial discrimination against blacks. She is not going to move against them. It will be suicidal. If I were you, I'd just find another job and leave quietly. Believe me, you will be happier elsewhere. In fact, that is what I have experienced every time someone in your situation has left the university. They have been happier with their new jobs. Even if we could find something else for you on campus, I don't think you will be happy working here after this experience. You will always be resentful and angry about the way you've been treated. Believe me. I don't know what else to tell you."

Sensing I was getting nowhere with her, I said, "Unfortunately, I will have to file a complaint with the EEO office and take additional actions to get this matter addressed. I may even go to the press with this story because I believe this story is even more important than the allegations of discrimination in the athletic department. There are many credible witnesses, including those I have been talking with about the activities of the SBA for many years."

"Well, that is your choice. But I don't think it will lead anywhere," she advised.

"Thanks for your efforts," I said as I left her office.

I went immediately to the affirmative action office to file an official complaint. The staff that normally took the initial complaints explained to me that she wasn't certain they could take my complaint.

In a voice filled with anxiety, she said, "The affirmative action office was recently reassigned to report to the provost. If am right, that would pose a serious conflict of interest for us if we were to undertake any discrimination complaints against the provost himself. I need to check with Lisa Crist for advice on how to proceed before I do anything and get into trouble. I will contact you as soon I know something."

"I really hope the consultation doesn't take long. I need to proceed with the complaint before the statute of limitation expires," I added.

A few days later, I received a telephone call from the affirmative action office informing me that my complaint had been referred to the federal EEOC office downtown for investigation. She also informed me that, because of my position in the university and the seriousness of my allegations, she had recommended the university retain an outside investigator on behalf of the general counsel's office to determine if there is prima fascia evidence to support the allegations. But, to her disappointment, she said the president rejected her recommendations.

A week after that, I received a telephone call from the EEOC office staff inviting me for a preliminary interview. I arrived early in the morning and spoke for an hour with a Cuban woman who described herself as the intake clerk.

"What is your full name?" she asked as we sat down in the interview room.

"Samir Dyfan," I responded.

"Is that your real name? Are you Spanish? What does your name mean? Are you Spanish?" she asked again.

"No, I am not," I responded.

"Well, what are you? I mean what is your race or ethnicity?" she asked again.

"I don't have one," I responded.

"What? Look, everyone has a race and ethnicity. So tell me, and quit kidding around. We only have one hour to finish this interview," she added

"I am not kidding. I don't have any racial or ethnic identity," I added.

"Look, mister, stop kidding. I have been working in this office for twenty years, and I have never met anyone who doesn't have one, except for mixed race individuals. But even they would usually choose black, Hispanic, or one of the other groups. Seldom do they choose 'other' or say they have don't have any identity," she advised.

After a few minutes, she entered the word "other" in the space provided on the form for race or ethnic identity.

"That's not my identity either. I have told you that I sincerely don't identify with any group. I am not 'other' either," I explained.

"Look mister, I have to put something down, and that is it. The form will not be complete if I don't put something down for that question," she said in a tone of voice that suggested she was getting frustrated with my response.

I decided to let her continue with the interview without questioning her choice of designation for my identity. After I was through explaining the charges against the provost and the SBA, she informed me the charge would be "Race and Color Discrimination for Title V11 Protective Activities." By then, we had run out of time. She informed me that, after they received ESU's responses to the charges, the director of the EEOC office would review the case and make a decision about whether or not to investigate the charges.

She said, "It doesn't look good. We already have several cases we are investigating from that university. We can't spend all of our time devoted to one organization. This office is not the EEOC for ESU. It is for everybody. We have other cases to investigate. That school is going to hell in a handbasket. You know what I mean? Why do you guys have so many problems in that place? God, that place is in the newspaper everyday. Now you show up with an unusual name and no race or ethnicity. This one beats me though. I know the director is going to have a good laugh with this one. Good luck!" She then left the room.

A few weeks after the initial interview, I received a letter from the local EEOC informing me that, because of the complexity of my allegation and the limited resources of the EEOC to investigate my charges, they had granted me permission to file a lawsuit in federal courts within ninety days of the date on the letter. The EEOC letter also noted that my allegations of race and skin color discrimination were not valid because my racial designation of "other" was not a protected category under federal law. This sounded like they were saying that anyone who did not choose one of the racial or ethnic EEOC categories was fair game for discrimination in America. I could not believe this statement was true. My understanding was that no one could be subjected to discrimination because of reasons related to, among other things, race or ethnicity. This, to me, means discrimination against anyone, even those who have no racial or ethnic identity, was technically racial discrimination because the decision is based on reasons related to race. Astonished with the shabby way the EEOC had treated my case, I decided to telephone the EEOC to inquire about the rationale of non-protection. My inquiry was forwarded to the very intake clerk that I saw earlier during my first visit.

"Mr. Dyfan, this is Blanco. I have your folder here with me. You have been given ninety days to file suit in federal courts. We had recommended mediation to ESU, but they rejected it because they rightfully claimed your racial category of 'other' is a non-protected category and is really not within our jurisdiction. So, you see, they feel they have nothing to mediate. With regards to the Title V11 Protected Activity charge, we could not find any evidence of that to warrant further investigation. That is why we feel your best option is to take your case to federal courts. Let them sort it out for you. We feel the courts are the best places for complex cases such as yours," she said.

"I did not choose 'other' as representing my racial or ethnic classification. You did. I told you several times that I did not have any racial or ethnic identity to classify. You decided in your wisdom to classify me as 'other' because you claimed that, unless there was a classification in the intake form, the process would not be complete, and, therefore, my case could not be processed. I feel that was a setup for an easy dismissal of my case as you have done," I explained.

"Mr. Dyfan, I don't have a lot of time to go over this again with you. We have given you the right to sue. Go and find a good lawyer to fight your case in the courts. You seem to be a nice guy. Believe me, you have a good precedent-setting case. But we can't get involved in your case. It is too complicated for our resources. Please take it to court. You will see. Now I've got to go. Good luck!" she said as she hung up the telephone.

I was pissed. I just found out that not having a racial or ethnic identity or classification, which is what "other" means, left one unprotected from racial and ethnic discrimination. I could not believe this was the intent of the law. Even atheists and agnostics are protected from religious discrimination. Why wouldn't the law protect racial and ethnic "others"? Weren't we deserving of protection from discrimination by members of the groups that have a name? Weren't we a true minority? The government reported that twenty-three million Americans of mixed racial and ethnic descent classified themselves as "other." This is quite a lot of people without federal protection from racial or ethnic discrimination. I wondered how many of them knew they had no legal recourse against this sort of treatment. I decided to seek legal counsel and explored my options by consulting an attorney. The first item on my agenda was to find an experienced labor attorney.

My inquiry led me to a good friend who had taken it upon himself to talk with an old acquaintance who was a semiretired labor attorney about my case. He had recently gone into semiretirement from his job as a trial attorney to head a local bank he had started a few years earlier. He expressed interest in my case because of the uniqueness of my situation and the vagueness of the law as it relates to protection of individuals classified as "other." While he had tried dozens of cases involving individuals who were traditionally classified, he had never encountered one with the challenges of mine. It had the potential to break new legal ground. My concerned friend gave me his number and asked me to call him in one week after he retuned from vacation.

A week later, I called for an appointment with him. He asked me to visit his office the next day and expressed excitement about my case. He listened to my story with studious attention trying to discern the key issues, periodically asking for clarifications as he took notes. When I was through, he sighed.

He said, "Splendid. This is a fascinating and complex case that requires a law school professor who is familiar with the complexity of American demographics and the politics of diversity in higher education. I can't take this case because I won't be able to dedicate the time it would require. I am going to refer you to a very close friend and colleague of mine who is a labor attorney that specializes in discrimination cases. I have already talked with him about your case, and he is expecting your call. His name is Peter Harvey. Call him as soon as you can because you don't have a lot of time. Good luck, Samir. I heard a lot of good things about you and your efforts to protect people at the university. That takes a lot of heart and self-sacrifice for your principles. It's not everyday that you run into someone like you, and I am going to do everything I can to help you. I am sure Peter will help you even if you don't have any money."

I called Peter Harvey's office the next day and scheduled a meeting to discuss the referral. He and his partner met with me that very afternoon for an hour to discuss the details of my case. After the conclusion of my presentation of the facts related to my case, they informed me they needed time to think about the facts and best approach given that my case was complex with many issues. He indicated there were many issues that appeared to be violations of employment laws, and they needed me to write down a brief account of only the critical issues I would like to focus on involving my immediate supervisors. They advised me to avoid most of the other issues that are not directly related to the immediate issue of my termination. He took a copy of the EEOC letter of permission to sue and asked me to bring it along when I talk with him again and any relevant documents I may have that relate to any of the charges or events in my written account. He also asked me for permission to speak about my case with Berthan Allred, the attorney for the athletes that were suing ESU for racial discrimination. I told him I was fine with it, but I wanted him to know I believed the allegations of racial discrimination in the football team were unsubstantiated and orchestrated for political leverage by the SBA. He said he had surmised that much from my presentation.

A few days after the meeting with Peter Harvey, I received a telephone call from someone identifying himself as Jim Kuti, president of the League of Black Government Administrators or LBGA.

"Is this Mr. Dyfan?" he asked.

"This is Samir Dyfan. What may I do for you?" I asked.

"Well, this is Jim Kuti of LBGA. You may not remember me, but I have attended many of your seminars on emotional intelligence over the past few years. And, boy, did I enjoy them. You are really an energetic and mesmerizing speaker. I have learned a lot from you and am very grateful for that," he added.

"I am glad you have found the information useful," I said, sensing he was up to something other than just to express his gratitude.

"Mr. Dyfan, I am calling because I have heard what has happened to you at ESU. I am not sure whether you are aware that LBGA or, shall I say, I am the one responsible for referring the ESU athletes' case to the attorney, Berthan Allred, who is now representing those poor football students in their discrimination suit against ESU," he pointed out to me.

"No, I am not aware. How did you get involved in this matter?" I asked.

"Well, a black administrator high up in the administration contacted me about the problems in the football team and asked for our help. He also indicated that racial discrimination was endemic and widespread in the university and that no one was addressing any of these problems because the administration was involved in a massive cover-up. We then contacted Berthan Allred and asked him to represent not only the students but any black person in the university who wants to join a class action suit against ESU," he said proudly.

"I am not sure that I qualify given that this is a case for blacks. Besides, I have grave reservations about the claims of massive and endemic racial discrimination against blacks at ESU. Having said that, I don't see how I can be of help to their case," I explained.

"Well, we believe you can help us, and we want to offer you free representation in your case against ESU if you will agree to cooperate with us in our case. You won't have to pay a penny because Berthan Allred will represent you completely free in your lawsuit. All I am asking is for you to meet with our attorney to explore how we can work together. You will find it in your best interest. Please, just a meeting without any preconditions. Let's meet and talk, and we can decide how to proceed," he appealed.

"Well, I am not sure. I will have to talk with my attorney to see what he recommends, and I will get back in touch with you tomorrow. But, before you hang up, I would like to know who in the administration contacted you. Are you willing to tell me?" I asked.

"No, I can't, but you will be surprised if I told you. Let's say this. It is someone you would consider most unlikely," he responded.

"What about the person who recommended that you contact me?" I asked.

"I can't tell you that either because the person asked that we keep his or her name confidential. But he or she believed you have information that is critical to our case. Let's leave it at that for now. Maybe I can tell you sometime in the future," he added.

"Are they two different individuals or the same person?" I asked.

"Different persons. The person who originally contacted us is no longer in the picture because he is in a delicate position and has asked us not to even try to contact him again. And we don't have any reasons to contact him again. I've got to go. I am driving in heavy traffic and running out of power in my cell phone. Talk to you later," he said as his voice faded.

I immediately called my attorney to tell him about the call from Jim Kuti and his advice about meeting with Berthan Allred. He informed me that he had not had time to discuss my case with Berthan, but he saw no harm in a meeting.

"I know Berthan very well and have worked with him in the past. Let me set up the meeting with him. I would like to be present when you meet with him. I will call you back with the date and time as soon as we can meet," he said.

He called back a few minutes later to inform me they could meet the next day if that was fine with my schedule. I was available and, as he had requested, went to his office a few minutes before the meeting. To my surprise, my attorney's office was located in the same building just a few floors below Berthan's office. We left my attorney's office immediately for Berthan's and were ushered into the conference room where we waited for his arrival. He arrived soon after with a cup of black coffee in his hand. He looked haggard, unshaved, and unkempt. He revealed coffee-stained teeth as he smiled. His suit looked as if he had slept in it for the past few weeks. His hair was uncombed and all over his face.

"Thanks for coming. I am delighted that we are going to have the opportunity to work together. I am Berthan. It is nice to meet you. I have heard so much about you and am so delighted to finally meet you, Mr. Dyfan. It is indeed a privilege and a pleasure," he said as he entered the room and sat down beside my attorney on the opposite side of the conference table.

"Berthan." said my attorney. "Samir and I are here today to have initial discussions with you about a telephone offer he received from Jim Kuti regarding your discrimination case against ESU. Do you know anything about this offer to represent him free of charge if he cooperated with you in your other case against ESU?" he asked.

"Oh, yes. I am willing to do that if we can find common ground. Certainly, but it is up to Mr. Dyfan. I am told he has information that can help us in our case. If he is willing to help us, we will work with him. And, if there is a fit, we don't mind adding him to our class action case," he added.

"I have agreed to assist Mr. Dyfan in his case, but I won't object if he is willing to work with you, but that is his decision. We have not signed any agreement as yet, so I am open. But a decision will have to be made soon because we are fast running out of time to prepare an effective case against ESU," said Peter.

"Well, I need to think about it. I suppose it all depends on what you are looking for from me. I am not sure I have any information that will help your case in any way. But we will see. I will call you tomorrow to discuss my decision with you. Thank you," I replied.

"Sure. Please, let's talk. Call me if you have any questions," Berthan said as we left the conference room.

Back in my attorney's office, he advised me to meet with Berthan, find out what he had to say, and go from there with my decision. It sounded reasonable. The more I thought about it, the more curious I became about his interest in me. I could not imagine how I could be helpful in any way to his case given the nature of my experiences with the SBA, the BFSA, and the PACB. I decided to meet with him to find out what he was after. He agreed to meet the next day in his office. My attorney wasn't present for that meeting, but he had another attorney present during the meeting. His physical appearance did not improve one bit. He still appeared haggard, wearing the same rumpled shirt and dandruff-covered navy blue suit.

"I am delighted you agreed to meet again. I believe you will find out you have made the right decision," he said as he walked into the meeting room. A black female attorney followed.

"Please, let me introduce Tammy Allen, a colleague who has been helping me with the ESU case. She will be the one working with you in your case, if we agree to work together. You will need a black attorney to pursue your case for strategic reasons, and she is very experienced with racial discrimination cases like yours," he assured.

"Well, let's get to business. I understand Peter will not be meeting with us today. Is that correct?" he asked.

"Yes," I replied.

"Good. I hope that is okay with you? If not, please let me know because he is just downstairs. I can call him," he added.

"I am fine with it," I said.

"Great. Now, Mr. Dyfan, may I call you Samir?" he asked.

"Yes, that is fine." I replied.

"Please tell us everything you know about the case involving the ESU football team," he requested.

"From what I know and have heard so far, there is no hard evidence to support the charge of racial discrimination. My experience with the student that was dismissed from the football team was not a pleasant one. He appeared to have an attitude problem and had been rude and disrespectful to me in the presence of other students. I've talked to several people involved in the initial investigation, and they could not find any evidence of racial discrimination. I feel the same way about the charges of segregating the players in hotel accommodations during away games. The coach consulted with me several years ago about his attempts to force team members to room with someone different, but the black players were against the idea. We discussed several strategies for integrating hotel rooming of the players during away games. So the accusation the coach forced them into segregated rooms is not valid as far as I am concerned," I explained.

"I disagree with you on that. We have a lot of solid evidence to prove our case, including staff in that department who came forward to support the allegations. But that is not what I am after today. What I need from you, Samir, is anything you may have in your files—e-mail, letters, notes from meetings, recordings, or witnesses that will corroborate what we already have. Do you remember anything that will help our case?" he asked.

"No, I don't have anything that can be of help to your case. I am sorry. I have checked my files in preparation for my case, and I don't remember seeing anything relevant to your case. The only thing I found that I don't think will help your case are the evaluations of the workshop I conducted for the football team. There is nothing that I believe will help. I have already turned them over to the EEO office," I responded.

"What about anything Anthony Day has? He is critical to this case. I've heard he is a nice guy and a close friend of yours. Can you get anything that he may have that can help our case? We are aware that, even though he is incompetent, it is not his fault. He is just not smart enough to realize the white administration is manipulating him to turn his face away from all the discrimination that is taking place in that university. He is doing their dirty work of covering up for them. And let me ask you this. What did he do to protect you? Nothing. You see what I mean? This is the guy that is supposed to be protecting blacks from racism, but he fails miserably because he is in league with the racist white administration while his people suffers. Talk to him as a friend, and see if he is willing to help us. We will go light on him if he helps us quietly. Just get him to tell us what he knows or where to look or give us anything he has that can help us," he pleaded.

"I am sorry, but I am not willing to do that. You may want to find someone else to do that," I responded to his appeal.

"You don't have any choice, Samir, but to help us. If not, you will find the cost of litigation so expensive that you will not be able to take legal action. We are offering you a great deal. Let's face it. While you may think you don't have any axe to grind with the white administration, they are really the ones running the show. You made a serious error in judgment when you filed your EEOC complaint against the black provost and vice provost. They are just Uncle Toms doing the bidding of the white administration. You should have gone after the head of the beast, not to the asshole where the crap comes out. Those guys were only doing the biddings of the whites at the top of the fucking administration. You should know that. When have you ever seen blacks with real power in America? Whites will never give real power to blacks. They always find a cover for their dirty work. If anything, the SBA is in cahoots with the SWA, the senior white administrators. I am only sorry that I didn't go after Debbie Franklin, the real culprit here. She was in charge when all of this racism was happening at ESU and did nothing about it because she had her cronies guarding the EEO office to ensure that everything was swept under the rug," he pontificated.

"You are right about one thing, Berthan. The SBA was in cahoots with the SWA, particularly during the Franklin administration. She was the enabler of SBA activities and, in many ways, welcomed it. I have always felt she encouraged it because she still harbored political ambitions beyond ESU. And she was laying the groundwork for black political support in the event she decided to run for political office again in the future. Everything I tried to do to stop the SBA from harming others or promoting their political agenda failed because she refused to do anything about it, even when there was ample evidence of illegal activities. So, in a sense, you are right that white complicity in the university administration was partly responsible. But I believe the SBA members were independent actors with only self-interest as their only motive," I responded.

"Why do you think they, the senior SBA members, have refused to lend their support to our efforts to have the administration address these legitimate grievances? We are not asking them to do anything extra except to forcefully condemn the racism in the athletic department, but they won't because they don't want to offend master," he added.

"Now, I don't believe for one minute their refusal has anything to do with being Uncle Toms as you are suggesting. I believe it's the opposite. The white administrators are afraid of the SBA because of their coercive power. They are afraid to do anything about illegal SBA behaviors because they are afraid of being labeled racists. Which is the modus operandi of this group. These guys are not Uncle Toms at all. They are aggressive in the pursuit of their agenda," I added.

"Let's talk about you for a minute. Why do you think of yourself as 'other' or telling people you don't have a race or ethnic identity? People are just laughing at you every time you say that. Let me tell you this, if you don't already know it. In America, you're black if you have one drop of Negro blood running in your veins. Quit telling people you are not black because you are. They think you are either an Uncle Tom or are in denial about your racial heritage. Blacks are familiar with people like you who are in denial, that is, are trying to pass as white. That's how they see you. Accept your racial heritage, and be proud of it. In America, there is no such thing as being race-less or ethnicity-less. It is all bullshit to me. You are black whether you like it or not," he explained.

"What does all of that, what you just said, have to do with your case? I see no connection. I don't have any interest in debating your idiotic opinions with you," I said contemptuously.

"Well, I think it was foolish of you to have identified yourself in your EEOC complaint as 'other.' You should have identified yourself as black and made the charge against the whites that really run the university. You would have had a better chance with your case. That's all I am trying to say," he explained.

"Well, that's the reality of the case whether you like it or not. I filed the complaint against individuals I believed were involved in illegal activities in violation of Title V11, and they were the provost and vice provost, both SBA members. In fact, one of the associate vice presidents and SBA members recently had a hostile workplace complaint filed against him by a white secretary for yelling and cursing at her," I explained.

"How is cursing and yelling at your secretary or staff a violation of the law? I do it all the time with all of my staff if they don't get the fucking job I am paying them to do completed as I expect. If that is a violation of any law, then I am also guilty," he said.

"Samir is right, Berthan. It is a violation of OSHA laws because that kind of behavior creates stress and can lead to accident and injuries in the workplace," added Tammy Allen.

"Let's get back to our case against the football team. Are you going to help us or not? Why don't you think about it and let us know tomorrow?" he suggested.

"Sure, I will be back in touch with you after I consult with my attorney," I promised.

I left his office disappointed with his attitude and unprofessional behavior. As I entered the elevator, I decided to stop by my attorney's office before I left the building. He was in and agreed to speak with me even though I didn't have an appointment. After I was through telling him about my experience talking with Berthan, he informed me he was hoping I would agree to work with Berthan because he was my best opportunity to get legal representation for my case against ESU. In addition, he informed me he was not willing to take my case on a contingency basis because he didn't think he would have adequate time to do justice to the case. He explained that the case was very complex and would be difficult to win. He wished me luck and said they had handled a few discrimination cases in the past several years against ESU and knew how difficult it was litigating cases against the state universities because they have unlimited taxpayer money to spend and can make cases very expensive to litigate by tying things up in knots. I thanked him for his efforts and left.

At this point, I estimated that I had spent almost half of the ninety days the EEOC gave me to sue. I realized I didn't have much time left. Finally, I began to search for an attorney that was willing to take my case on a contingency fee basis. A few weeks later, I found a local attorney willing to take the case. As I prepared for my meeting, I received a telephone call from Berthan Allred.

"Hello, may I help you?" I asked.

"Yes, Samir, this is Berthan. Do you remember me? I am sure you do. I am calling to ask if you have given some thought to my offer. Let me take a moment and explain specifically what I need from you. I would like you to serve as an adverse witness against ESU. I think this is important because, as the vice president for diversity, you were on the inside and knew what was going on. You have a lot of information and credibility. I know that is your strength. Everyone I have spoken with has told me that people have a lot of respect for you because of your integrity," he explained.

"What do you mean by adverse witness? And what do you want me to do?" I asked curiously.

"Well, let me explain. First, I want you to give a sworn statement in the form of responses to several questions I will ask. In the event that we go to trial, you will then serve as a witness during the trial. But first, I want you to give sworn testimony to a few questions. Let me tell you what I am getting at. I might ask you a few questions. For example,

I ASK: Mr. Dyfan, are you currently vice president for diversity at ESU? And how long have you been in that position?

YOU SAY: Yes, I have been vice president for eight years.

I SAY: During those years, have you seen cases of racial discrimination at ESU?

YOU SAY: Yes.

I ASK: Is it true you tried but failed to get the administration to deal with these incidents of racial discrimination?

YOU SAY: Yes.

I ASK: Is it true you went on several occasions to the provost, vice president for personnel, general counsel, vice president for EEO, and even the president of the university to get them to stop racial discrimination and the use of racial epithets against blacks, but they refused to do the right thing?

YOU SAY: Yes.

I ASK: Is it true you were present on several occasions when senior administrators used racial epithets against blacks? Is it also true that senior administrators at the university frequently use racial epithets? By that, I mean they frequently referred to black faculty and staff as goddamned niggers?

YOU SAY: Yes.

"I don't want you to say anything else. Just answer the question with a 'yes' or 'no' with no explanations. I don't want you to say anything else. Do you think that is something you can do?" he asked.

"Let's suppose I agreed to do what you are asking. Do you think this approach will work during a formal deposition or during the trial? What do you think the defendant's attorneys will do? Will they permit you to ask leading questions? Or do you think they will just let me give partial answers to your questions because they would already know it was the senior black administrators exclusively who used racial epithets and the ones that were involved in most of the cases of racial discrimination that you referenced in your questions. What do you intend to do about these concerns during the trial?" I asked curiously.

"We will cross that bridge when we get to it, if it gets that far. And, if it does, I doubt they will be willing to out the SBA and the allegations you are talking about knowing we will be following with another suit involving you soon after. They may just let your answers slide. Besides that, can you imaging what scandal they will get into if your allegations against the SBA get out into the press? I seriously doubt they would take the risk," he responded.

"I am not sure that I am willing to entangle my case with yours. It is obvious to me that, if the full story of my case comes out, it will undermine the veracity of yours. But, beyond that, I have this strong feeling that you don't intend to go to trial. You just want to use the skewed testimony to strengthen your case for a settlement. What's after that then? Let me be frank with you, I am not willing to do what you are asking," I responded.

"Well, just think about it, and let me know. If I don't hear again from you, I won't call back. Thank you for your time," he said as he hung up the telephone.

The next day, I went to talk with my new attorney and gave him all of the documents I had that related to my case. I was surprised that, during my search for related documents, I had found an old e-mail from Alfred Pratt in which he was demanding I pay (in cash) a $13 fine for missing a scheduled SBA meeting at the Big Trees Country Club. The fine was for confirming that I intended to attend, which, in his mind, was an non-cancelled reservation for which the SBA was billed. My attorney was amazed at the tone of the e-mail and the fact the vice provost was unconcerned about the legal propriety of what appeared to be a "fine" for missing a SBA meeting. My next task was to write a brief description of the critical issues and events related to my experiences with the SBA, the provost's office, and my firing.

After I completed the report for my attorney, I decided to write a statement documenting my allegations against the SBA and the failures of both administrations in light of ample evidence of illegal activities. My intent was to call a press conference in front of the Administration Building at the university, read a detailed list of allegations against the provost and other SBA members, and ask the governor for a thorough investigation and their removal from office. At the conclusion of the press conference, I would distribute the statement to the press and all of those present for maximum exposure.

I was on my way to Lisa Crist's office at the university when I inadvertently ran into Lucy Dalembert. I hadn't seen her since my notice of nonrenewal in January, and she was anxious to talk with me about my search for another job. She even encouraged me to use her as a reference because she had been my supervisor for a brief interim in the early 1990s after Maryann Cole was removed from office because of SBA activities described previously. She was also interested in knowing how I had been treated by the provost's office since my termination and hoped they could find something else for me within the university or in one of the regional campuses, as they had done so many times for others.

"If they can find something for Vernon, whose behavior created so many problems, then they should able to do something for you because I believe you have done an excellent job over the years since you came to ESU. Has the provost said anything about another appointment?" she asked.

"No, he said there is nothing else for me at the university and advised me to look for employment at black schools. He even said he would not consider me for the downgraded diversity position of director of diversity he intended to create after he abolishes my current position. It is clear to me that they don't want me around because they feel threatened by my presence in the provost's office.

"I can't believe they can't find something for you at least until you can find something else. They do it for others all the time," she added.

"I am in the process of filing a lawsuit in federal court this week, and I intend to call a press conference soon after the suit to publicize the case and the charges against the administration. I also intend to discuss the failures of the general counsel's office and the former vice president for personnel to act, even though they were both given actionable evidence on many occasions about SBA activities," I informed her.

"Well, you are right about failures because I knew you and Anthony Day had spoken with her on several occasions. And you know what? Judy Krup failed to do many things that she should have taken care of as vice president and close friend of President Franklin. Let me do something because I don't believe the president and the executive vice president, Frank Hazan, are even aware of your credibility or the value of your work on this campus. All they even know is what the provost has told them, which may be self-serving. I don't think they even realize the potential for a bigger scandal if you go public with these allegations. They are also not aware that you have been talking openly about the behavior of the SBA for several years. Let me talk with Frank. I will get back in touch with you," she promised.

"You should also know that I intend to publicize my experiences with the SBA and the complicity and failures of the Franklin and Judge administrations over the past several years, beginning with the Maryann Cole affair. I intend to tell everything I know," I informed her.

"Well, I will be back with you soon. When is your ninety days to sue up?" she asked.

"I still have a couple of weeks left. My attorney intends to file with the courts next week," I responded.

A few days later, I received a telephone call from the general counsel's office with a request to talk about my case. But, before I left for the university, I talked with Lucy about her discussions with Frank Hazan about my case. She informed me the president and executive vice president had talked, and there was an interest to work with me to resolve the problems to avoid an expensive litigation and even more costly bad publicity from another scandal involving the university's vice president for diversity. She asked me to work with the administration to resolve the matter without harming the reputation of the university. I promised to do the best I could to work with them.

I arrived for the meeting with Lisa Crist that very afternoon to discuss the renewed interest in the case. To my surprise, when I arrived, another attorney was present with Lisa for the meeting.

"Welcome, Samir. I hope you don't mind that I have asked one of my colleagues to join us this afternoon?" she said as I walked into the meeting room.

"No, I don't mind. In fact, I welcome it because I have worked with her and feel comfortable with her," I responded.

"Well, I have good news. I have been asked to do what I can to work out a resolution that is satisfying to you. Isn't that good?" she asked, smiling and looking pleased.

"Does that include removing the provost, vice provost, and other JDA members from their current positions in the university? Is she willing to start an investigation regarding their efforts to violate Armando Segundo's civil rights?" I asked sarcastically.

"Unfortunately not. But that's what we would like to discuss with you. Samir, we have known and worked with you over the years. We know you have done an excellent job trying to address what I must admit were very difficult problems. And both the president and the executive vice president understand that. You must understand the president is under tremendous pressures because of the football case and all of the other problems you have read about in the papers. She cannot do anything about your allegations right now. She has heard what you had to say, and I can guarantee you that they will carefully look into it in the future. But, right now, it is going to be difficult to go against six senior black administrators given the current climate. I hope you understand so that we can work together to resolve this matter to your satisfaction. Let me also say this. I know you will be happier elsewhere when you find another job. That is always the case with the people that have been in similar situations. Believe me. That has been my experience. What do you think?" she asked.

"I am not thinking. I am trying to listen to what you are saying. Can you help me understand why the past and present administrations failed to do anything about these issues even though there has always been ample evidence that something was wrong?" I asked.

"Well, as I have said in the past, I don't know. All we can do is to report it to the president. She decides how and when to proceed after that. I think you yourself hit the nail on the head. They are powerful and well-organized. As a result, it is not easy to go against them. Besides, you are only one person going against eleven or twelve people who deny the allegations. No one else has been willing to come forward to corroborate your allegations. Most of the time, you had no concrete evidence except things that were said and done in your presence. Now, the issue of Armando Segundo is different. There were others present. And, if they come forward, I guarantee you that we will look into it and take action without creating big problems. Just wait and see," she promised.

"Will you do something to keep them from firing Armando Segundo? You know that I have already told him of what the SBA are planning to do, and I have given him the names of all those who were present during the provost's staff meeting should he need witnesses in the future. I have also promised to serve as a witness if the need should arise. I want assurance that Armando is safe. Can you guarantee that?" I asked.

"Well, let me say this. I think they would know you have said something about it, and everyone is watching. I really don't think they will do anything," she assured me. "Now, with that said, let's get down to how we can help you. First, let me ask you about the status of your right to sue. How many days do you have left? And are you going to be working with Berthan Allred? We need to know the answer to these questions before we can proceed. Because if you are going to serve as a witness in his case, then we cannot continue because it might be potentially construed as witness tampering."

"I have decided not to do it because I cannot do what he is asking me to do. Besides, I don't believe any discrimination was involved in the case involving the football players. I also believe the coach's firing was unjust and illegal. I think he was sacrificed in the altar of expedient racial politics. On your other question, I believe I have approximately two weeks left," I responded.

"That's good. Well, here is what we have to work with. You will be given an extension of a couple months on the date of your termination. This means your contract will not expire until September 30. After that, you will have an additional six months in which to find another job. In the event that you find a job within thirty days of October 1, you will be given five months' pay as severance. If you find a job within 60 days, you will get four months' severance pay and so on. Do you get the idea?" she asked.

"Yes. Will this offer be put in writing?" I asked.

"Oh, yes. Everything will be put in a formal agreement. But that's not all. We intend to retain an executive search firm to help you find another job. We will pay the fee for six months. How does that sound? But it even gets better. We will also ask you not to use the name of the university or its employees in any future publications, including radio, television, or print interviews. We also ask that you not discuss the issues with anyone. We are willing to allow you to discuss the events in educational programs. Only then, we ask you not use the real names of the parties to these events. How do you feel about that?" she asked.

"Where will I be working? What will I be doing during the interim until I find another job? Have you thought about that yet?" I asked.

"Yes, you will be on this campus, if you want, until the end of September. And after that, we will, on paper, transfer you to one of the regional campuses. But let me say that you are not under any expectation to show up on campus. You may work from home. We are doing this to help you out Nobody will say anything to you if you never again show up on campus. Technically, you will be reporting to Lucy Dalembert, and your pay will come out of her department's budget. Now what do you think?" she asked.

"What does the provost's office think about this?" I asked

"They are not involved in this in any way. Frank took care of this directly with the president. Please don't say anything about this to any of them. In fact, the agreement calls for nondisclosure. This means you can't tell anyone about the agreement," she added. "Let me just add one thing, Samir. This is a great offer. We have never made this kind of offer before. I know how hard it is to accept the current situation because I have been in a similar situation before I came to ESU. A new boss took over the firm I had worked at for almost fifteen years. All of a sudden, I was given notice. I had not done anything wrong. In fact, I was one of the best lawyers, but he didn't like me. And there was nothing I could do about it except leave. If I had stayed and fought him, it would have destroyed my career. Now I have a better job, and it pays more than I was making. I don't think you have done anything wrong, but that's the way it is. You served at the pleasure of the provost."

"Well, I understand that, but there is a difference between the two situations. If there wasn't a history of illegal and unethical behaviors, I would have accepted the termination without any questions. That is why I refer to what happened to me as 'firing' instead of 'nonrenewal.' At any rate, I do appreciate your efforts to help resolve this matter. When will the agreement be ready?" I asked.

"It should not take long at all. Maybe in a few days. How is that?" she asked anxiously.

"Okay. Why don't you get it ready? I will read it and discuss it with my attorney. If the terms are as you have stated them, I will sign it and return it to you as soon as possible. Time is of the essence. I would prefer to conclude this before my right to sue expires," I informed her.

"I will contact you as soon as it is ready for your signature," she promised.

"Now, before I leave, let me say something. I trust the administration will follow through on your promise to protect Armando Segundo and to look into the allegations. I am hoping that, if corroborative evidence is found, appropriate actions will be taken to remove these guys from office before anyone else is hurt. I assure you I will ignore whatever agreement I have with the university and go public if anything happens to Armando during Daniel Marks' tenure as provost," I explained.

I left the meeting with a deep feeling that, even though I had not succeeded in beheading the SBA beast as I had hoped, I had alerted the new administration to the cabal's modus operandi sufficiently so that they would have a harder time forwarding their ambitious agenda of capturing the presidency of the university, which, as the ultimate prize, was now within the group's reach. I hoped that, by looking into the evidence of the most recent attempts to get Armando fired, the administration would discover the brazen nature of their illegal actions of targeting someone because of the person's ethnicity and national origin. I gave them a list of at least ten individuals who were present in the provost's staff meeting when SBA members openly discussed their efforts to fire Armando.

A few days later, I was notified that the agreement was ready for my signature. I picked up the agreement for my attorney's review and suggestions. He suggested the agreement clarify the agreement covered past events related only to SBA activities and not future events and other activities. This distinction was important because he did not want to prevent me from writing or discussing other events that happened in the past or the future, and this may include future SBA activities. They made the changes, and the agreement was signed. Now I hoped for the best.

I continued my search for another job as I lived out the rest of my contract with the university conducting workshops and doing research. At the end of September 1998, I was reassigned to one of the regional campuses an hour away from the main campus and my home. In order to keep the agreement "kosher," I was asked to go to work at least once a week for a few hours "so that we were not in violation of the state's pay for work policy." This meant that I had to drive to the regional campus one morning a week for a scheduled meeting so that there would be a record that I was at work. This was accomplished by scheduling a weekly meeting with the campus dean to discuss progress on my search for another job.

In early November 1999, I was offered a position of dean of the faculty in a proprietary school of allied health just a few minutes from my home. I accepted the position and began work in the school in early December. Ten months later,

I was offered another employment opportunity, bringing my academic career in higher education to a close. I was ready for the change, and I have never regretted it. My new position was ordained in heaven. I continue there to this day and have never been happier in a job. I have a large staff, sufficient budget to do my job, and the support of the senior administration.

In early February 2000, I received a telephone call from Anthony Day at ESU informing me that he too had been fired in late fall from his position as assistant vice president for affirmative action by Daniel Marks. He was given one year to find another job and reassigned to the School of Education as assistant to the dean. He had consolidated both my and Anthony Day's position to create the new position into which he had now hired Regina Washington. This meant the SBA had finally succeeded in pushing Anthony and me out of the university. He also informed me the new associate vice president, Regina Washington, had expressed an interest in meeting with me to learn more about my experiences at ESU. He wanted to know if I would be willing to meet with her sometime in the next few weeks before she formally started at ESU. I found the request interesting and expressed a willingness to meet. The meeting was scheduled for early in the morning the next day at a local Panera Restaurant. As I walked into the restaurant, I realized I had forgotten to ask for a description of her so that I would recognize her

I almost left when I saw her. But she had already been given a description and advised to look for "a weird-looking and racially ambiguous person." Apparently, the description was helpful because she called out to me as I walked into the restaurant from the north entrance.

"Samir Dyfan," she called out to me as I walked in.

"Yes. Oh, Regina!" There sat this beautiful woman who identified herself as Regina Washington.

"Well, I am glad you are willing to meet and talk. I know this must not be easy for you to do," she said.

"To be frank with you, I am delighted to by here to talk. I have no hard feelings toward you. I want to help as much as I can safely without creating problems for you," I replied.

"I must say I've heard a lot of great things about you and decided I should talk with you to find out as mush as I could about the university before I dive into things. Let me ask you this. Why did you leave ESU?"

"It's a long story. But what I believe you should be aware of is there is a highly organized, secretive group of senior black administrators on campus that you will have to contend with as you try to do your job. They are highly organized, powerful, political, and destructive. At first, they will try to co-opt you by getting you to join the SBA and eventually to buy into their political agenda. If you fail to go along with their political agenda, then you become their enemy. And they have successfully destroyed their enemies," I cautioned her.

"I mentioned to the provost when I interviewed for the position that I did not have any experience dealing with diversity issues and wondered why they were letting you go. I asked why they were keeping Anthony Day in the EEO office and not you since I didn't think the university needed two EEO experts. I asked if it was still possible to keep you instead of Anthony Day. I got a very suspicious response from the provost that left me wondering what really happened. He said it didn't work out as he had expected," she added.

"As I said earlier, to make a long story short, I refused to go along with their political agenda and became a threat. You should know they have been the ones behind the termination of every EEO director the university has ever had and the one responsible for the termination of each one of them. The reasons given for the termination in each case were always the same: the EEO director was incompetent and inept. The attacks always came from SBA members in the provost's office and led by Alfred Pratt, Vernon Machiavelli, and Daniel Marks. Then they positioned themselves to lead the search for a replacement, hoping to find someone they can easily co-opt. In one case, they pushed for the hiring of a close friend and college buddy of the vice provost, Alfred Pratt. They were hoping he would be easily influenced to go along with their agenda, but, after a nasty confrontation with the associate vice president for academic affairs, Vernon Machiavelli, over the direction of a discrimination investigation, they pushed for his firing just a year after he was hired as a complaint investigator in the EEO office."

I continued, "How are they able to get away with it? They are highly organized and collectively know how to work the administration's fears. They are also adept at using the BFSA to increase the level of pressure on the administration when they need it. Remember there are eleven SBA in the university. This number includes the provost, vice provost, one vice president, two associate vice presidents, two assistant vice presidents, one academic dean, and three associate deans. That's a powerful group, especially when they are highly organized," I explained.

"I am glad I had an opportunity to speak with you. Please don't let them know I have met with you. I don't want to start off on the wrong foot with them. I suspected something was not right with the response I received from the provost when I tried to convince him to retain you. I mentioned to him that I had seen your name over the years as a major institute presenter at the premier national conference on diversity. I told him that you are one of the experts on diversity and would like to keep you instead of Tony, but he wouldn't budge. But I am glad you are doing well. I will try to stay in touch with you," she said as I was getting my briefcase ready to leave for work.

As I drove to work that morning after the meeting, I couldn't help thinking what a neat lady she was. She was intuitive and courageous enough to speak with me about my experiences. I wondered how she would get along with them and how long it would take before she too became a threat to the SBA. She certainly left me with the impression that she was a principled person. I knew that would create problems for her, especially now that the position reported to Daniel Marks.

Sometime in early September 2000, I received a telephone call from the former provost, Ron Liste. He informed me he had taken a new position in the medical school at ESU, heading a research institute on traumatic brain injuries.

"I am sorry about what happened to you at ESU," he said. "I did not know what had really happened until someone explained it to me the other day. I was under the impression that you left because you had found a better job. That's what I was told by someone in the provost's office. I didn't realize the SBA was a highly organized interest group. I had heard something about your allegations against them, but I could not believe it. Or should I say I didn't want to believe it. I thought I knew these guys in a way that kept me from believing what I had heard. I suppose President Franklin convinced me the SBA thing was nonsense. She explained the SBA away by assuring me she knew Daniel Marks well enough to know that it wasn't true. And I believed her. I should have known better. How are you doing, Samir?"

"Well, I don't know what to say. I am doing fine," I replied.

"I am glad to hear that. I wanted you to know I am willing to serve as a reference for you at anytime. Samir, I have the utmost respect for you and the work you did at ESU. I heard from hundreds of faculty, staff, and people in the community praising the work you were doing. I received telephone calls, letters, and e-mail from people from all over the United States who are impressed with your work and ideas. So, I want you to know that everyone I have spoken with believes you were fired because you had become too much of a threat to the SBA and their political agenda," he added.

"Well, thank you for your kind words and support. I might take you up on the reference offer one of these days. Say, Ron, did you share with Alfred any of the letters, e-mail, or telephone calls you received about the quality of my work?" I inquired.

"Yes, every time. I sent him copies of all the letters and e-mail and spoke to him about the telephone calls I received. The telephone calls were from people high up in county and state government. Some of them went directly to the president's office and were forwarded to my attention. Others came directly to me. The letters were mostly from individuals who spoke of you and your seminars in amazing language. One woman equated you to Mahatma Gandhi and Deepak Chopra. Why do you ask? Didn't Alfred share these with you?" he asked curiously.

"Once or twice at the most. He made a comment once in a meeting with black students that some of us 'did not realize we have thankless jobs at the university and, therefore, there was no need to go around asking people to write letters to the president about how wonderful we were.' I suppose he was referring to me in that comment that came from out of the blue. I only now understand what he was getting at," I explained.

"I can't believe that. I must have given him over 100 letters and e-mail. Well, those guys don't have any integrity, particularly Daniel, Alfred, and Vernon. You won't believe what they did to me after I left the provost's office. You know that I hired those bastards. I hired Daniel Marks as dean of the School of Arts and Sciences and Alfred for the vice provost's position when I first arrived at ESU," he said.

"Did you recommend Daniel for the interim provost position?" I asked.

"Yes, I was the one who recommended Daniel for the interim provost's job just before I retired. He knew before I left the office that he was going to be appointed to the interim position and made several promises to me before I left. He promised to help fund some of the projects I would be working on at the medical school and to fund a secretarial position and furniture for my new office. But when I called to schedule a meeting to discuss the funding, both he and Alfred refused to take my telephone calls or to accept any appointment for a meeting with me. I must have called a dozen times, but I didn't receive a single returned call from them. Even when I went to the provost office to speak with them, they refused to meet with me. Imagine that, I am provost emeritus, and they treat me this way. I was so embarrassed and upset. Soon after that, I began to have health problems." He spoke in dejection and disbelief. "You know what? I was discussing this with someone in the administration who is a supporter of yours. Do you know what he said to me? He said, and I am quoting him, 'I am not surprised. Samir Dyfan spoke openly to anyone who would listen that these guys had no integrity and should not be trusted.' That's what he said. He then went on to explain to me what they had done to you soon after I left office. They knew they could not have convinced me to go along with firing you when I was in the provost's office so they waited until I had left before they did it. I just don't understand why the president did not consult with me before she authorized it."

"After I was fired, I tried but failed to get an appointment to talk with her to encourage her to speak with you and some of the other vice presidents," I explained.

"Well, Samir, let's stay in touch. Please use me as a reference any time. Thanks again for listening to me. I really appreciate it," he said as he hung up.

I continued to monitor the situation at ESU without much effort because I received frequent calls from many faculty and staff at the university. In early February 2001, the chairman of the ethnic studies department, Bobby Terrell, came by my home to pick up documents I had donated to the department's library.

As we loaded his pickup truck, he asked, "How have you been doing, Samir?"

"Splendid and wonderful," I responded.

"You appear relaxed and fine. I am glad you were able to find a better job. I am told you are doing better than you were at ESU. That is great, and I'm glad for you," he asked.

"Fine, thank you?" I asked.

"You know that a lot of faculty and staff were sad to see you leave ESU. Let me tell you, they are very angry about the treatment you received in the hands of the SBA in the provost's office. It is not clear to me, but what really happened?" he asked curiously.

"To make a long story short, I refused to go along with their political agenda and attempts to ruin the careers of faculty and staff they perceived as threats to the SBA agenda," I responded.

"Well, I know you will be interested in my experience with Daniel Marks and Alfred Pratt. They tried on two occasions to get me to provide them with information they needed against two black administrators. It was never clear to me what they had against these individuals, but they were out to get them," he explained.

"What happened? What did they want you to do?" I asked.

"They tried on several occasions to get me to fabricate information against a close colleague in my department and Jack Okun in the Center for Blacks. In the first case, they tried but failed to get me to fabricate evidence of mismanagement against a black administrator. In the case of Jack, they wanted me to provide them with ammunition they could use against him by promising they would merge the Center for Blacks with the ethnic studies department, if I helped them. In both cases, they were looking for information that proved their allegations that these individuals were incompetent. My experiences with these guys corroborate yours. It appears as if this is the way they operated. But I could not figure out why they were going after these two individuals. What did they have against them?" he asked.

"Well, I know they were trying to get rid of Jack because the previous director of the Center, Ruby Brown, the wife of former the dean of Fine Arts, a SBA member, is back in town and wants back her old job. She and her husband are back because he was fired after a year as president of a historically black university. Since their return, she has been pressuring the provost and vice provost to get back her old job. She has been going around the campus referring to Jack as incompetent and incapable of running the Center. Her main vehicle for pushing Jack out of the center's directorship is the BFSA. When that effort failed, she accepted a one-year appointment in the fund-raising office while she waited for the provost to find a way to get rid of Jack Okun," I explained.

"What about the other person, do you know why they are after her job?" he asked.

"I am not sure who you were referring to in your earlier comments," I explained.

"Well, you know who I am talking about. Even though I refused to cooperate with their efforts to fire her, they did anyway. Daniel Marks got rid of her soon after you. All he told her was that he would like to make some changes in the leadership of the department. That was all he told her," he explained.

"I think I know who you are referring to. She must have become a threat to the SBA agenda because she was always talking about the need to increase the representation of black women in the university administration. That's the only thing I can think about. Remember that the beast only strikes when it is threatened and/or hungry," I added.

"Well, thanks for the documents. This is a fantastic collection that even the university library doesn't have. Thank you again, and good luck in your new position," he said before he left.

A few months after my conversation with Bobby Terrell, ESU settled the case involving the football team out of court. Soon after that, Berthan Allred was headlined in the local newspaper after he was jailed because of contempt of court charges involved with his financial assets in a nasty divorce case. He had declared bankruptcy when it was discovered he was hiding most of his financial assets in a secret bank account in Singapore. He remained in jail as of summer 2002.

As it turned out, what goes around comes around—at least sort of and for some people. Three years after I was forced out of my position, eight of the top

SBA administrators were gone from their positions. This included among others, the provost, vice provost, associate vice president for academic affairs, vice president, associate vice president and assistant vice president for student services, and dean of the School of Fine Arts. The five-headed beast had been beheaded. The most senior black administrators had been fired. Two resigned, one retired, and the top five senior black administrators had been slowly fired one after another until most of them were gone.

The demise of the SBA began slowly as the new administration began to realize that many of the things I had told them about the lack of integrity among SBA members were true (whether they identified them with my warnings or not). It turned out the problem began when that president discovered the provost had not been honest about the reasons for transferring Vernon Machiavelli to one of the regional campuses. The dean of the Vista campus had given the president a copy of the report written by an outside attorney that the provost had hired to investigate complaints of excessive abuse by Vernon's secretaries.

The report found that the abuse was even more egregious than first appeared and went unaddressed for twenty years. The investigator recommended that disciplinary action be taken against Vernon, including psychotherapy for anger management. But, instead of following the recommendations of the investigator who was also black, the provost conspired to transfer him to the Vista campus with his salary and title intact to sweep the problem under the rug. It turned out the provost had not been forthright with the president about the reasons for the transfer. In fact, he had not mentioned the investigation or the report to neither the president nor the executive vice president. According to my sources in the administration, this discovery raised serious questions about the integrity of the provost and lent validity to some of the issues I had raised about the SBA as a "Mafia" type organization, as someone in the administration put it.

From this point on, the beast began to turn against itself. As it turned out, the provost tried to blame the vice provost for the decision to transfer Vernon to the Vista campus. He explained to the president that the vice provost had direct supervision of the associate vice president, Machiavelli, for over seven years and had failed to address the problems during that time until a formal complaint was filed by his current secretary for creating a hostile work environment. He also blamed the decision for hiring the outside attorney and keeping the report under wraps on the vice provost. Daniel Marks claimed he was not aware of the Machiavelli report until the president mentioned it to him and explained he only recently found out about the outside attorney. But the president did not buy his excuses because the general counsel had already contacted the outside attorney, only to find out the provost knew about the investigation from the beginning and had initiated the investigation. In fact, the letter of transmittal for the final report was addressed to the provost.

The motto among the top SBA members had always been that one of them "will take a bullet for the old man" if the need arose. The old man and "Don Corleone" of the SBA had always been Daniel Marks. Because of his age, administrative seniority, and faculty rank, he was viewed as the one with the most potential to ascend to the presidency. In addition, he had demonstrated he could get whites to trust him and appeared less threatening to them because of his halting manner of speaking. And now that Daniel expected Alfred to take the bullet and cover for him, Alfred was unwilling to become the fall guy. All of a sudden, the old man was in trouble, and no one in the SBA was willing to sacrifice his or her career for him. To add insult to injury, the executive vice president's probing of the provost's staff regarding Daniel's discussions about firing Armando Segundo during the provost's staff meeting was confirmed by some of those present during the meeting.

As the provost's credibility dropped, the president began to distance herself from the provost by channeling her communications through the executive vice president. In turn, the provost was expected to communicate with the president through the executive vice president. In the culture of higher education, this was a clear signal that the provost had lost the president's confidence. In reality, it meant the provost was a dead duck. From this point on, the relationship between the provost and vice provost became tense and strained. As the provost's relationship with president went from bad to worse, Daniel Marks began to complain to some of his deans about the president's behavior as arrogant and demeaning. One of the deans he frequently complained to about how the president was treating him was the individual he had hired from among his department chairs to replace him as the dean of the School of Arts and Science. According to my sources, he quietly complained to the president that the provost's office was in turmoil and that the deans were all complaining about the provost's indecisiveness. He also mentioned the provost was badmouthing the president to the deans. This sealed the provost's fate. From this point on, the president made it clear that she was not happy with his leadership as provost. Word spread that Daniel was incompetent and incapable of carrying out the responsibilities of the provost's office. Incidentally, the dean who reported the provost's behavior to the president eventually succeeded Daniel as provost.

As the relationship between the provost and vice provost continued to deteriorate, the vice provost began to search for another job within the state university system (so as to maintain his years of service toward retirement). By late fall that year, his search began to bear fruit when he was interviewed for the provost's position at State Ebony University (SEU). He needed a reference from the provost to seal the deal. The provost agreed to serve as a reference, but he eventually did not give him an enthusiastic reference.

In the end, Alfred was not offered the position at SEU. Soon after the interview, Alfred found out that the reason he did not get the job was because he had received a lukewarm job reference from Daniel Marks. This discovery sent him into emotional orbit. He became very angry and made his feelings known to the provost. He declared war on his fellow SBA member, Daniel Marks.

At about the same time all of this was going on in the provost's office, the Student Services office was going through its own turmoil. The problem began soon after Erica Bolton, assistant vice president of student services, an SBA member, retired. The expectation was that a BFSA vice president and campus activist, Jenny Davies, would be promoted to Erica's position as Al Richards, vice president for student services, had promised two years earlier. But, when Erica retired, Al Richards announced to the campus community that the position would not be filled because of budget cuts. He appealed to the BFSA for patience and understanding. He promised to fill the position as soon as the budget situation improved. Thinking she was eventually going to get the job, Jenny Davies agreed to support the vice president's appeal for understanding in the hopes the budget situation would improve sooner than later.

But several months later, word leaked from the personnel office that Al Richards had secretly appointed a Latina assistant, Marina Rodriguez, to Erica's position without a search. This "act of betrayal" was the final straw for most BFSA members who had always been deeply suspicious of SBA intentions. From this point forward, all hell broke loose. The BFSA leadership declared war on SBA members Al Richards and Sheryl Hendrix, Al's associate vice president for student services. Word began to spread again around campus that Al and his assistant were having an affair in violation of university policy, that Al Richards was incompetent and an Uncle Tom, and that Al hated black people. Others wrote to the president demanding the vice president and associate vice president for student services be fired from the student services office. Clearly things were not going well for the SBA and its agenda. The vipers had turned against one another, and the end was near.

Fearing his job was on the line, Al called an urgent and secretive meeting in his office conference room with a number of black faculty and SBA members to appeal for help and support. He explained the president had relegated him to report to the executive vice president and had refused to meet with him. He hinted this might be because of his race and the fact that the president was a white Republican. He asked the SBA and BFSA unite to protect the gains blacks had made at the university. He insisted the new administration was targeting senior black administrators for elimination from their positions and urged blacks not to stay quiet about it. But his appeal fell upon deaf ears. Those present were not inclined to get involved to "save his ass," as one person put it.

A few months later, Daniel Marks announced he was retiring after just two years because of deteriorating health. Soon after that, the president announced the dean of the School of Arts and Sciences would replace him as interim provost. Immediately after that announcement was made, Daniel Marks saw this as perfect timing as an opportunity to get even and fired Alfred Pratt. He wanted to get Alfred fired because it was his refusal to help Daniel Marks run the provost's office as his surrogate that finally exposed Daniel's incompetence and inability to carry out his responsibilities as provost and chief academic officer. In reality, his inability to do his job and dependence on Alfred probably stemmed from his bad health.

But it didn't end there. Angry and determined to shake down the administration, Alfred threatened to file a discrimination complaint and take legal actions if his demands were not met. He wanted to keep his full salary, be promoted to full professor, and be given a year's sabbatical as compensation for the "racist treatment" he had received. The administration was not inclined to give in fully to the shakedown, but it quietly negotiated a partial settlement with him that included the sabbatical to get him away from the campus for a while.

A few months later, Al Richards announced that Sheryl Hendrix was leaving her position for health reasons and reassigned her to the student health services office as assistant director. She had absolutely no experience in the health field and no responsibilities in her new position. In fact, her new office took up precious space in an already overcrowded facility. Exactly a month later, Al Richards announced he would be retiring as vice president of student services. He claimed he had planed to retire at age sixty-five and had informed the new university president about his intentions two years earlier. Of the eleven SBA members in the university, one resigned because of frustration with the administration and rude, aggressive behavior of Alice Pratt, the wife of the vice provost. Another retired. Six were fired or forced out, and one was transferred to the Vista campus. Only four of the eleven SBA members remained in the administration. The beast had been beheaded.

Beyond the remaining SBA members, the newly appointed athletic director, Roy Johnson, resigned from his position within two years because of health problems. His resignation preceded the firing of the provost and left SBA and BFSA members speculating about the "true reasons for his departure." His departure fueled rumors the "Republican president [of the university] was planning to rid the university of blacks in the administration, and Roy Johnson was just the first." But the rumor was self-serving and emanated from the provost's office. Knowing he was already in trouble with the president, Daniel Marks and Jim Aaron, the SBA point man with the BFSA, began spreading rumors of "ethnic cleansing" as a way of rallying the BFSA troops for a shakedown of the administration in the event that the provost was fired. As rumors of the impending mass firing of blacks spread among BFSA members, campus activists became even more paranoid and began reaching out to the leadership of the local NAACP and Urban League for support. Soon after the prediction of ethnic cleansing began, the provost was fired, followed by the firing of the vice provost. By then, the die was cast. The prediction was coming true, and everyone was waiting for "the axe to fall on the next victim." And it did.

By the time the last SBA member was fired, the campus was rife with talk about "the Republican's conspiracy to fire every black administrator" as a fact, and they could cite the evidence of four of the most senior black administrators being fired within the same year. This was incontrovertible evidence to those who were fanning the flames of racial hatred in an effort to find a bargaining leverage to coerce the "white administration" into promoting from within the existing SBA or BFSA ranks into the vacant positions in the name of diversity. That's the way they had always done it, and BFSA members knew it would work because it had in the past. And they were prepared to try again. But first, they knew they had to get the "whites" running scared of another scandal for the politics of blame and the psychology of guilt to work again this time. The game was on again.

A few weeks after the vice president of student services was fired, an e-mail accusing the administration of racist practice started circulating among blacks on campus. To everyone's surprise, the first copies were hand-distributed by Al Richards during his last student services staff meeting in early June. After that, it began circulating to all black faculty and staff on campuses. The first shots had been fired. Now, they were waiting to see how the white administration would react. They knew it was only a matter of time before the mail got to the administration, even if they didn't send a copy directly to the administration.

The circulated e-mail made the following points:

- Morale and the climate at ESU are at an all-time low. People continue to speak quietly about their disgust regarding the level of incompetence, hypocrisy, elitism, and the Machiavellian administrative style of the administration. Faculty and staff are fearful, intimidated, bullied, and demoralized by their vindictiveness and are afraid to speak out for fear of retaliation.

- The president has only given lip service to diversity issues at ESU. Her definition of a diverse executive leadership team excludes African-American and Latinos as demonstrated by the president's cabinet, president's office, provost office, and executive vice president's office. Additionally, in the past two years, all of the senior black administrators have left their positions. Some have indicated health concerns as a reason for their departure. Others have remained silent regarding their reasons. While rumors have suggested they were all terminated by the president, it is clear. It is also clear they were inequitably paid. Clear salary disparities exist between the salaries of the former and current leaders.

  - Former Provost Daniel Marks = $220,000

  - Provost Tammi Luxor = $265,000

  - Former Athletic Director Roy Johnson = $195,000

  - Athletic Director, Bill Zoolander = $275, 000

  - Former Vice Provost Alfred Pratt = $155,000

  - Vice Provosts Wales and Xiang = $177,000

- The largest salary disparity is between Roy Johnson and Zoolander. It is difficult to believe a pillar and well-respected member of the community that brought prominence, recognition, and notoriety to the ESU Athletic Program could be so inequitably paid for his services. It's shameful that Roy Johnson was not compensated for his talent and contributions to ESU. Because of Roy Johnson's professionalism, the community may never really know how he was pressured to leave.

- Consistent with the inequitable treatment of minorities, Al Richards, former vice president for student services, was the lowest paid although he managed the largest student services office in the state university system. He created a vibrant campus life that changed the negative image of the university, built an exceptional student housing program, developed exceptional retention services, and successfully enhanced student and staff diversity at ESU. He even led the building of the new athletic facility. Given the great contributions he made to ESU, his resignation was quite sudden and surprising. According to the announcement of Richards's departure, he (Richards) had expressed a desire to leave the university four years ago. In other events, the president has alluded to the fact that Richards' age and health may have prompted his retirement. It is unacceptable the president of the university would make statements that could be interpreted as discriminatory. Why is it that poor health is given as a reason for every senior black administrator that leaves the university? This appears to be her way of quietly ridding the university of black men without controversy? It would be interesting to read Richards' resignation letter and Judge's acceptance to determine what really happened.

- Currently, there are no Latino or black senior administrators at ESU. The president has failed to implement a successful minority recruitment plan to increase the number of minorities.

- ESU employees are very angry about these failures as well as the hostile, inequitable, and elitist climate that exists at ESU. The trustees cannot continue to ignore the incompetence of the administration. Eastern State University belongs to all of the people of this community, and the institution should not be made exclusive by these individuals.

Soon after this e-mail started circulating, speculation started as who wrote it. Many dismissed Al Richards, former vice president for student services, or Provost Daniel Marks as the authors because everyone knew neither one of them could write at the level the letter was written. This led to speculations that Alfred Pratt and Vernon Machiavelli were the authors. The consensus among blacks on the campus was that Alfred and Vernon were the authors because of the style, knowledge of salaries, and the giveaway, the extent to which the e-mail praised Al Richards for allegedly doing an excellent job. It was commonly known that Alfred and Al were very good friends and Alfred had previously made similar comments about Al's performance in his position. Knowing as I do the modus operandi of the SBA, I am certain that Al Richards, Alfred Pratt, Vernon Machiavelli, Johnny Brown, Sheryl Hendrix, Daniel Marks, and Jim Aaron met in one of their homes to discuss the content of the e-mail and to draft it.

It was no surprise that the first copies appeared on campus when Al Richards distributed it to his staff during his last meeting before his departure from the student services office. This e-mail was typical SBA strategy of appearing to be fighting for minorities or blacks when they really cared less about them. In fact, SBA members were collectively hated by Latinos and blacks on campus for ignoring their concerns until they needed them to promote their exclusive agenda. In addition, Al Richards, Alfred Pratt, and Daniel Marks had a reputation, to quote one particularly reviled individual on campus, for having "done more harm to other blacks and Latinos than even the Grand Dragon of the KKK could have managed to do in the time they were in office." It was also commonly known that Alfred Pratt, Daniel Marks, and Jim Aaron were so hostile to other blacks on campus that they frequently referred to them in their conversations as "goddamned niggers." I was not the only person who had observed this behavior. Now, they were at it again, rallying the troops for another self-serving fight to shakedown the white administration for a few positions for their cronies.

As it turned out, the president found out about the above e-mail and became alarmed about it, just as they intended. In her state of panic, the president called a meeting with the remaining SBA members, the leadership of the BFSA, a few community members, and Roy Johnson to discuss allegations in the e-mail that senior black administrators had been pushed out of their jobs. According to my sources (who were at the meeting), the meeting didn't go well because BSFA members Tom Strung and Jenny Davies and the community members refused to accept Roy Johnson's explanation that he wasn't pushed out of his job but left for genuine health reasons. Talk about respect for a community icon. The meeting was frustrating because the BFSA members refused to accept the president's assurances she was committed to diversity in her administration. They were adamant she should not have appointed an African faculty member as interim when there were African-Americans like Ruby Brown or the retired Erica Bolton that could have filled that position.

The president tried to explain to them the African faculty member she appointed, Ibera Clove, had been a faculty in the university for thirty-five years and knew the institution and student needs very well. She also tried to explain the fact she had appointed a black person to the interim position was proof of her commitment to diversity. But they were not pacified. They demanded she assure them she would eventually hire an African-American to fill the position, but she refused to commit to their demands because it would be illegal under federal employment laws. They viewed her refusal to give them a wink and a nod assuring them she would meet their demands as proof that she was not committed to "black diversity," as one of them put it during the meeting. After the meeting ended, BFSA member were heard referring to Roy Johnson as an "Uncle Tom for trying to undermine their bargaining position."

Even though they left that meeting disappointed the president could not reassure them she would hire an African-American to replace Al Richards, they felt confident she would not dare disregard their demands. Now, all that was left for them to do was to influence the selection of the search committee chair and membership so that they could get their cronies in the search committee in order to influence the search outcome. They had the university president exactly where they wanted her—panicking and afraid of another racial scandal in the university.

To make matters worse, the newly appointed associate vice president for diversity and equal opportunity, Regina Washington, resigned less than two years after her appointment. She indicated she had been frustrated and disappointed with the politics of diversity in the university since the first few months of her appointment. Now, the last black vice president in the main campus was leaving, complicating racial matters for the president. What would the departure of Regina Washington mean for the politics of racial and ethnic diversity on campus? What would the BFSA do now that the university had lost the last of the senior black administrators? How much coercive power would they derive from this latest development? How much more would the president give in to BFSA demands for a black vice president for student services?

A few weeks after Regina Washington resigned from the university, the BFSA succeeded in getting their ideal choice as chair of the search committee for the vice president for student services position. The president appointed Associate Dean Jim "the Snake" Aaron as chair of the search committee and asked him to recommend others to be appointed to the committee. This was an invitation to stack the committee with BFSA members and their sympathizers who would be more predisposed to going along with whoever the BFSA wants for the position. It goes without saying that the BFSA was very pleased with the president's gesture, and it signaled her willingness to play ball with them. Now the true test would come later. After they had chosen the candidate they wanted, would the president go along with their choice?

In early September 2002, to the astonishment of those who knew him on campus, the president appointed Jim Aaron as interim associate vice president for EEO/AA and diversity. What was astonishing about Jim's appointment was the fact the university administration knew he frequently used racial epithets against blacks that opposed the SBA agenda. But this was not all that stunned the campus community.

While many faculty and staff were pleased the SBA had been decapitated with the removal of its leaders from office, many managed to coerce the university administration to cut sweet deals for themselves before they left office. In summary, Daniel Marks, the former provost and head of the beast, returned to his academic department with a fat annual salary of $185,000. Alfred Pratt demanded and got an annual salary of $129,000 and a promise of promotion to full professorship as he returned to his academic department. Al Richards, former vice president of student services, extorted an annual salary of $170,000 for a minimum of four years and the option of a faculty appointment in the School of Education. His girlfriend, Sheryl Hendrix, former associate vice president for student services, also demanded and received an annual salary of $150,000 and a faculty appointment. And last (but not least), Vernon Machiavelli, former associate vice president for academic affairs, was transferred to one of the regional campuses with his $140,000 annual salary intact, a reward for abusing his secretaries for twenty years. And finally, Jim "the Snake" Aaron, associate dean for diversity in the School of Medicine, managed to up his salary to $143,000 for being the loyal lapdog of the SBA beast.

It is important to note that, as long as these guys remain on campus, they cannot be counted out completely. As I write, they have used their coercive power to influence the outcome of the search for the vice president for student services. Indeed, it was not surprising that the president passed over a Latino candidate who was more highly rated by the search committee and hired an black candidate in an effort to appease the BFSA at Eastern State university. And, as I write, they have managed to get Jim Aaron appointed as the chair of the student services vice presidential search committee and have him appointed associate vice president for EEO/AA without a national search, even though he lacks even the basic understanding of EEO/AA function, processes, and policies. In short, he is not only unqualified for the position. But, in my opinion, he lacks the ethical and moral qualities essential to the position. This is the same person who frequently referred to blacks as "goddamned niggers" and served as a coconspirator with the SBA in my firing. A black racist and the most unfit person ever appointed to that position. They have again repositioned themselves to reemerge for another round of coercive politics albeit with new faces leading the charge of the politics of blame and the psychology of guilt in their selfish game of self-aggrandizement, at the expense of all.

Epilogue

After we completed this manuscript, someone raised an important question: Is the diversity mechanism hopelessly corrupt? As a parting shot, we would like to return to the point where we started. Diversity is invaluable for a number of reasons. First, diverse inputs lead to high-quality outputs, whatever the activity is. This constitutes an opportunity whether we are talking about our children's education, our work, or our governance. Second, the United States is the most diverse nation in history, no matter how you measure diversity. This constitutes a mandate to understand and embrace diversity and to facilitate inclusive and fair processes. Nobody should conclude from this book that active and assertive diversity programs should be abandoned or eliminated. Nor should any charlatan put our story to use in advocating such a position. On the contrary, we hope to incite outrage among all people at the corruption of such a noble and necessary cause.

Samir Dyfan is a real person. He came to the United States from Africa because this was a nation where he could fail or succeed on his merits. Despite the many tragedies of this epic, he has succeeded at making a good living, marrying, and raising a family. He has children who lack ethnicity and race even more than him. He lives in an upper middle-class neighborhood where his neighbors care more about his character than his race or ethnicity. He became a citizen of this nation, a privilege not even afforded him in the land of his birth. He has achieved all of these things despite the corruption of the system meant to ensure equal opportunity for people of minority. On the other hand, Samir is fortunate. Many fall through the cracks because the system meant to ensure opportunity is too busy with self-service.

We believe profoundly in the value of diversity and all its related activities: civil rights, equality, justice, fairness, and equal opportunity. It is true we have come a long way since the 1960s, let alone the 1860s. Maybe the mechanisms of diversity that were born in the age of the civil rights movement have simply outlived their relevance. The mandate our book presents is to reinvent this system in a way that fits twenty-first century needs for community and belonging. Toward this end, we currently are engaged in creating a manuscript that charts this direction.

Denys Blell and Bob Kreisher
January 16, 2005

978-0-595-34061-
0-595-34061-X

Printed in the United States
34492LVS00004B/184-207